the SUMMIT

Eric Alexander

New Leaf Press

First Printing: November 2010

New Leaf Press,
P.O. Box 726, Green Forest, AR 72638

New Leaf Press is a division of the New Leaf Publishing Group, Inc.

ISBN: 978-0-89221-701-4
Library of Congress Number: 2010937082

All Scripture quotations in this book, unless otherwise noted, are taken from the New International Version of the Bible.

Cover and interior design by Diana Bogardus

Front cover photo by Charles Mace (Luis Benitez atop the Hillary Step at 28,800 feet, leading out in front of teammates Erik Weihenmayer, Jeff Evans, Eric Alexander, and Ang Pasang Sherpa). Title page photo by Erik Weihenmayer. Back cover photo by Eric Alexander (Jeff Evans).

Please consider requesting that a copy of this volume be purchased by your local library system.

Printed in the United States of America

Please visit our website for other great titles:
www.nlpg.com

For information regarding author interviews,
please contact the publicity department at (870) 438-5288

New Leaf Press
A Division of New Leaf Publishing Group

Dedication

Echoing the words and heart of David, I would like to say:

I love you, O LORD, my strength.
The LORD is my rock, my fortress and my deliverer;
my God is my rock, in whom I take refuge (Psalm 18:1–2).

Acknowledgments

It is with a most humbled heart that I gratefully thank all of those who have stood by me in the process of putting into writing these adventures and stories that have become such a major part of my life story. Even more so, I would like to thank the people who have shared their vision for setting off for distant places with unlikely goals, invited me along to dream big, boldly, and passionately, unafraid of the voices declaring the task insensible and impossible.

I would like to thank my friend Joseph Chonko for always believing in me and giving me the courage to continue while showing me what a godly man of integrity should look like.

Thanks to mentors and friends like Steve Cyphers and John Kanengieter, who took the time to care about a bunch of young, punky kids, of which I was one, and give them a passion for the outdoors. Many other friends have stood by me amidst my fears and struggles and urged me on or joined me in it: J (James Whorton), the Bakers, the Stephens, Rick and Julie, as well as my entire church family in the Vail Valley.

Then there are those who put their necks and dollars on the line along with us on these adventures — the sponsors: Mountain Hardwear and the National Federation of the Blind. Without these groups, many of my summits would still be dreams.

To those who dared to dream big and included me in it: Erik Weihenmayer for being a blind man with vision and not giving up on your little buddy Erie (me), and showing me what possibilities lie within us all. To John Davis and his 2Xtreme dream and Dave Shurna and the Global Explorers group — I admire your leadership and yet your servitude. Thanks for giving me something worthy about which to write.

I am thankful to all the members on the Everest team for giving of themselves to something greater than themselves. Thank you for the brotherhood on the mountain.

Thank you to Darlene and Ralph Dokken, who have endured so much yet found time, strength, and energy in the middle of the fight to pray for me ever so faithfully on these adventures, and even when safe at home. You both have been an inspiration and example to me. Darlene, you prayed for this book to be written, and now take that little piece of the summit from 29,000 feet with you as you have departed. I know the Lord is happy to see you and is holding you close. I hope you are enjoying your new legs and a new life without wheels.

Thank you to the Byrnes family for letting me use your "cabin in the mountains" as a quiet escape to get work done.

A huge thanks to the New Leaf Press team for all of your help and daring to adopt this project; and to Becki for introducing me to them.

Mostly thanks to my family: my mom, Anita; dad, Richard, and his wife, Rosie; sister, Lisa and her husband, John; my in-laws, Rob and Nancy, for all of your support and help from highs to lows and everything in between.

Finally, thanks to my dear and lovely wife, Amy, who with the help of my two-year-old daughters, Karis and Aralyn, was able to read through this and help me along. Thank you for believing in me, in all I do and all I am; you mean the world to me. I love you and look forward to climbing many summits with you.

Our Journey to the Summit

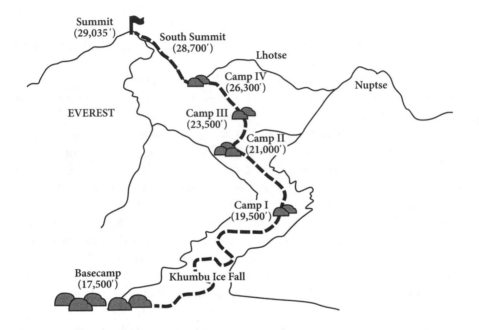

Members of the
2001 National Federation of the Blind (NFB) Everest Expedition

Eric Alexander, Erik Weihenmayer, Pasquale Scaturro, Brad Bull, Jeff Evans, Mike O'Donnell, Chris Morris, Luis Benitiez, Didrik Johnk, Charlie Mace, Michael Brown, Sherman Bull, Steve Gipe, Kevin Cherilla, Kami Tenzing Sherpa, Ang Sona Sherpa, Lhakpa Tsering Sherpa, Pemba Choti Sherpa, Ang Pasang Sherpa, Phurba Bhote Sherpa, Ang Kami Sherpa, Lhakpa Tshering Sherpa, Chuldim Nuru Sherpa, Tenzing Sherpa, Mingma Sherpa, Mon Kumar, Reba Bull, Maurice Peret, Pasang Sherpa, Ang Pasang Sherpa and Tsering Sherpa.

Contents

Introduction

This book is a byproduct of encouragement. Over the last few years, I have given hundreds of speeches, talks, lectures, presentations, and keynote addresses. More times than I care to count I have been asked, "Can I buy your book? When is it coming out?" I have been told, "You need to put this into a book." While I had aspired to do, that even if only for my daughters, the project was slow to move forward largely due to lots of time traveling, getting married, having kids, and so on.

My friend Erik Weihenmayer has written a brief chapter in his book about our Everest climb, and a few short magazine articles had been written on it, but I realized that nothing of any length had been written about our historic journey to the summit of Everest. I especially wanted to share what an amazing faith journey this was as well. This story is important because I believe it truly speaks to the underdog in us all.

I had the privilege of climbing with a great group of guys that laid it all on the line for the sake of someone else, a dream that Erik Weihenmayer thought possible. What he needed was a bunch of believers to accompany him on the journey. Not everyone who was asked went along, because not everyone who was asked could believe. I have learned a lot from the journey to Everest about friendship, loyalty, trust, relationships, adventure, goal setting, and the list could be a mile long, but most importantly, I learned how to climb with Jesus. No, He doesn't need crampons or a permit, just trust and devotion, love and obedience, and a high level of commitment that leads to rewards far higher than the summit of Everest.

We were up against it with a blind teammate. It was hard work, it was trying and testing, but it was a moment I will never forget. A moment standing on top of the world that has inspired this group of guys to go out and live lives that encourage others to go and seek out their own Everests, whatever that may be.

Ed Viesturs said, "It will be the hardest ever guided ascent of Everest,"[1] and it probably was. He was right. If it wasn't hard, we would not have gained so much, and I believe we would have had less to give.

As you read, each chapter will begin with information on a climb significant in this book, but not necessarily related to the pages that follow in that chapter. These pages will give insights into mountains and treks around the world, bringing the reader on a Seven Summits adventure and more. I offer too, as a heads up, that after chapter 3 the story will divert from the Everest climb to discover stories of other places and people. I do this for two reasons: first is that most people climb the Seven Summits having Everest as their last — it was my first. But this will give you insight into what the quest for the seven summits is like. Secondly, as the book is entitled *The Summit*, I wanted it to end on earth's highest summit, as well as on the one which has had perhaps the greatest impact on me that a climb could possibly have.

At the end of each chapter, I would like to offer a reflection on a subject pertaining to something I gleaned from the experience. A deadpoint is a climbing move where momentum is used to achieve a higher handhold, so these will be *Deadpoint Reflections*.

 I will call the struggle we face the **Crux**. As it pertains to climbing, the crux is the most difficult part of the climb. It will make or break the ascent, and usually is the piece of the puzzle that takes up residence in the back of one's mind begging the question: "Do I have what it takes to overcome this difficulty?" The crux will relate to "the climb" that takes place away from the rock and ice of the mountains, but in the heart and the struggle which is often daily living.

 The **Hold** will be the next portion that will serve as an answer to the crux. The hold is that which keeps you attached to the next piece of the puzzle, what to cling to, and what we need to utilize in order to solve the problem. In climbing, sometimes holds are as small as the edge of a dime and sometimes a truck can be parked on them; either way, they present the path for overcoming the crux. What is presented is just one hold, and just like in climbing, sometimes we need to be patient and wait for the next one to appear, or search for a better one. I know there are better ones, and more than what I present, but the key is to not lose sight of the anchor.

The **Anchor** is the support should the hold fail. I can think of no better anchor than a giant monolith of uplifted granite: the Rock. "The Lord is the Rock eternal," and is the one true anchor. This portion will give a scriptural answer to the crux, allowing the reader to look for a solid hold knowing the anchor above is solid.

There is a glossary in the back of the book to help with terms that may be unfamiliar.

Endnote
1. "Tenacious E," *Outside* magazine (December 2001), quoting Eric Weihenmayer, *Touch the Top of the World* (New York: Dutton, 2001), afterword.

Everest and Beyond

The Eight-Thousanders

The tallest of 14 mountains around the globe are referred to as "eight-thousanders" because they are taller than 8,000 meters. These are listed below from highest to lowest:

Name of peak	Location	Height in meters
Everest	Nepal/China	8,848
K2	Karakoram	8,611
Kangchenjunga	Nepal/India	8,586
Lhotse	Nepal/China	8,516
Makalu	Nepal/China	8,485
Cho Oyu	Nepal/China	8,201
Dhaulagiri I	Nepal	8,167
Manaslu	Nepal	8,163
Nanga Parbat	Pakistan	8,126
Annapurna I	Nepal	8,091
Gasherbrum I	Karakoram	8,080
Broad Peak	Karakoram	8,051
Gasherbrum II	Karakoram	8,034
Shishapangma	China	8,027

Climbing Grades

Grading climbing is a complicated matter, and people around the world are unable to agree upon a universal measure for difficulty. There is the American, French, Russian, Australian, Alaskan, Scottish, and probably Pig Latin system of rating. I will do my best to briefly give an overview of how climbs are rated. Nothing is worse than coming home from a difficult climb that required every ounce of strength, balance, focus, and determination, becoming one with a sheer mountain face only to have someone ask, "How was your *hike*?" Here is something about the two systems I have used to rate the climbs in this book:

Yosemite Decimal System (YDS)	The French Alpine Grading System
Largely in America and around the world people understand the Yosemite Decimal System of grading, which divides all hikes and climbs into five classes.	The French Alpine Grading System addresses the technical difficulty, length, and level of commitment required for a climb. It is a fairly common measure.
Class 1: Walking on flat, even terrain	F (Facile/Easy): easy angled snow and ice, with glaciated terrain. Ice axe and crampons are normally required. Not steeper than 35 degrees.
Class 2: Easy scrambling, occasional use of hands	PD (Peu Difficile/ Not Very Difficult): longer routes, scrambling on glaciated terrain of 45 degrees.
Class 3: Exposed scrambling, risk of fall, with increased use of hands	AD (Assez Difficile/Fairly Difficult): committing routes, steeper snow and ice at 55 degrees.
Class 4: Hands are necessary, potential for fatal falls, and rope may be needed	D (Difficile/Difficult): snow and ice with slopes of 75 degrees, use of two ice tools, very exposed, steep fifth class rock.
Class 5.0 to 5.15: Progressive scale of technical rock difficulty and further classified by a,b,c,d from 5.10 to 5.15.a. Rope and equipment become necessary to avoid fatal falls and severe injury.	TD (Tres Difficile/Very Difficult): Very serious sustained sections of ice climbing and difficult rock climbing.
	ED (Extreme Difficile/Extremely Difficult): Don't go here if you wish to go home.
	ABO (Abominablement difficile/ Horribly Difficult): Meant only for Yetis and Abominable snowmen.

Why? Why Climb Mountains?

"The answer cannot be simple; it is compounded of such elements as the great beauty of clear cold air, of colors beyond the ordinary, of the lure of unknown regions beyond the rim of experience. The pleasure of physical fitness, the pride of conquering a steep and difficult rock pitch, the thrill of danger — but danger controlled by skill — are also there. How can I phrase what seems to me the most important reason of all? It is the chance to be briefly free of the small concerns of our common lives, to strip off nonessentials, to come down to the core of life itself. Food, shelter, and friends — these are the essentials, these plus faith and an unrelenting determination. On great mountains all purpose is concentrated on the single job at hand, yet the summit is but a token of success, and the attempt is worthy in itself. It is for these reasons that we climb, and in climbing find something greater than accomplishment."[1]

---

1.   Charles Houston, K2, The Savage Mountain (Canada: The Lyons Press, 2000), p. 24.

Summit or Plummet

[Ama Dablam]

ELEVATION: 22,493 feet

HOW LONG TO CLIMB: Three to six weeks; as fast as one day to summit if sighted and acclimated

HOW MANY IN THE TEAM: Eight Americans and three Sherpas

RATING: D+, YDS 5.8

BEST TO CLIMB DURING: April to May (before the monsoon season) or September to October

ALSO KNOWN AS: Name means "Mother's jewel box" or "Mother's necklace"

Notes:

This is the 3rd most popular mountain to climb in the Himalayas.

April 2000: A team of climbers has been assembled for a climb of picturesque Himalayan peak Ama Dablam, with the purpose of using it as a springboard for Everest the following spring. One of the team members is blind.

For he will command his angels concerning you to guard you in all your ways; they will lift you up in their hands, so that you will not strike your foot against a stone. — Psalm 91:11–12

There are only three real sports: bull-fighting, car racing and mountain climbing. All the others are mere games.[1] — Ernest Hemingway

April 14, 2000, Day 29 — The relentless storm only added to the drama of retreating that day. With 4,000 feet of air below us, we would descend in what we call "full conditions," meaning the foulest of weather, over the jagged, rocky, extremely exposed terrain that now had a coat of ice and snow, not only on its surface, but on our ropes as well. It was slick, at least the parts angular enough to collect snow on that steep and often vertical terrain. Rappelling, climbing, slipping, sliding, and banging our way down the ridge in what at times was a whiteout, gave me a new perspective on what it would be like to be in my blind climbing partner, Erik Weihenmayer's shoes.

The three of us, Chris Morris, Brad Bull, and I, had just grunted our way from the 20,000-foot perch of Camp Two to the lower and more comfortable accommodations of Camp One at 19,000 feet on Ama Dablam. We were tired and very relieved to see our tents just yards away. My tent was one of the farthest from the fixed lines leading us down onto the platform terminating just before camp. My tentmate at this camp would be Dr. Steve Gipe, who had remained at Camp One as the team ascended. Dr Gipe's intentions were to attempt the summit from Camp One as the team fixed the route up higher, then later rejoin the team as everyone was leaving Camp Three for the summit. As I approached my tent I could almost feel the warmth of my bag and a nice cooked meal, and was already beginning to think of sleep. In fact, I may have been half asleep and daydreaming when it happened. Chris Morris said he thought I was a "goner" and Dr. Gipe kept yelling, "Stop! Stop! Self arrest!" Brad Bull started to pray. I know God heard his prayer.

Camp One is perched at the top of a 600-foot, mostly smooth, yet steep slabby rock face. If you are familiar with the rock formation outside of Boulder, Colorado, called the Flatirons, it would be similar to this with little blocky features that would give a falling person flight at times. I was ten feet from my tent and scrambling over the rocks, which were scattered all over the top of the face. As I made my final few steps to the tent, one of these rocks shifted, toppled over, and caused me to lose my balance and fall to my stomach on top of it. I was caught off guard to say the least, because I had stepped on this particular rock a number of times before, but it was my heavy load and the thoughtlessness of my step brought on by fatigue that caused it to turn over.

I felt like I was Coyote in a Roadrunner cartoon. My body started to drop, yet somehow my head seemed to linger in space. I hugged the rock and as I did, it started to slide over the edge with me on top of it. I knew that if I didn't let go I would tumble some 600 feet down, being crushed by this rock that was now in my arms. So I decided to let go, and take my chances, hoping that I would be able to grab on to the ledge in front of me as my feet began their way down. With gloved hands hitting the loose and partly snow-covered edge, I had no chance as my hands deflected like a soccer ball off the goal post in a botched goal attempt. This wouldn't be a completely vertical fall. I would, in some moments, be afforded the luxury of abrasive granite shredding me and my clothes.

My head smacked the rock, and as I began my freefall and slide for life, all I could think of was a series of four-letter words. Words like: "Stop! Help! Grab!" And then over again: "Grab! Grab! Stop! Stop! Help! Help!" Perhaps one or two other four-letter words were spoken, but I can't recall what they might have been. People often ask me what I was thinking in that moment. I have to laugh because it's not as though I could have paused in mid-flight and reflected on the matter, concerning myself with the various methods I would have employed to bring myself to a complete stop. In fact, I kid and tell them, "I was thinking what anyone would have been thinking: 'Do these pants make me look fat?'"

The fall was sudden and quick, yet it seemed to last all afternoon. I slid, crested a precipice, landed again on my belly not far below, repeating this endlessly during the course of my rapid plunge. Fortunately, I was still wearing my helmet, multiple layers of clothing, and my backpack, which at times padded me from the impact of the hard granite. During the course of this tumble, had I caught my foot on a ledge or begun to cartwheel, I most certainly would have fallen the entire distance to a rocky death below.

I believe very strongly that it was a miracle I landed on the small, coffee table-sized ledge 150 feet below Camp One. It was as though I was surrounded by angels, and the hand of God Himself caught me at that moment. I sat stunned in disbelief, waving my hand in the air, to signal to the team that I at least thought I was okay. I reached down and felt my legs, was glad to have them both, palpated my arms and knew they were not broken, and lastly, examined my head, at which time I confirmed that I had indeed lost it. The team up above, notably our Sherpa Pemba Galgen, threw a rope down to me. Pemba descended on that line, helped me to my feet and onto the rope. He then climbed up alongside me as I was able to "Batman" (tug and pull on the rope instead of the rock, like Adam West as Bruce Wayne in the original Batman TV series) my way back up to the tent.

Dr. Gipe put me into our tent and told me to lay low as he made dinner for both of us. Shortly after we ate I fell asleep, only to be awakened at 4:00 a.m. gasping for breath. I began to cough, knowing all too well that this was not a good sign, and rolled over to nudge Gipe awake. He put a small pulse oximeter on the ring finger of my right hand. This device, commonly used in hospitals, will tell not only your heart rate, but by shooting a beam of light through your finger is able to determine the amount of oxygen your blood is carrying. At sea level, most healthy people would have an O_2 saturation of between 95 and 99 percent. My O_2 saturation was near 45 percent. Clinically speaking, it's the next best thing to dead. Gipe told me at that moment what I already knew: that I needed to get down right away or I could die.

Meeting Erik

I could say that it was a blind person that got me into this mess, but that would be inaccurate. Erik Weihenmayer, my blind friend E. W., or Big E, as we like to call him, had merely invited me to be a part of this expedition to 22,493-foot Ama Dablam in the Himalayas; I was the one responsible for the mess I was in. I had met this blind adventurer a few years prior when I returned home from work only to be greeted at my door by a strange and giant German Shepherd named Seigo (pronounced see go). Erik had been invited by my roommate, Darol Kubacz, to crash on our couch after the two had spent the day skiing.

Darol, who broke his back in a motorcycle accident, is in a wheelchair and still skis with Erik, but does not ski as his guide. As Erik and I talked, we discovered a common passion we both shared for climbing. My first thought was that this guy must not know what he is talking about. He must enjoy hiking and maybe the occasional rock gym style of climbing. The funny thing is that he was sizing me up in the same manner. It was the middle of winter in Vail and the frozen waterfalls were well formed.

I invited Erik to come up again and join me out on the vertical ice in East Vail. I had worked with a number of blind skiers in the past and was excited to see exactly how blind climbing was going to work. I thought I would run Erik through the paces and maybe educate him a little bit on what real climbing is like, so I started easy. I quickly ascended an easy climb, less than vertical, and he quickly ascended right behind me. *Okay*, I thought, *This guy knows how to use the gear, but let's try something harder*. I set up a line on a harder, now vertical, climb right next to us and quickly he ascended that one, too.

The last climb was a super-skinny pillar, as big around as a ballerina's leg, which wandered upward, getting fatter and steeper until it ended 75 feet up at a powdery snow-covered break over. I went up and must admit that I struggled a little while breaking a sweat, delicately placing my feet on the pillar so as not to break it off and make the climb impossible. The sweat continued to linger on my brow as I now had a clear view of my thin 9.5 mm rope (about the diameter of a Sharpie marker) posing as a target for Erik's two sharp tools being swung wildly by a man who could not see. This is his lifeline, so if he should hit it that could be the end — of him and my rope. With a great deal of effort, he made it to the top of this challenging climb.

I asked, "Hey, what if you hit my rope? You sure came close, you know."

He said, "That's why I told you to keep it tight, because I can feel the pressure on my harness and then know the direction of the rope in front of me. When it looks like I am hitting the rope, I am actually scanning with my tools to feel where it is so that I won't hit it, but sometimes I miss. And if I miss, I'll buy you a new rope, how's that?"

I said, "But you'll be dead!"

He replied, "I'm good for it." This was the beginning of a great friendship and climbing partnership that would take me around the globe on expeditions often led by a blind man.

A little over a year later, I was again out on a climb with Erik. August in Colorado is not really the time that one is concerned with snowstorms; however, it is not unheard of to have a blizzard in August or even on the 4th of July. On this day, Erik and I were in the Elk Range near Aspen, and our objective was a route on one of the better-known peaks in the state; a steep and technical rock climb up the north face of Capitol Peak. Erik and I would hike the five or so miles in to the base of the peak the night before so that we could get an early start on the face, and planned on being off the peak before any storms hit.

As we went to sleep that night, it began to rain, dousing our hopes of climbing just as much as it doused the rock. When we awakened the next morning, our route was covered with snow and hail, making it dangerous if not impossible for us to climb. We settled for a later start on the easiest route on the peak — "the knife-edge." As we climbed slowly toward the summit on this beautiful, now snowy August day, my friend Erik and I began to get a bit cold, as we were not quite prepared for a blizzard of this nature. So standing at the edge of the knife, I made a decision to turn around and forego an attempt of this beautiful, prized summit. I figured I had three good reasons: first it was cold, snowy, and slippery; secondly, it was getting late in the day; and finally, my friend Erik is completely blind and that usually slows us down a little.

What I didn't know at this time was how this day and the decisions we made on this day would change not only both of our lives, but also make a dent in the history of climbing. On our descent we spoke of desires, dreams, and goals, of things we had done and mountains we wished to climb. Sliding our way down through the scree (loose, chossy rock on the side of a mountain which resembles thousands of chards of broken dishware) of little K2, which is Capitol Peak's neighboring summit, Erik told me of a man named Pasquale Scaturro, who was putting a team together along with Erik himself to go climbing in the Himalayas. To me it sounded exciting, the trip of a lifetime, of which I had always dreamed. I would wish him luck and be jealous of his adventure. I wouldn't get to go because I had never climbed in the Himalayas, or so I thought.

Just as I awakened from my daydream of the greatest mountains in the world, Erik asked me if I would want to be a part of his team. At first I thought maybe I should play it cool, saying, "I might have to think about it." Then as my heart attempted to pound its way out of my chest I said, "Does a one-legged duck swim in a circle? Heck yeah, I want to go!"

"We're going to try Ama Dablam, near Everest," he said, "and if it goes well we may even try Everest the next year." I was beside myself thinking of the possibilities, the adventure, the great fun it would be to climb halfway around the world with my blind friend, to think of new ways of moving over a difficult route, and to do something that no one had ever done before, possibly never even thought of before.

Erik and I packed up our wet tent and started the hike out, a bit frustrated that we had not made our summit, but now entertained by the idea of a warm meal and an amazing adventure. It got dark as we walked down the narrow trail, and at one point I led Erik right into a wash where he fell and slid down into the river below. I thought, *If I can't even get this guy down a mellow trail in Colorado, how on earth am I gonna get him through the Himalayas?* It seemed to bother me more than it did Erik, and at this point I knew that with a good attitude a person can go a lot further toward success than by focusing on the problem; keeping one's eye on the goal and not the minor setbacks, and looking past them to keep making tracks.

Throughout the following winter, we would get out on the ice in East Vail and climb its vertical frozen pillars as a means of training and getting to know others on the team. In those times of training, we would also discuss logistics, plans, budgets, and strategy; just another day at the office. I would bike, ski, climb, snowshoe, and run as a part of my training, and it was on one of those colorful fall runs through the golden aspen, which seemed as bright as fire, that I had a poetic moment, giving me this:

> *As the trees reach for heaven all afire,*
> *It is only the mountains all aglow that can reach higher.*
> *So as I run and live this story*
> *It is to God above, whom all creation sings the glory!*

The Team

Before we knew it, all our planning was done and it was time to hit the highway, to put up or shut up and go for broke. It was March 17, 2000, and after days spent buying gear, organizing, and then packing it into five-gallon buckets and army duffels, we were leaving on a jet plane for Katmandu, Nepal.

We would leave with an eight-man team, and one woman who was our Base Camp support. Half of the team I would be meeting for the first time on our flight over the sea. This could be a bit scary, climbing one of the world's great peaks with guys I had never met before, but it really allowed us to develop trust and learn to rely on each other's good judgment.

With the exception of Jeff Evans, Michael Brown, Charlie Mace, Sherman Bull, and Base Camp manager, Kevin Cherilla (these five would join us the following year on Everest), the team roster included the following:

Luis Benitez resides in Boulder, Colorado. He has spent more than half his life in the mountains, working both as a senior course director for Outward Bound's mountaineering programs and as a professional guide for Alpine Ascents International.

Bradford Bull is a level-headed architect and climber from Denver, Colorado. Brad had been on four previous Himalayan expeditions, summiting Mt. Everest in 1995, and the world's fourth-highest mountain, Lhotse, in 1998. Brad would be known on our team, and become world-famous, for his perfect hair.

Jeff Evans moved from the Blue Ridge Mountains of Virginia to the Rocky Mountains of Colorado when he was 18, and began his pursuit of high places. He has spent many seasons in the Alaska Range, guiding expeditions and working search and rescue on Denali, often known as Mt. McKinley. He is now a practicing physician assistant in Denver.

Didrik Johnck is a global citizen. Didrik would be the designated team photographer. After a successful climb on Cho Oyu in 1997, and running Base Camp for an Everest expedition in 1998, this would be Didrik's third expedition to the Himalayas.

Chris Morris, formerly of Wasilla, Alaska, now resides in Boulder, Colorado, where he works as a personal trainer. Chris is known for his endless energy and his ability to hop around from boulder to boulder like a chimp on caffeine, even at 20,000 feet. Chris also keeps heavy situations light with his ability to be positively pessimistic. An example of this would be speaking of how Erik climbs and saying, "He might be blind, but at least he's slow."

Michael O'Donnell hails from Ouray, Colorado. Mike comes from a guiding background with a lot of experience in big wall and ice climbing. He has climbed in nearly every major mountain range throughout the world.

Along with Adrian and Alan Burgess, he made a bold attempt on the south face of Lhotse in 1983. With his penchant for storytelling and his fiery Irish demeanor, he would keep us entertained over the ten weeks we were away.

Steve Gipe, from Bozeman, Montana, would be our team physician. Steve, at age 50, has worked as an emergency physician in Bozeman since 1984. He is also medical advisor for the Bridger Bowl Pro Ski Patrol, county search and rescue, and Jackson Hole Mountain Guides. Gipe is a slow-talking, slow-hiking freight train, and a friend to everyone on the expedition. He would take care of everyone's emergency medical needs no matter how small or how large, and was always there to dish out a dose of medicine and a dose of calm encouragement. He was an instrumental part of the team's success as a whole.

Pasquale "PV" Scaturro, of Lakewood, Colorado, was our expedition leader. PV has a story about everyone, everywhere, and everything. He has been there and done that. He tells so many stories that most of the time you think he is full of it, and just when you are about to call him on it someone will come down the trail, greet him, and say, "Hey, PV, good to see you. I haven't seen you since that time you tried to castrate that wild bull in Mozambique with your car keys!" A veteran of seven Himalayan expeditions, including summits of Mt. Everest, Cho Oyu, and Pumori, Pasquale also has over 20 years experience running and guiding white water rafting expeditions throughout the world, logging a number of first descents of rivers in Africa, which includes the first full descent of the Nile, which was made into an IMAX movie. Though he is of Italian descent, PV looks like he could be from anywhere east of Spain to the edge of Mongolia. With his thick moustache, unshaven face, and wild mountain hair, PV at times looked like Saddam Hussein after getting caught in a spider hole.

Kami Tenzing Sherpa was from Khumjung, Nepal, is a climber and our expedition sirdar and climber. We have nicknamed Kami the "King of the Khumbu," as he is known for leading some of the largest expeditions in the region. Kami is a very quiet and kind man who is able to procure just about anything at anytime in a place as remote as Base Camp.

Erik Weihenmayer is husband to Ellie and father to Emma and Arjun, living in Golden, Colorado. He is a writer, adventurer, and the first blind person to climb the Seven Summits: Denali, Kilimanjaro, Aconcagua, Mt. Elbrus, Mt. Kosciusko, Mt. Vinson, and Mt. Everest. Erik has become a great friend and consistent climbing partner in numerous adventures around the globe.

Kevin Cherilla, who was our Base Camp manager, is a physical education teacher at Phoenix Country Day School and lives in Phoenix, Arizona. Kevin is married and has two children. He has actually been back to Everest since our trip, and in the spring of 2007 made the summit from the north side as a part of a small international team. As we climbed the mountain, Kevin would keep us laughing, not always intentionally, by the nature of his comments over the radio from Base Camp.

Reba Bull was a helper to our Base Camp manager (she was aka Brad's newlywed wife). Reba came to help with the organization of Base Camp as well as to give moral support. It was a joy having her at camp not only because she was kind and supportive, but because she figured out high altitude baking and was able to make birthday cakes, pies, and other treats even at 18,000 feet on a slow-moving glacier — Martha Stewart, eat your heart out!

Michael Brown, from Boulder, Colorado, a filmmaker, director of "Vision of Everest," and three-time national Emmy Award winner for cinematography. Mike came on to the team originally just as a filmmaker, but as time went on it wasn't long before he was really a member of the team. The documentary he made of our Everest expedition, "Farther than the Eye Can See," would win him awards and honors internationally.

Kim Johnson Morris, from Boulder, Colorado, is a documentary filmmaker, and was the Base Camp camera operator and production manager for "Farther than the Eye Can See." Kim has worked on a variety of international documentary films, live television, and Web productions.

Charley Mace is both a climber and cameraman from Golden, Colorado. So far, he has summited three 8,000-meter peaks (about 26,250 feet), but this would be his first visit to Mount Everest. His photo graces the cover of this book. He was the first American to summit Manaslu (26,751 feet). He also climbed the Abruzzi Ridge of K2 (28,244 feet), and Gasherbrum II (26,355 feet). He is the very proud father of three: Steven, Kelsey, and Ben. Charlie has a knack for just appearing out of nowhere, and likewise has an affinity for speaking in the same way he climbs; that is, he can surprise you with a thought or a word from out of the blue.

The Sherpas were the unsung heroes and those who made up the remaining members of our team. Pemba Gyalgin, along with Kami Tenzing, would be our main help on the trip to Ama Dablam, and would again join us on Everest with Ang Pasang, Chuldim Nuru, Lhakpa Tsering, Ang Kami, Phurbu Bhote, Pemba Choti, Lhakpa Tsheri, Ang Pasang Lhakpa Tsering, and Ang Sona Sherpa. These men added strength, ability, calm, kindness, and the ability to work as hard as oxen to make our Himalayan climbs possible.

There was an air of excitement as the five of us from Colorado met at Denver International Airport all dressed in our Mountain Hardwear team jackets. Immediately, we bribed the personnel at the check-in counter with team t-shirts, hats, and books, hoping they would overlook the fact that our bags were oversized and overweight, thereby saving us some money for our expensive journey. We were very fortunate to have sponsors such as

The National Federation of the Blind and the now defunct Quokka Sports. Without this sponsorship and the hard work of Pasquale and Erik, the expedition would never have happened.

It was a 40-hour trip from Denver to Katmandu International Airport in Nepal, yet it didn't matter that we were tired because we were all so excited to be here, realizing a dream of climbing in the Himalayas. Back home, people often said we were crazy or didn't know what we were getting into, and tried to discourage us from going after our dream by saying things like, "Erik is going to die, and he is going to take you with him." I could guess, perhaps, these statements came from the fact that many people feared to live up to and pursue their own dreams, and therefore could not accept that a blind man might accomplish something that they would never accomplish themselves.

Other comments truly did come from sincere concern for all of us involved in this endeavor. The criticism extended beyond the average naysayer to well-known world class Himalayan veterans. John Krakauer even sent Erik a personal letter that read, "I am not at all enthusiastic about your trip to Everest next spring. It's not that I doubt you have what it takes to reach the summit. You've already shown that you have plenty of what it takes. It's just that I don't think you can get to the top of that particular hill without subjecting yourself to horrendous risk; the same horrendous risk all Everest climbers face, and then some. It's a totally different world above 8,000 meters. All kinds of things go haywire up there, and the consequences are so much more serious when they do." I can't fault John for saying this because at times I think every person who climbs at high altitudes must ask themselves, "What am I doing here? Am I crazy?" John Krakauer's experience on Everest alone, from the 1996 tragedy that claimed numerous lives, should warrant that he speak caution to anyone with aspirations of going to the "Death Zone."

While John said he wasn't enthusiastic about the idea, another famous Himalayan vet said he supported Erik, but thought the risks were so great he would want no part in it. I have to say that as a commercial guide, without the bond of friendship, I probably would not want to work so hard and take such a risk either. Ed Viesturs, the first American to climb all 14 of the world's 8,000-meter peaks, was quoted in a men's journal as saying, "More power to him, and I support his going, but I wouldn't want to take him up there myself. Because he can't see, he can't assess the weather or the icefall or the ladders you have to crawl across. There are areas where he will have to move quickly. Trying to dance through them will be very difficult. When I guide, I like people to become self-sufficient. With Erik, they will have to be helping him, watching out for him every step of the way. For me, the risks are too great. It will be the hardest ever guided ascent of Everest, if they pull it off."[2]

Ed was right. Erik can't see or assess the weather, but neither can most guided parties on big mountains and even guides get it wrong many times. Erik would rely on our judgment and be a part of the decision-making process. Erik was as self-sufficient as most climbers on the mountain, carrying his own pack and gear, standing on his own feet. I was just his eyes, never his pony — though there were times I would joke and tell people, "I got him up there by cutting holes in my pack for his legs to go through; an adult version of the baby Bjorn."

We did listen to the voices of doubt, but did not let them dictate the direction we would take, for we were all experts with the right amount of experience, and this told us that failure would not come because this was a crazy idea, but because we could not, or would not, work together to achieve our goal. It would be failure due to lack of cooperation either from the team or the weather — not from being blind dream-chasers. The criticisms, doubts, and fears of others, and even of ourselves, only added fuel to the fire of desire.

Still a question that remains for so many people is why would a blind man want to climb a mountain described as one of the most starkly beautiful mountains in the world, due to its dramatic and awe inspiring features, and how would a blind man live up to the technical challenges at over 20,000 feet? Erik had come a long way over the years and made huge leaps in his knowledge of the mountains and evidenced it by saying, "I knew being crushed by a refrigerator-sized piece of ice would be a bad thing."

As for the view that would come in many different forms along the journey, and the motivation needed, Erik said, "I climb for the pure love of it, but a wonderful side benefit is that it redefines people's perceptions about what is possible for blind people and sighted alike. I truly believe that if a blind person can be seen succeeding on some of the most arduous mountains in the world, it will do more than reshape people's perceptions; it will literally shatter them."

We would be climbing for the love of the sport and for the exhilaration of the mountains, not to be a circus sideshow telling the world, "Look what he can do!" Rather, what the world would see and perceive would just be a wonderful result of what we would hopefully accomplish. What excited me most was to be a part of something that would be greater than myself. We, as a team, would of course be committed to the climb, but even more so, we would all be committed to Erik and to the well-being of our team. Early on we realized that our success and our strength would be attributed to our ability to work together as a team for a common goal.

Walking off the plane and into the streets of Katmandu for the first time was a shock. The international airport was being renovated brick by brick, and all by hand at a snail's pace. We lugged our 50 huge duffels through the dirt to the bus that was waiting for us. As we made our way over, we were marauded by kids, beggars, and taxi drivers all trying to get a little bit of money to ease their pain; the average annual per capita income in Nepal is $218. The giving side of me wanted to hire each one, and almost allowed me to believe they all had good intentions. Then from out of the chaos arose some trustworthy faces, this we knew because the t-shirts they had on had the same logo as the ones we wore.

Faces, like that of Norbu, who had come to greet us, gave me a feeling of security so that I could relax and take in all that was going on around me. With bags sticking out all over and people crammed in the overloaded bus, we hit the streets of the city, making tracks for our hotel; a refuge in this off-beat city. Rickshaws and tuk tuks, bicycles, pedestrians, cars, cows, chickens, and goats all made the streets their own. In the middle of all this disorder would be a police officer waving his arms and blowing his whistle, dancing more to his own tune than controlling traffic. He looked to me like a man on a boat trying to control the waves in a storm at sea. After a few near misses, some fancy driving, and a few, "Oh, oh, whoa!" moments, we made it to our hotel, the Marshyangdi, with its fortified walls and its nice, little garden full of flowers and small shrubs.

Stepping inside to the faded sound of car horns made me smile, thinking that my first experience in a third world country wouldn't be quite as rough as previously imagined. We'd unloaded all the gear, found our rooms, taken a nap, and now it was time to go out and explore this wonderful, dusty place of Katmandu. Taking a right out of the hotel driveway into the narrow over-crowded street, I encountered a young teenage boy asking me, "You want hashish? I give good deal, best hash!" Before I could say no, he was asking another team member if they would want some; my ghastly look must have given me away as a non-sale. Two steps later it was the same thing, only this time it was, "You want tiger balm?" A few more strides and then, "You want . . ." something else and something else. It took all of about two minutes to learn to say an emphatic NO before the other person even opened their mouth or to give a distant glance as if you never saw or heard them give their sales pitch. Aside from the aggressive street people trying to hock their wares, I did find that the people of this city were indeed very friendly, humble, kind, and giving; something I would experience to a greater depth upon entering the mountains.

Early the next morning we all went for a run to the Buddhist stupa, known as Swayambhunath Temple, or as we called it, the "Monkey Temple," which resides high on a hill in the middle of the city. Legend states that it rose out of a lake as a self-created lotus flower, and similarly, the monkeys residing on its flanks came from the head lice of Manjushree Bodhisattva. Hitting the streets before all the vehicles and peddlers were out gave us a different perspective on the city. We saw residents cooking breakfast on the sidewalks, children in their uniforms preparing for a day at school, and butchers slaughtering goats in the streets. Running in this smog couldn't be too good for us, but for only a couple of days we could manage.

We ran up the steep wall of 1,000 stairs (365 in reality) that lead to the stupa. At the entrance we ran past concrete statues of Buddha with people prostrated before them. Behind these same statues we would see children sleeping on straw mats and our hearts would break, knowing that these kids had most likely spent a number of nights out on the streets and that their hopes were being put into these statues made of concrete that could never fulfill them. Monkeys screeching above us and chasing each other through the trees took our attention from the children out onto the streets and up the steps leading to the temple. The small monkeys would line the steps jumping onto people's backs, as if to assert their territorial authority, and were allowed to have their way because they are considered to be sacred reincarnated relatives.

I discovered the speed and grace with which some of the Sherpas climbed, soon almost believing myself that these had to be Chris Morris's relatives. Atop the stairs sat a large white dome with a towering stack of 13 blocks representing the path to enlightenment. With the painted eyes of Buddha looking in all four directions, this dome was surrounded by close to 100 small cast scroll-like wheels, the size of coffee cans mounted into the walls all the way around. These wheels are filled with prayers written on bits of paper, and when spun it is believed these prayers go to the heavens where they are heard. Many of the team took the opportunity to make clockwise circumambulations and spin these wheels, with Erik running his hands along the side of them to feel the shape and cast inscriptions.

Because of my personal faith in Jesus, I forewent the ritual of spinning the wheels, and instead quietly prayed for the people of Nepal, my team, and our safety. This was a religious ritual to an idol and not something that I could participate in. I didn't advertise the matter, and wasn't asked to participate, so no conflict ever arose. I simply felt that even in these small matters, thought to be of little consequence, I could honor God, so I sat back and took in all that was around me and had engaged my senses.

Erik had no trouble using the rest of his four senses to experience Kathmandu. It was alive with smells (pollution and incense), sounds (car horns, people, chanting, animals), tastes (Nepali food), and things to touch (prayer wheels, flags, monkeys, and dead rats in the street). From here we would run to the Hindu side of the city. It is the Hindus that really govern it, and with the king in power it is somewhat of a monarchical democracy, with Hindus making up most of the city's population.

Entering the Patan District, where the largest Hindu temple for Shiva exists, Pashupatinath Temple, really gave a quick snapshot of this culture when we saw, though first smelled, bodies being cremated in public. The bodies would be burned and then dumped into the Bagmati River; the same river in which children would be playing and women washing clothes. We wandered the area and were very impressed by the people we saw; some looking very authentic and some just out to make a buck. There were men with 27-year-old dreadlocked hair 30 feet in length, and other men painted, covered in ash meditating high on a wall or concrete block. Some were charging for a photograph of themselves. One even claimed to have had nothing to eat or drink but milk for the last 15 years of his life, calling himself the "milkman."

It would take us a couple of days in this city to get all of our permits, visas, trekking groups, and gear organized. We set up our tents on the rooftops and tied on new stronger lanyards by which to lash them down. We laid out all our fuel, stoves, climbing hardware, and compiled and inventoried all of it, packing it up in a suitable fashion for zopkios, yaks, naks, and porters to carry.

A couple of days in this city was plenty for me. It was time to trade the smog and congestion for clean air and unnamed peaks of 20,000 feet and higher. It would be a small plane that would carry us from Katmandu to Lukla at just under 9,000 feet. Flying in to begin our trek, we all sat cramped in the same small plane with our packs on our laps and nothing stowed under the seat in front of us. This "cowboy" style of flying didn't provide much comfort, as it demonstrated that the air service was just as crazy as the ground transportation.

Bouncing our way through the rough mountain air into Lukla, we caught a glimpse of the dirt strip that was to be our landing zone, perched on the edge of a huge precipice overlooking a valley; the entrance to these majestic peaks unlike any other range of mountains on earth. The landing strip, running uphill at an opposite angle from our approach, ended short of the town of Lukla, which was under construction and in the middle of a huge growth spurt. This airfield had seen its share of catastrophes, and Pasquale attempted to put us all at ease when he said, "Brad, dude; look at that! They cleaned up all the old plane carcasses that used to line the airstrip. Guess they thought it might scare away the tourists!" How nice.

We held our breath as we went in for the landing, and when the pilot pulled up the nose at the last second, turning what was our dive into a climb, he put us in perfect position to hit the upward-angling strip. We all cheered and clapped as we hit the dirt with huge grins and high fives, all of us feeling as if we had just landed the plane ourselves.

More spectacular than the flight in, and even the landing, was the first sight of these mammoth mountains. After we got out of the plane, I asked a Sherpa standing next to me, "What's that peak there?" pointing at what I thought was one of the greats.

He replied in a carefree tone, "Oh, it doesn't have a name." And thus I became acquainted with the Himalayas.

It was the first time we would meet a lot of our Sherpa support and porters. Sherpas are a tribe of people who years ago emigrated from Tibet to the
east. *Sher* actually means east and *Pa* means people. They occupy primarily
the high mountains of Nepal, and are known for their strength, endurance,
patience, and peaceful, humble nature. People often confuse the word *Sherpa*
as synonymous with the word *porter*. Though many Sherpas work as porters,
this is not the case. The job of porter is often filled by Sherpas and people
from the lowlands as well, sometimes young in age and rarely women.

In the city, many of our Nepalese staff were able to meet with Erik. They
thought the blind guy got along well enough, but for them this first day in the
mountains would be very interesting to see. As a team, we all knew that Erik
had already climbed Denali in Alaska, Kilimanjaro in Africa, Aconcagua in
Argentina, El Capitan in Yosemite, and Polar Circus in Canada — a resume that
would look good for any sighted climber — but this meant nothing to the Sherpas. Even though the Sherpas accepted Erik for who he was, and how he was, he
was going to have to prove himself on this peak if he was to get a shot at Everest.

We would take ten days to reach Base Camp, stopping in villages along
the way and staying in teahouses from time to time, though not exclusively,
as this is so often how people get sick in the mountains. Viruses are passed
from other trekkers and climbers as well as from the unwashed hands of the
cooks. A few days into the trek we found the comforts of home in Namche
Bazaar, where there now exists an Internet café and even a coffee shop. A
total surprise was to see the exact jacket I was wearing in a shop of this high
mountain village.

Moving forward, we went on up the valley passing Ama Dablam, heading instead toward Imjatse, which means Island Peak. We would really begin
the process of acclimatizing here with an easy ascent and later be able to
progress more quickly on the technical slopes of Ama Dablam. On day nine
of our trip, we would stop by the monastery of Tengboche. Here we would
spend one night, have a quick visit, receive a blessing, and then continue on
toward Island Peak Base Camp.

While here in this beautiful setting, a lama invited us in to the monastery
to observe a ceremony that was taking place. The setting was surreal, with the
ornately decorated building brightly painted, and standing atop a prominent
point, but still well below the backdrop of the icy domes and steely crags of
the mountains twice our elevation. The gate led to a courtyard where the
chanting monks and cymbals could be heard. Rising from the courtyard into
the dimly lit entry of the cold building was a long series of stairs. Here visitors
are asked to remove their shoes and quietly go inside, being sure to sit on the
floor to the side of the room. Here on the floor, visitors would be in a position

lower than the monks, elevated side-by-side on one long bench covered in pillows. The benches lining each side of the room faced in toward a vacant aisle.

At one end of this aisle was our group sitting on the floor near the door, and at the other end was a giant imposing golden statue of Buddha. Some of the instruments that the monks played reminded me of what I called noise-makers when I was a kid. Little drums, cymbals, a large gong, and a large drum all filled the room with sound that seemed to have no score or melody. I sat still and observed for as long as I could, but when the chanting began, I began to feel uneasy. The chanting is a deep guttural monotonic groan that seemingly continues on forever, with monks rarely taking breaths. It may be that they have trained themselves how to breathe through the process of making this chant.

To some, this experience is something of a beautiful inspiration, possibly even one of conversion. I have to admit, for me it was one of aversion. I felt my stomach knotting up, and a wave coming over me like the darkness of a storm. The air was getting heavy, and it became hard to breathe. This is called a spiritual place, and I agree it was spiritual, so much so that I had to leave. I quietly but swiftly got up, put my shoes on, and exited the gates of that place. Immediately, the heaviness lifted, my breathing became normal, and the storm clouds rolled away. I stood there pondering this matter and wondering how such an oppressive spirit existed in the midst of such kind, servant-like, humble, and genuine people like the Sherpas. Moments later I was joined by two other guys, trekkers, Jim Doenges and his friend Dave Lesh. I looked at them, they looked at me, and almost at the same time we asked each other, "Did you feel that?"

"Feel what?"

"That heavy, oppressive feeling that nearly took your breath away!?"

"Yes, that's why I left!"

"Me, too!" Then I asked, "Are you by chance a Christian?"

To which they both replied, "I am."

The Sherpas believe that there are mountain sprits and that Mt. Everest is the goddess mother of the earth. They believe that certain things must be done to appease these spirits for good living and for safe passage through the mountains. While I do not believe that Everest is a god in any form, I do believe that these people are indeed captive to many spirits; deceptive and controlling. This experience showed me two things: who my fellowship would be with on this trip, and the reality of what forces I could well encounter here in the mountains. Many people travel from the West for this religious experience, and many mountaineers are drawn in by the piety, karma, and teaching that it offers. I made it a point now more than ever to be reading the Scripture, taking Jesus to be what He said He was and is, "the Way, the Truth, and the Life."

To this point all was fine and I wasn't too worried about my sore throat slowing me down as we readied to depart the following morning for Island Peak's 20,000 foot summit. I was worried, however, about Jim Doenges, the trekker with our team who had developed a nasty cough, something commonly referred to as the "Khumbu crud."

March 29, Day 13 — Departing at four a.m. for the summit of Island Peak, we made good time and were up to our high point at 19,900 feet well before noon. By this time it was starting to heat up, and so was Jim's cough. He had to get down, as the cold dry air of this altitude was aggravating his cough, and I was amazed at the guy's toughness. It became so bad, in fact, that he broke two ribs just from coughing and the next morning had to descend to Katmandu, heading home earlier than planned so that he could heal and prevent further injury. At this altitude he would not heal, making a rapid descent his best medicine.

Island Peak, though we did not summit due to the poor conditions just below the peak, taught us a lesson about contentment, acclimatization, and obstacles. In a blind man's words, "It was a scree nightmare. I was thinking this peak might have been a little out of my element. If it was rock climbing I could handle it, if it was a snow couloir, no matter how steep, I could handle it; but this was jumbled-up steep rocks, and it was miserable." If he only knew what awaited him in the coming days.

Only two days of trekking away was Ama Dablam Base Camp. We were so glad to be on our way toward this magnificent peak and zeroing in on our real objective. It had been a long time both trekking and in Katmandu, and we wanted the good stuff. Making the final approach to Base Camp, coming down the trail in the distance, we spotted an old friend of P.V.'s and decided we would play a joke. I would pretend to be the blind Erik, and Erik would go on trying his best to not be noticed, posing as a sighted climber.

I stumbled my way up toward this Himalayan veteran, making sure to look like an idiot so Erik would be embarrassed. When he reached out his hand to introduce himself, I reached right toward his kit and caboodle at which he jumped and said, "Whoa there, friend, try my hand up here." I had a hard time keeping a straight face after everyone else started howling with laughter, so the trick was over at that point. This kept us laughing until we broke over the ridge onto the flat football-like field that was our Base Camp.

At first sight of this camp, my jaw dropped. In all of my years of climbing, backpacking, and traveling I had never seen such a great site as this. It was perfectly grassy, as if mowed on the weekends, flat and level with a small stream running right through it for fresh water, direct from perhaps the most beautiful mountain on earth. Now standing directly above us with its arms stretched out as if to embrace us and welcome us to its home was Ama Dablam. In Nepalese, *Ama* means "mother" and *Dablam* means "jewel box." The mountain stands tall like a mother and has a hanging glacier just below the summit, which looks like a locket of sorts earning its name as the jewel box.

The mountain also has two ridges going off in opposite directions, hanging like outstretched arms covered by a long, flowing white shawl of snow. Directing my glance downward from the summit, I now saw the camp coming into view — almost as impressive as the mountain itself was Kami Tenzing's creation of our little mountain village. On one end was the kitchen, made with walls of stone and covered by a large yellow tarp. Next to this was our dining tent; a MASH-style tent with tables and chairs inside. From here, stretching out in a semi-circle, were our eight individual tents, each suited for three people. The semi-circle ended in a large dome tent we called the "love dome," because it is where we communicated with the outside world via satellite phone and Internet, "sharing the love."

On bad weather days, it was big enough for us to be inside playing hacky sac, and cranking tunes. Beyond this, we also had a gear and food storage tent. Himalayan veteran Brad Bull described it as "the most luxurious and thoughtfully master-planned Base Camp that I have ever experienced. In fact, I think that Thomas Jefferson would be impressed," referring to our interpretation of Jeffersonian architecture and its implementation into our design. One added great feature is that the toilet tent was just far enough from our campus to make it accessible without worry of complications odiferous in nature.

Up to this point, I had been able to avoid the "Khumbu crud," and other ailments that usually cause one to run for the outhouse. The trip had been most impressive, and I knew that the most spectacular bits were still ahead. The climbing team and the trekkers who accompanied us had been getting along great, considering that we shared tight tents, teahouse rooms, and a small dining tent without much time apart. Instead of arguments typical of many large groups, most nights we would go to bed with a stomach ache from laughing so hard. For the most part, the weather had been great. Temperatures in the day were sometimes warm enough for just a t-shirt, ending in the evening with small snow flurries and high winds.

Having time at the Base Camp in such beautiful surroundings causes one to reflect a bit, and inevitably the question comes as to why we climb, and how success is defined. Climbing and the outdoors had always played an important role in my life from the time I was introduced to it as a teenager. It gives me a chance to play in and appreciate creation, to leave the worries of everyday life behind, and to focus on the task at hand step-by-step up the mountain. We are forced in this way to rely on others and just as much to dig deep inside for personal strength, and for strength from above in order to achieve success or just to survive, as I would come to find out later.

Some people think that choosing a blind climbing partner is unsound. Erik, however, is stronger than most sighted climbers I know, especially when it comes to mental toughness and maintaining a positive attitude, which in the mountains is the key. For us, obvious success would be to reach the summit, but we preferred instead to define the summit as teamwork; collectively making the best and safest decisions at the right time.

Everything was set, and the first carry to Camp One was underway. Half the team made the slow climb from Base Camp at 15,000 feet to Camp One at 19,000 feet, and then down again to Base Camp, which, all told, was a nine-hour day. While that half of the team was working hard to carry heavy loads up high, I was working hard below to digest my words. The night before, what I thought was a routine trip to the smallest of our tents became a violent attack of giving back to the earth what had come from the earth. All I needed to do was open the door to this small, smelly tent, stand inside, and hover briefly over the five-gallon, Hefty sack-lined bucket. Seconds later, I was sprinting out into the open, painting the lawn with all that was inside me.

The day before I was so proud of how I was one of the few that had not been sick, and now here I was unable to climb because of a stomach bug. The good thing was I was commiserating with Erik, who also had a virus with which he was wrestling with. Dr. Steve Gipe gave us a bit of Cipro, the Himalayan miracle drug, and soon we were ready to get outta Dodge and head for Yak Camp (the first camp on the way up, named after the high point to which our beasts of burden could carry; not after what Erik and I could potentially be doing).

We left for our ascent, with Erik, Gipe, and I staying at Yak Camp while the others would go on to Camp One. The next day they would try for Camp Two as Erik, Gipe, and I would negotiate the boulder field and 600-foot slabs below Camp One. Erik and I made it through the boulder field unscathed, which is amazing since this is without a doubt the hardest kind of terrain for a blind person to negotiate. Erik said, "If I really hated a blind guy, I'd drop him in the middle of this boulder field from a helicopter and say, 'Have fun.'"

Speaking rhetorically, he said, "Who talked me into this climb? Shouldn't I have done a little more research on this mountain and terrain?" He called me "patient" for getting him through this "1,000 feet of rocks piled on top of each other, ranging in size from baseballs to trucks, with treacherous gaps in between each one." I would tap my ski pole on each rock for him to hear where he should step and/or scoot on his backside just as often. He would hear the sound of the small bear bell I was ringing and it would give him an auditory clue as to the general direction to follow, along with my voice and verbal instruction.

Sometimes, due to these strong aural abilities, I joke and call him Batman. Climbing with his custom-made Leki poles, Erik would probe and jab, slide, scoot, and walk awkwardly across the field of boulders. Once we'd reached the slabs, smiles hit both our faces as I could see the tents above and the end of this nightmarish struggle to get there. I was worn out from the effort, and my patience was worn thin, just like my voice. As we strolled into camp, we overheard via the radio what the rest of the team was doing: fixing the yellow tower for our ascent to Camp Two. They would also set up some tents so the next day when we made our way to Camp Two, 1,000 feet higher, all would be established; one of the joys of teamwork.

April 7, Day 22 — It was a good night's sleep, considering we had a drop of 600 feet on one side and 4,000 feet on the other. I suppose it was due to the fact that we were so drained from fighting our way through the boulders below.

What for most people is the hardest part of the climb, and the scariest, is exactly the part to which my blind buddy was looking forward. I was also excited to uncover the more technical difficulties of the mountain. Moving away from Camp One, the terrain began to steepen and we would begin using ropes. Still with Erik, I helped him negotiate the terrain and let him know when to clip into the rope and when it was safe to climb without. It went smoothly and faster now that he could use his hands and feet to feel the rocks and had to rely less on the people and voices around him for guidance with every step.

Before I knew it, I was glancing up a vertical piece of rock that towered at the already obscene height of 3,000 feet above the deck. I knew these would be our last moves before we could settle in for sleep. Didrik Johnk described the sequence of moves just below Camp Two in this way, giving rise to a new name for this part of the route: Abject Terror. "The southwest ridge presents many climbing challenges including an intense traverse with one move we call 'letting it all hang out,' because you step out onto a wall with about 3,000 feet of air beneath your feet; there are two bomber handholds but no footholds. To make the move work, you must grab the handholds, let your butt hang out over the ledge, and smear the bottoms of your shoes against the vertical piece of rock. Some call this spot 'abject terror.' " For me, watching Erik negotiate this was indeed abject terror. I would hold my breath until he had completed each move.

Soon came my turn to trust that skinny bit of rope and climb in my big boots with a heavy pack. Just above this is a part of the route called the Yellow Tower, which in technical terms is 5.6 to 5.8 in difficulty. At sea level it would be a cruise, really pretty fun, but at 20,000 feet with a heavy pack, big boots, and no eyes (prosthetic anyway), it would be a little stressful. Here we began to practice something called positive pessimism, a gift from Chris Morris that would keep us amused for years to come. It works like this: One takes a bad situation or negative element and adds to it another negative situation, but saying it in a happy way that contradicts rational thought. Climbing the Yellow Tower with its aged skinny ropes we would say things like, "The drop may be 3,000 feet, but at least I can't rely on these weathered, old ropes." Another example: "It sure is cold, but at least it's windy!"

I would look up and offer suggestions to my friend saying, "Reach up, a little higher, now out left, six more inches. Trust me on this, lunge straight up for the hold!" In this manner we would move up the tower. Erik made the last few moves in such a way that I thought he had been yanking our chain about being blind. We cruised up the Yellow Tower without a hitch. From there, it was just a few paces to Camp Two. The best way to describe this place is to think of what the Base Camp was in all its glory and splendor, and think of the extreme opposite.

Perched on a little ledge thousands of feet above anything was our humble, little home. It was literally like camping on a cloud; a very small cloud. I looked at it and thought, *That is our tent, huh?* It has a rope right to the front door so blind Erik can grab it when he needs to take care of business, leaving the tent without making a wrong turn and meeting his Maker sooner than expected. At closer inspection, I noticed that one of the corners of the tent was not even touching earth. This observation led me to think, "Cool, Erik is blind. He can sleep on the left side (the side overhanging the abyss)." He isn't stupid, however. While I was out observing the scenery and the site, EW was in the tent getting situated, being sure to leave his foul and rotten underwear on the right side, which I would not touch, as he knew and admitted, forcing me to then take the left with just the thin nylon wall separating me from forever. As we made ourselves comfortable in our lofty abode, the rest of the team descended to Base Camp to get more supplies.

The team got down and the storm came in. Big E and I were pinned to the side of this mountain alone at Camp Two for what would turn out to be six long days. The pressure on me was extremely high. If the storm worsened, if I was hurt, or if one more thing should happen to him, that could be it. We had to be cautious, and just like any partnership, we had to share duties. I wasn't exactly scared, but I was well aware of the burden of responsibility this put on me. I also could not help but think of Erik's pregnant wife back home and how she must be feeling. Lucky for him he remembered his book on tape, which could take his mind off the stress of the situation.

Six days — and I had left any form of entertainment below, trying to keep the load light. No problem, I thought. Since the rest of the team is 5,000 feet below and can't climb in these conditions, I will take advantage of the solitude and the beauty around us. These are, after all, the most beautiful mountains in the world. How often will I get to enjoy such a view, and what a great place to contemplate the complex profundity of life. I sat outside the tent in the cold air and enjoyed what moments I got of the view through breaks in the storm. By day two, I was so bored I was pleading for Erik to share his book with me. It didn't help my cause when I made fun of the fictional book based on the old Roman Empire because Erik said, "Hey, I didn't exactly force you to read this. You can go back outside and contemplate life if you'd rather!" So I would shut up for a while and listen to the story, dozing off to sleep quickly. Given the altitude, a boring story is like being put under heavy anesthesia at the hospital, and is the reason I think he liked the story to begin with.

Being just the two of us, it became my responsibility to do all the cooking, cleaning, and camp management. Erik would go on short forays, gathering snow and ice to melt for water, which enabled us to cook and stay hydrated. I didn't worry too much that if he went the wrong way he could tumble thousands of feet. No, the camp was rigged with fixed lines, so as long as he stayed attached, there would be no problems. It was also by staying attached to these fixed lines that Erik could answer nature's call all by himself, and in answering that call one day, I took one of my better pictures of him and the view. Looking as though he was ready to take flight off the edge of the cliff, I thought EW was commencing a bombing raid on Nepal, and it turns out I was right. I got a picture of four cheeks, and he even cracked a smile. I still use the photo for blackmail to this day.

Earlier on, before the storm, the team had attempted to go higher and shuttle some gear and supplies up the mountain only to have to turn back, leaving a cache of food and fuel higher up the icy slopes. On our fourth day, our food and fuel began to run low and we needed to do something. Our only option was to climb higher and retrieve the cache. This was good, as we needed to stretch the legs anyhow. We took off with a rope and worked our way over the corniced cliffs to the place we knew the cache would be. With EW anchored to the bottom of the face, I climbed up the steep, choppy ice pitch, happy to find the food 75 feet higher. What a perspective it offered to climb higher and peer down over the dramatic and sheer west face.

We made our way back to camp, though at times I would get caught up in looking at the view, forgetting about the place where Erik may need to place his next step. I turned around to see him veering off toward the edge of a cornice and a bottomless void, and I calmly said, "Turn to the right just a little," knowing that if he had eyes he would have just filled his britches having seen where he was headed. There was no real grave danger since he was clipped in to the fixed rope, nonetheless, it sure keeps things exciting when your partner at 21,000 feet on a knife-edge ridge can't see a thing. Funny that this alone would put most expeditions into a desperate state of emergency, wondering how to evacuate the sightless one. For us, however, it was just business as usual.

We made it back to our camp, and to our surprise were soon briefly joined by a Sherpa who dared to brave the elements and iced-over slopes to bring us some more gear, fuel, and food. This also served as a mission to stockpile the camp, as the team would also soon be joining us. For me it was great because he brought me a little gift from Brad Bull — a copy of *The Hobbit* by J.R.R. Tolkien. I read it in no time, and from that moment on thought of myself as a Hobbit in a strange land on a strange adventure. The smell and the hair growth made this a very small stretch of the imagination.

Two days later, the rest of the team rejoined us at Camp Two to plan our bid for the summit. By now we had used a lot of our reserve food and fuel, and didn't have a lot of time to waste. Either a small party would go to the summit, taking their time while the rest of us went down, or we would all have to move upward right away. We chose to move on as a team, and Chris Morris took off leading the charge. For a couple of hours he struggled to push the route forward. But, with the new snows and the thin ice left on the rock from the constant melting and freezing, this was not easy and pushed the limits of the risks we would be willing to take on this expedition.

It was time to make a tough decision, and I am glad that it did not rest solely with me, because I would have wanted someone to reach the summit, if for no other reason, just to show the doubters back home that we could. Pasquale made the final call along with Kami taking input from the team, then said, "Fellas, we have done our best to climb this thing. I have never been with a stronger team, even on Everest, but as much as I hate to say this, it's over." Just that quickly, and without argument, we turned from this beautiful peak and began our descent, somewhat dejected but trying to remain optimistic.

Into my brain shot the words I was sure to hear upon arriving home: "We told you so! What made you think you were worthy to try a Himalayan mountain? Everest, not a chance! You couldn't even succeed on this lesser peak, how will you succeed on Everest!?" I put it out of my mind but was not at all looking forward to returning home having "failed." The reality of the situation, however, was that we had been terribly successful. Even with a blind climber, we had fixed 90 percent of the route for other teams, and as a team, we got along tremendously well. We had all put a Himalayan experience under our belts, and learned that we, as a team, had what it takes to succeed. It was the weather and conditions that contributed to our not reaching the summit, not our abilities or even blindness.

In the eyes of the world, success is so often seen and measured only in dollars, distance, time, firsts, titles, position, power, status, and summits, whether they be corporate ladders or mountain peaks. Our success had now been defined on a much more personal level of brotherhood and wisdom. We had become good friends and exhibited the excellent decision-making capabilities in extreme pressure situations. Without arguing or even raising voices, we cooperatively made the best possible decision: abandon the climb. Consequently, only two teams made it higher than we did. A Mexican team made it to Camp Three, but in the process two of their team members received concussions, and the other I believe to have been Russian, putting a man on the summit, though he lost a number of fingers to frostbite.

April 14, Day 29 — Engulfed in a storm, we began our descent from Camp Two to Camp One at 19,000 feet. I threw a rope down over the yellow tower from which we could rappel, and having just spent six days at Camp Two, I was one of the first ones down, along with Chris Morris and Brad Bull. Just as we made it to the bottom, the others who had been standing still in the storm with lighter shoes on began to succumb to the cold. Though we had just packed up camp, they decided to go back, and erecting tents once again, spend one more night. I felt bad for EW that he had to go back and make it eight days at this island in the sky. Meanwhile, the three of us fought our way down the slick rock and frozen ropes carrying extra weight, which pulled us this way and that, but at least it was snowing sideways.

This is when it happened. After a long day descending in these poor conditions with Brad and Chris, I was tired and relieved to be at a lower camp. Detached from the fixed lines, I was making my way across the slabs of boulders moving perhaps a bit less cautiously, excited by the prospect of a good night's sleep and a warm meal. Here I was, just steps away from my tent, when one of the boulders overturned beneath me, sending me into a fall down the steep rock face. Miraculously, after the 150-foot fall, no bones were broken or major injuries sustained. With the help of my team, including Pemba Sherpa, I made it back up to camp. It was during the night that my breathing became labored, and with the careful attention of Dr. Gipe, I was brought to the realization that my life was in danger and that I needed to descend immediately. Still tired from the day before, and now with high altitude pulmonary edema, this would not be easy.

High altitude pulmonary edema (HAPE) is a condition where fluid accumulates in small air sacks in the lungs, known as alveoli. The blood is able to seep out from the capillaries and into the lungs themselves, causing a person to drown in their own body fluid. The only cure is rapid descent and supplemental oxygen, and if left untreated, it is fatal. This should not be confused with HAFE, another altitude disorder from which everyone on my team was suffering, myself included. Though never fatal, HAFE can sneak up on unsuspecting people and is usually noticed first by those near the victim with a keen sense of smell, and not the victim himself. High Altitude Flatulent Expulsion is caused by the decrease of pressure on the transverse colon resulting in expansion of gasses and their immediate and often untimely release.

A helicopter rescue at this particular camp would not be an option due to the rugged terrain, altitude, and inclement weather. A descent of the very slab on which I had fallen would be my only way down. I began shoving my sleeping bag into the stuff sack, but this task proved to be too difficult and I knew I could not get down quickly with a heavy load. Gipe said, "Take only what you need, leave the rest here, and we'll take care of it." So I left the tent, and started to rappel down the long, steep slab of granite alone.

This wasn't a time to panic, and thankfully the words of Philippians 4:7 were in my heart: "And the peace of God, which transcends all understanding, will guard your hearts and your minds in Christ Jesus." Perhaps the strangest thing through all of this as I faced my mortality was that the words of that verse sank in and I was not afraid. I felt lifted up. Fear is what I naturally should have felt after death had now knocked at the door twice in two days. I could attempt to explain it away and say that it was my focus on the solution and what needed to be done instead of panicking on behalf of the problem. Really, I think that through prayerful intervention God gave me His Holy Spirit as a comfort. In those two days, He was beside me lending His peace.

I would descend 30 feet at a time, stopping to catch my breath, sometimes barely having enough strength, as I would get light-headed holding the rope tight below my belay device. I would pray, "Please Lord, give me the strength to get down, don't let me pass out here on the face." After what seemed like hours, I was finally down to the boulder field and traversed slowly through this half-mile section of rock that had been so difficult on the way up for EW to come through. Thinking of this, I could now relate a little bit more to his situation. Just after the boulder field, Gipe caught up to me, with bottled oxygen that we'd had stashed at one of the higher tents. Immediately I felt better as the pulse oximeter showed my O_2 saturation to now be 62. Together we walked down the remaining 2,500 feet to Base Camp at 15,000 feet.

By now the news had reached home via the Internet, and I knew for sure my family was not taking this well at all. It was the one time when I wished communications were down so they wouldn't know what just happened. The good part was that I knew they were praying for me. I crawled into my tent and tried to sleep. However, whenever I laid down the fluid in my lungs would begin to choke me and I needed to sit up. The fun thing about this was that as I would hack and spit up, I was discovering a variety of new colors that

I had never seen before. It would have made Walt Disney proud.

The rest of the team began their second attempt at a descent from Camp Two, to rejoin Chris and Brad at Camp One. They added the supplies of Camp One, including my gear, to their already heavy loads to complete the descent into Base Camp, finishing in a snowstorm late that same evening. After what proved to be a 12-1/2 hour day, we celebrated the fact we were all off the mountain together with dinner and a few beers. I abstained, going back to my tent, but could not sleep. I was sure my condition was improving, but in actuality, it was not.

Early the next morning, after a night awake reading the Psalms and hacking, Gipe assessed my condition and determined that the best thing for me would be to be placed in the Gamow Bag and be evacuated by helicopter. This hurt my pride as I was hoping to be able to stay with the team and hike out in style. A Gamow Bag is a 15-pound polyurethane chamber sealed closed by a zipper, invented by Colorado astrophysicist Igor Gamow. Only slightly larger than a sleeping bag when fully inflated, the bag creates an environment for the affected person that is pressurized and simulates a lower altitude, thereby reducing the swelling and leaking in the sufferer's capillaries, thus offsetting the symptoms of HAPE. It is a person on the outside who inflates the bag using a foot pump to a pressure of one atmosphere above the ambient air pressure (about 2–4 psi).

Speaking pessimistically in the positive sense; this device could save my life, but fortunately, no one had yet used it. I would be stuck in this small space for a few hours and was sure thankful for the fact I am claustrophobic. My fondest memory of these hours is peering out through the clear plastic window of the chamber and seeing my teammates reading the user's manual. With my altimeter watch on, I could see now that we had this life-saving device working, and that it was as if I was descending thousands of feet. In all but the most severe cases, symptoms will clear up in a couple of hours inside the chamber. After two hours, mine were not resolving.

As I lay helpless inside listening to my walkman, I could hear over my music the loud shouts via the radio in Nepalese between Kami Tenzing, our climbing Sirdar, and the company that operates the rescue helicopters. The shouting match lasted for half an hour, and was terminated when the helicopter pilot agreed to fly into our Base Camp in spite of the storms, which were still lingering in the area. I had a hard time believing that I really needed a helicopter rescue and thought that I could hike out the 20-plus miles to Lukla for a flight to Kathmandu. I kept these thoughts to myself, as I knew I must be somewhat delirious and probably did not hold the best judgment, therefore leaving this decision to Pasquale and Gipe.

Strange as it may seem in the midst of all of this, I felt deep inside that everything was going to be fine. I can attribute this to a good team that worked tirelessly and was concerned for me, but more so, to the fact that people at home were praying for me. My family and my church were praying, and God was granting me the benefit of their requests. First Thessalonians 5:17 says, "Pray continually." Should it really take this to get me to do so?

The next year, when I saw Kami in Colorado, he shook his head and looked at me in disbelief, remembering how the events transpired after this. He could not believe even a year later how I was retrieved and flown from the mountain. It was the second miracle of the trip for me. As the helicopter entered Base Camp, the still unsettled sky cleared, giving the pilot a narrow window of opportunity to land in what was otherwise poor conditions. With the help of my teammates, the Gamow bag was unzipped and I ran to the helicopter with only a few of my things and Cynthia, our Base Camp assistant manager; she was going to look after me in Kathmandu. As we flew away, the sky again closed up over camp. In the mountains, a clearing like this is often referred to as a sucker hole. It means you are a sucker if you chase the summit with only a hole in the clouds to ascend into.

As we made the three-hour flight to Kathmandu, I would look out at the giant peaks, and even back down at the trail we had come in on, with a feeling of shame. "Loser! Lame! Letdown! How could you do that?!" were things I would shout to myself inside my head. I could not help but feel that I had been a burden and had let the team down, as well as letting down my friend Erik. I was disappointed in myself, for needing to be a strong climber, I fell. I could understand if blind Erik had fallen, though if it were due to a fault of mine I would never have been able to live it down. But me; how could I fall? I was really beating myself up; I let me "have it good!"

I checked in to the Hotel Marshyangdi and promptly went to the hospital for x-rays, which showed there was still fluid in my lungs. By now, my O_2 saturation had gone up to 89 but the hospital still wanted to keep me overnight for observation. I hyperventilated before the nurse came in for the next measurement to give her a false reading so that she would let me go. Ninety percent is the cutoff; if your O_2 sat drops below this, you are required to stay in the hospital until it gets higher. I really did not want to stay in the hospital since our hotel had hot showers, there was pizza to be eaten, and sleep to be had. Besides, I had just spent a lot of time on the mountain living just fine with an O_2 sat in the 80s, so this was nothing.

April 19, Day 34 — Upon arrival back home, I was certain this was the end of my high-altitude climbing career, and if not, certainly the last time I would climb with this team since I felt like such a failure. It was nice to have had the chance, but now it was all over. To be honest, I felt somewhat relieved.

Deadpoint Reflections

Nobody trips over mountains. It is the small pebble that causes you to stumble. Pass all the pebbles in your path and you will find you have crossed the mountain.
— Unknown

The mountaintop is not meant to teach us anything, it is meant to make us something.[3]
— Oswald Chambers

Crux: Success. Three of my most notable successes in the mountains have come from climbs in which I did not reach the summit. I believe all too often in our culture, standing on top of that proverbial mountain is what defines success more than anything else. We define success by winning, earning, status, achievements, possessions, by having well-behaved children who get good grades, by how we look, and even by being well known or well liked. An accurate measure of success is to look at results based upon the goals we set for ourselves. I pride myself on being a safe climber, and safety is my primary goal on any climb, superseding summits, and not influenced by financial investment or reward.

May of 2007, on a climb of the Maroon Bells with my blind friend Erik, we spent hours driving, then riding a fully loaded tandem bike with a trailer carrying all of our climbing gear to then sleep at the trailhead, hiking miles in to the peak in darkness, and then climbing to 13,500 feet. There we were greeted by funky May weather just shy of the summit. Erik was driven and wanted to continue to push on toward the summit. I wanted it too, but looking through the saddle of the Bell Cord Couloir, I could see the squall coming and he could not. I would need to make a decision and he would have to live with it, not really being able to provide much input. I knew the rugged terrain above would slow us down and though it was still early in the morning, turning around at this moment was the right choice. I could discern that Erik was disappointed and frustrated, questioning my decision. I was disappointed too, and really had no guarantee that this weather wouldn't just blow over. We headed down the steep, snowy trench, and just as we removed our crampons at the bottom of the slope, a loud, thunderous boom filled the air as a crack of light flashed around us. Hail and rain began to fall, and we hustled to get down below the tree line. High on the ridge of this peak, bolts like these are often fatal. We made the right decision, we got down safely, and it was a success as defined by my goal of being safe. We don't always get what we set out for on the first attempt. That is one thing about success — unless we set our sights very low, it does not come easily. One year later we made the summit of this peak by the same route and were able to experience the beauty of this climb again. I think the summit was even sweeter due to the fact that it did not come easily.

The other climb I consider a success is Amadablam; a success because it knit our team together and showed the team's character, communication skills, selflessness, and lack of greed for the summit.

Finally, on a climb of Kilimanjaro, I saw four blind students make the summit while I remained behind at high camp with two others who had become ill. Success for me was doing the thing that was best for everyone else and stuffing my pride, which wanted to say I was responsible for their summit. The truth is that they were the ones who carried out each step courageously.

Hold: We must understand that life is a process that God uses to refine and reshape us. We should set goals and be willing to adjust them as life comes at us, and as God reveals the chart for our course. We need to seek and live by success as God would see it, and as more than an accumulation of trophies meant to impress others. God gives us ambition and puts desires in our hearts, and success is not letting the pursuit of those things rule our lives.

Anchor: This is what we can hook, clip, and tie ourselves onto, being confident in its security. What would biblically defined and exemplified success look like? What makes a person a successful Christian? "Love the Lord your God with all your heart and with all your soul and with all your mind and with all your strength. The second is this: 'Love your neighbor as yourself.' There is no commandment greater than these" (Mark 12:30–31). Biblical success shows nothing of being perfect; rather it is the humble acceptance of God's grace in admission of sin and failure. That is step one. Step two is living a life of obedience out of love, revealing an effort to emulate godly character. It is a process of relationship, striving, and refining.

Endnotes

1. Historically attributed to Ernest Hemingway; research also shows the source might possibly be "Blood Sport" by Ken Purdy, which originally appeared in the July 27, 1957, edition of the *Saturday Evening Post*.
2. "Tenacious E," *Outside* magazine (December 2001), quoting Eric Weihenmayer, *Touch the Top of the World* (New York: Dutton, 2001), afterword.
3. Oswald Chambers, *My Utmost for His Highest* (New York: Dodd & Mead Co., Inc. 1935), October 1.

Into the Gray

[**Mount Everest**]

ELEVATION: 29,035 feet

HOW LONG TO CLIMB: Seven to ten weeks

HOW MANY IN THE TEAM: My team had 23 which included 10 Sherpas

RATING: AD; YDS AI 2

BEST TO CLIMB DURING: April to May (before the monsoon season) or October to November

ALSO KNOWN AS: *Chomolangma* or *Qomolangma* means "Saint mother" in Tibetan and *Sagarmāthā* means "Holy mother" or "Saint mother"

Notes:

The tallest of 14 mountains around the globe referred to as "eight-thousanders" because they are taller than 8,000 meters tall.

"For I know the plans I have for you," declares the Lord, "plans to prosper you and not to harm you, plans to give you hope and a future."
— Jeremiah 29:11

I went to the woods because I wished to live deliberately, to front only the essential facts of life, and see if I could not learn what it had to teach, and not, when I came to die, discover that I had not lived. I did not wish to live what was not life, living is so dear; nor did I wish to practice resignation. The mass of men lead lives of quiet desperation and go to the grave with the song still in them.[1]
— Henry David Thoreau

Re-entering the states was not a fun time. It was nice to have the comforts of home and of loved ones, but this was overshadowed by all the questions and concerns people had and then the doubts that I too began to have. People would ask why I wasn't roped, and what if I died, and what about this and what about that; all these questions making me feel like an utter failure. It was really bad when a person who had spent time on Ama Dablam would say, "I know the place you are talking about, that would stink to fall there. How exactly did you fall there?"

I would reply with, "Yes it did, and I am still trying to figure it out." In fact, after giving a presentation in Crested Butte, a man approached me with some photographs of a helicopter rescue on Ama Dablam. He said, "Here, you can have these. I think they are of you." He had been at Base Camp during the rescue. He added, "I didn't think they would be able to land a chopper considering the weather; you got lucky." No luck about it, I was blessed.

This mountain gets climbed with some regularity and I know my skills are greater than what this incident would surely communicate, but this is hard to convince people of, especially Mom. Most would not be overly quick to judge me, especially my team, which I would later find out. On this climb of Ama Dablam, I had placed my trust in the Lord and I knew that I would need to seek His help for strength, guidance, wisdom, and patience. I had been taken care of well, and in the fall did not cast any blame on God. During the entire event of the past spring, I never felt overwhelmed by fear but was soothed by the confidence of knowing that, dead or alive, I would be taken care of.

It is amazing what peace and assurance there is in knowing, not assuming or believing or guessing, but actually knowing that my fate was and is in God's hands. I would realize this again over the next eight months as I recovered from what had now turned into pneumonia. The fluid in my lungs from HAPE had caused greater problems because of a virus that I had as well, thus causing the pneumonia. Visiting a doctor here in the states for a second opinion I thought was a good idea, and sought out a specialist in Boulder to see how I might best recover. During these months I was able to climb, ride, ski, and stay active, but not at all near the level for which I had hoped. Each time I would try to push myself, I would only get frustrated by the meager pace I could keep or the short distance I could cover.

I did take some time off to rest and recover, but couldn't keep that up for long without becoming restless. At this point I didn't think I would be going to Everest, so it didn't really matter what I did or if I trained, I just wanted to feel better. On one particular bike ride here in my home of Vail, I was heading up over Vail pass pushing hard, but not like I once could. Upon reaching the point where the real ride begins, I was forced to pull over due to a sudden inability to breathe. I got off my bike and it was all I could do to keep from falling over and passing out. Ten minutes later my heart rate had dropped, my vision cleared, and I could breathe again. I knew I had better give it some more time before trying again. I was done, off the Everest team, and inside I really thought this would be the case. I needed to work but wasn't willing to settle into a desk job as I still wanted to be outside and pursue something active which would help me to stay in reasonable shape.

I got a job as a ski instructor at Beaver Creek, working primarily with people who had disabilities since I had experience as a guide for blind skiers from years past. This would provide me with a free ski pass and give me a chance to be outdoors, enjoying people that indeed had challenges in their lives that most of us never have to face.

That winter at Christmas time, I met a boy of 14 who had severe MS. I was asked to ski with him because it could very well be his last day to ever ski. His disease was in such late stages that he could barely hold his own head up, and he could not ski under his own power or even balance without help. We would transfer him from his wheelchair to his monoski, a bucket like seat attached to a single ski beneath which it can be held upright by a guide, or used with outriggers on the arms, if the skier has the strength. We were off.

My job wasn't to teach him to ski better or to even entertain him, but to give him a feeling of freedom that everyone needs to feel at some point in their lives. I spent the day skiing with him, and when I heard him laugh and saw him smile from his monoski, which I was guiding and keeping upright, I knew this day really mattered to him. When we had finished the day, greeted by his family who showed their tremendous support, it was apparent that he knew, and that they were aware, that he had just lived a dream.

Climbing Everest had been a dream of mine since I was a little kid. I had heard the stories, seen the pictures, read the books, and wondered if some day I would have what it takes to do that. It was the place of legend, not a real place, and I was afraid to dream a dream as big as that mountain. When I was in elementary school, my dad came home one day with three very large prints he had won at a golf tournament. Each large silver frame was filled with a print that had a title and a pencil sketch below of a climber dressed in the garb of the Hillary era. He hung these prints on the wall, not realizing I would see them and dream of being like them. The first print said "PRE-PARE," and showed two men stuffing their backpacks with gear and going over their oxygen systems, while the mountain loomed in the background. The second print proclaimed "ASCEND!" The two figures were swinging an axe into the ice, roped together, their fates dependent on each other. Engulfed in a storm, the peak was no longer visible. They were now entrenched in battle, the climb of their lives. So many of us long for a battle like this in our lives and never seem to find it by pushing papers. Instead, we find it in TV, or the heroes of the silver screen as a form of escape. These are the people living the adventure and fighting the very battle I wished I could fight, for this battle would demand everything from me. Choosing not to face it, I instead looked longingly at the picture of the climbers who were proving that they were man enough to defeat whatever the enemy is or was.

The third print stated boldly: "TRIUMPH!" A climber stands alone next to the flag, obviously on the summit of a great mountain. Eyes wide open and breathing hard, I would snap out of the dream that had me standing there in the cold and wind holding that flag. It had taken a team effort to get there, but each person had to make it on the strength of his own legs. The battle had been won. Thinking of these prints and of the battles that many of my students faced, and the one that EW would be facing, I couldn't let the dream die. The feeling of hope and possibility would awaken inside again. I would share this desire with my closest friends.

Throughout the winter I would meet with a good friend of mine to shoot the breeze, pray, and climb. His name was Joseph Chonko, and these times would be great times of encouragement for me. He had a gift of making others feel important, loved, and more capable than we really were. The funny thing is he would believe his own misconception of others, so much so that others would start to believe them, too. He would tell our friends that I could climb 5.11c rock in my plastic boots and was a real "hardman."

In climbing, the term *hardman* refers to one who could eat rocks and poop sand, one that won't get rattled easily, and is always ready to take a challenge head on. If I wasn't careful, I just might start to believe him myself. I know all too well that the only time I will free climb 5.11c in my boots is in my dreams. It was his enthusiasm and faith in me that got us both up a number of climbs because his passion was infectious. Other times we might make the trip all the way to the crags and get so involved in conversation it would never matter if we didn't even climb, and sometimes we wouldn't.

Our friendship became very close, and Joseph became my biggest supporter. He would tell me that I had to go to Everest, or at least try. "I'll be your porter," he'd say, "yeah, your own personal Sherpa. Shoot, I would do anything to have a chance to go to the Himalayas even if it just meant schlepping gear for you." Only one and a half years before I had taken him on his first ice climb up the snake couloir on 14,000-foot Mt. Sneffles, where we had hid from lightning all morning and made the summit later in the day, putting a crowning moment of glory on his birthday event. We would later climb a number of peaks, towers, and icefalls together, building a great friendship.

It wasn't climbing this friendship was built on, but rather a deep faith in God, and it was through climbing that the two of us could easily connect with each other, but more importantly, connect to God. Joseph was indeed very human with his long, brown ponytail, tattered flannel shirts, and torn jeans, which would hang low over his faded brown army boots. However, in spite of his outward appearance, he was godlier than almost anyone I had ever met, and had a deep, earnest desire to seek truth in everything. He sought God and knowledge of God daily. He read the Bible and most impressively, took it to heart and practiced what he preached.

The great thing about Joseph was that you would never know he was preaching by his words, only by his actions. Passing by the skate park one day he saw a local kid without a helmet. He had obviously taken the time to get to know this kid before and was concerned since the kid wasn't yet much of a skater. He chatted with this ten-year-old boy and then said, "Come on down with me and lets go find you a good helmet." In my mind I was thinking, *Come on, man, we've got other stuff to do*, but this was important to him and he took some time out of his day to help this little kid. He was like this every day with everyone. Motives always pure, never second guessing, just doing what he could to serve another.

Besides climbing, studying the Bible, helping others, and skating, Joseph's passion was snowboarding, and for a guy who came from Pennsylvania and didn't really know what a mountain was, he became good very fast. In fact, it wasn't long before he was doing inverted aerials off cornices and becoming bored with the inbound terrain that Vail had to offer. He went looking to the out of bounds terrain to quench his thirst for adventure.

I think this is part of the reason I liked Joseph so much. Not much for conventional thinking, he was always looking for answers to tough questions and wouldn't accept a textbook answer. He had to find out for himself, and in any number of ways. He was really a non-conformist, not the kind that would non-conform together with other non-conformists, but a guy that had his own sense of style and being, who didn't care about what others or the culture might have to say about it.

My friend didn't own a car, here in the mountains, for the first five years I knew him, and the great thing about him was that he never made this someone else's burden. He was always eager to catch a bus or a ride to somehow ease the trouble of his friends. When he finally did save enough pennies to buy a vehicle (believe me he did, he knew every dollar by name and knew its destination and purpose as well), I was beside myself, if not a bit sad thinking that the old Joseph had gone. It seemed somehow, in my mind, to spell the end of the free-spirited, independent Joseph I knew and loved. This was odd because for most people, especially we Americans, the automobile does exactly the opposite. We can't wait to get our first set of wheels because it will mean freedom, exploration, and independence, with the promise of a more convenient life. Joseph had all these things without a car. He was happy living in this manner in the midst of the Vail Valley, a very wealthy community, and that was perhaps the most impressive thing of all about him. He was not influenced by *things*, and was able to ignore the pressures of a very materialistic place.

It was a way that I wished I could live; to let go of all the material things that tie us down and focus on the things that matter, such as community, neighbors, friends, and passion for the things and places you love, therefore creating those deeper relationships and not just deeper pockets or deeper garages. As much as I admired him for this quality, I was also driven crazy by it. When it came time to buy a necessary piece of climbing gear, he wouldn't just go to the nearest shop and get something that would suffice. No, he would have to weigh each piece by each brand, study the dimensions, capacities, weights, and then write a new algorithm to figure out which one he should buy, factoring in which place would have it for the lowest price, and coinciding with the maturation of the funds inside his piggy bank, so that he could afford to buy the perfect piece. Each purchase was exactly calculated to be the purchase of a lifetime based on need, and not lust fueled by marketers or instant gratification. Perhaps this is why his methods drove me nuts, because I was, and still am, less able to do this, and often fall victim to a slick scheme.

Joseph could see from a mile away when a woman was no good for him, and/or no good at all, and unless it had to do with his interests directly, he would keep his mouth shut. I was the opposite, being unable to tell when to stay clear and then opening my mouth in the affairs of others when it was not really my business. Even when your motives are good and "wounds from a friend can be trusted" (Proverbs 27:6) are the words you cling to, sometimes it is better to hold the tongue, which can do far more damage than a closed fist. Though he was younger than me, there was much to learn from my wise friend, and though he never knew, I did learn a lot from this very gentle, yet rugged and tough guy.

I learned about his passion for the Lord most of all, and was always encouraged by his insights, and the depth of the personal relationship he had with Jesus. His tenacity in study was stronger than that in climbing. And as I saw it was futile to spend days figuring out a boulder problem that got one a mere ten feet off the ground, he saw something else in it; in the same way, when it came to rereading a seemingly empty Scripture verse, he saw something else in it. There were always answers in Joseph's world but they were never easy to come by. Sometimes I still struggle with finding these answers and use the very tenacity that he possessed in an attempt to put it all together.

On the evening of January 29, 2000, I received a phone call from a rather distraught roommate of Joseph's, and mutual friend to us both, named Jeff Cerovich. Jeff called me as he had been calling all of Joseph's friends that evening, asking if he was with us or if he had been by, because Jeff had received a call from the ski shop where Joseph was working at the time. The manager had called their home looking for Joseph, since he was now a couple of hours late for work. I told Jeff I hadn't seen him all day and had no idea where he was, remarking on how unusual it was for him to miss a day of work, or to be even more than a few minutes late.

The times I had climbed with Joseph, when we would race back to get to work on time, he would always stop to call and say he would be late, and he never forgot a shift. It worried me a little, and I thought he must have just grossly underestimated the time of a back country trip and had no way to contact anyone. Then Jeff said he was last seen with some friends riding Vail Mountain and made mention of going home by way of the East Vail chutes. With this comment, my pulse began to race and my mouth dried out. Apparently, this had become Joseph's new way of commuting home from a day of boarding on the mountain to avoid the bus ride. He never told me he was doing this, knowing that I would scold him for going against his better judgment and knowledge of back country protocol, which is to say that you never descend alone. Joseph would go to the mountain by bus, board all day, descend the chutes to his home in East Vail, where he could then eat and go to work catching the bus just outside his door.

If indeed Joseph truly had descended the chutes by himself and had not since returned home or even to work, I knew that he was most likely in trouble. Jeff called the sheriff to alert them of the situation, and to ask if there was any information or sign of him otherwise. The sheriff's office said no, but that they would be able to commence search and rescue operations the following day sometime. Having spent five years on the Vail Ski Patrol I knew this out-of-bounds terrain fairly well, and also knew that if he was having a problem it would not look good for him as night was now well upon him and the temperatures would be dropping to single digits, if not below zero that night. Jeff and I rallied with two other friends, Amon Schwanger and Brian Taylor, in an attempt to survey some of the chutes that night.

With almost a foot of fresh snow and complete darkness, there was not a lot we could do from below other than hope. I held on to this hope that Joseph had injured a leg with a break or a couple of torn ligaments and was having to crawl out on his own, or perhaps he was buried in an avalanche, yet still able to breath. I kept thinking only of the scenarios that would lead to the possibility of him being alive. When a thought contrary to that would creep into my mind, I was quick to snuff it out; after all, it was still likely that he was not even out there. Jeff and Amon threw on their snowshoes and headed up on one of the chutes as far as they could with their headlamps beaming into the snow and darkness, all the while yelling and listening for a reply, faint as it might be.

Brian and I got in my truck and headed for some of the other chutes, doing the same thing, but to no avail. Our search at night with such a huge amount of land to cover would be in vain. It was hard to sleep, thinking that we should be out doing something, but there was nothing more we could do at that time. As time passed, we all became much more serious and determined about the search, knowing for sure that something was wrong and that there would now be no other explanation, save for him waiting out the night for a rescue the next day. Before the sun rose, I called a couple of my old ski patrol friends to see if they would be willing to go in to work early to help me search. They made a few calls to the director, and as the sun came up we were heading down the interstate looking for signs of an avalanche while others were on their way in, gassing up snowmobiles for us to take up the mountain.

Ski patrolman and friend, J. P. McInerny, and I saw no evidence of any slide activity anywhere in the chutes, which led me to believe that Joseph must have only hurt himself and was hunkered down somewhere waiting out the night. We came back to the lower patrol room where we met a few other patrollers and Tim Panza, another friend of Joseph's, who knew better than anyone where he would have gone and what possible routes he may have taken, since these two boarded a lot together. Well before the lifts began to run, Tim and I were being towed behind a snowmobile, up to the top of Outer Mongolia Bowl on Vail Mountain by way of Mill Creek Road and Mushroom Bowl for fast access and the possibility that he had struggled to find his way down to this road, as it serves as an out for many backcountry skiers and boarders.

The sky was clear and beautiful that morning, and the snow that had fallen the day before was still pristine, due to the fact it was bitter cold and extremely still. The sky was full of sundogs, crystalizations in the air that act as small prisms, diffracting light through the cold. It made this somewhat surreal as we made a game plan and awaited final approval from the sheriff for the ski patrol to descend out of the ski area boundary for the purposes of rescue. (I knew from prior experience that mountain rescue was not the group I wanted to trust in this effort, due to the bureaucracy it entails in order to get them out searching. If anyone is to have a chance of surviving an avalanche, minutes are all they have and Joseph had used his.)

Tim and I would not wait, and began to search out all of the tracks of different parties that had descended the previous day. We would see a party of three heading off in one direction and eliminate it by seeing that it had been three skiers, and then another set of two going together. Knowing that Joseph was alone, we kept searching for more tracks, knowing if we did not find his, the patrol was right behind us, and once they obtained permission could follow any of the tracks. Then we saw something certain — a single snowboard track headed into the woods toward two possible descents.

Tim and I followed this until it became a footprint in the snow, where he had removed his snowboard and began walking. At his point, Tim was certain it was Joseph, as he knew this was something Joseph would often do while others would choose to struggle, pushing or pulling themselves along in some other tiresome fashion. When Tim spoke with such certainty, I began to realize what this rescue attempt might end up looking like, and began to lose my composure. We broke over the edge into the steeper terrain still trying to follow this track, which now seemed to be two.

Just as we were making our decision as to which one to follow, the ski patrol came over the radio and said the sheriff had given them permission to help us but only in certain areas: the water tank and Marvin's chutes. This made the decision easy for Tim and me, as we immediately headed down a chute just west of the water tank following one of the two tracks. Minutes later we again heard a voice over the radio, "I see something like a snowboard sticking out of the snow, and we are halfway down the water tank chute."

Thoughts raced through my head as I tried to ski on Jeff's old skis, which I had borrowed. *It is just his board, don't panic, he is fine, it must have gotten stuck or broken and he had to leave it.* And then I heard the next call: "We found him." It became all I could do to breathe, let alone ski at this point, as I must have fallen six times trying to get down to where J. P. and Rick Walters were standing.

As we had all been trained, those already there started digging immediately and had Joseph uncovered by the time Tim and I arrived. Tim stayed high on the side of the gully, unable to make himself slide in closer to see if it was his friend. I felt woozy, as if I had not eaten for days, my stomach was weak, and my mind wanted nothing to do with getting a closer look. Without seeing, I would wonder if it was truly him, and even after knowing it was and that he was dead, I would probably not be able to grasp it and adequately process or accept his dying for some time to come.

Pale and weak, I slid down into the hole where he lay, head facing downhill, feet in the air with his board still attached. The moment I saw his blue jacket and red helmet, I knew it was him. I reached down, my face now streaming with tears, and grabbed hold of my friend, knowing it would be the last time. His body was hard and frozen and so lifeless, that I couldn't believe that this shell was all he was; and I knew it wasn't. My tears were now turning to hot needles that poked into my face and numbered in the thousands. I again knelt down beside my friend and whispered a prayer of thanks for him and for his life and that I knew he was now in a better place with the one true living God:

This is the place of a soul departed. . . . This is the place where my friend met God face to face. . . . Eternity's clock now started. Taken up in His hand. . . . To a better place. . . . Taken up in his hand, to the land now promised.

What surprised me as much as anything is throughout this whole experience, I never once got angry at God for taking Joseph at such a young age. Here was a man who was living so right, cared so much for others, and had so much to offer and live for, yet though I did not understand his dying so young, I was not angry that my best friend's life had been taken. Perhaps my anger toward God would not be justified, knowing that Joseph took the risk and put himself in this situation. Perhaps it was just delayed and would come later.

So often, people can't look past circumstances, so they blame God for these events, as if He is some mean kid on the playground torturing ants, and we are the ants. I was angry at Joseph, however, for taking a risk he should not have taken and that he knew better than to take alone. The terrain was not so steep or extreme that he was foolish to think he could do it; it was really no steeper than a black diamond at most resorts. However, this becomes quite another matter when obstacles are more difficult to see and there is no margin for error if you are alone, fall, and get hurt. For this reason, one always travels with a buddy just in case something goes wrong.

An expert can still tumble on an easy run and should never take anything for granted. I was angry that he had taken this backcountry place for granted, and it cost him his life. He had made beautiful turns down the western flank of the chute, down into the point where it narrowed, tightening his turns but still moving with considerable speed as was made obvious by his tracks, which abruptly ended near a group of small spruce trees. He didn't know what was on the other side of those trees. The snow had eroded away by running water of the creek, exposing a steep shelf of 50-degree rock. Joseph had plummeted through this, scraping his board on the rock and turning him upside-down into a terrain trap at the bottom of the cliff. It was a deep, twisted mess of fallen trees, snow, ice, rocks, and water, and Joseph was right in the middle of it, trapped in place by his snowboard.

In heavy snows, I had experienced skiers dying inbounds by falling over in the same way and then being unable to right themselves before friends or passersby could reach them for help. Their skis or snowboard acting as an anchor forcing them into the snow, which behaves like quicksand having no base from which to push against. In this way, a person can suffocate in a matter of minutes.

I'd like to think that Joseph died quickly and painlessly, without a terrible struggle, fighting the snow and fighting for breath. When Joseph was uncovered, there was a thin layer of ice near his face indicating that he had been breathing for some period of time while stuck in the snow. This is called an ice mask and forms as a result of condensation on the snow from a person's breath. It is possible for a short time to pull air from within the snow itself, but if a person is unable to increase the size of this air pocket in front of them it will soon freeze over from warm, moist respirations and create an ice barrier to the porous snow holding the air needed for survival. It was our assumption that Joseph died from suffocation. The coroner would later give us more information and other possibilities.

I spent a few minutes with Joseph in the five-foot deep hole, crying, staring in disbelief, praying, and trying to make sense out of this, as it had all happened so fast. The patrollers loaded him into the toboggan as Tim and I made our way slowly to the bottom of the chute to the awaiting Eagle County Sheriff search and rescue vehicle. At the bottom, we waited for the team carrying Joseph to arrive and load him in the truck for transport. It was one of the hardest days of my life, and I was, and am still, thankful that I live in a community where I am blessed with a lot of friends who support one another in many great and heroic ways. . . like my former co-workers and friends on the ski patrol, and the others who were below at the house in East Vail where Joseph lived.

Sharing the news with his family, whom I had never met, was something I certainly was not comfortable doing, especially since they had been phoned the night before that we were concerned and were organizing a search effort. I knew, like me, their hopes were also high that their son was just stuck somewhere and in need of assistance. It was Roger Anderson, a friend and elder of the church, who made this call and was able to speak calmly and lovingly to the family, sharing with them this news of their tragic loss. A group of us would travel to Pennsylvania for his funeral, and shortly after his family would come to Colorado for a mountaintop memorial service on Vail Mountain. I will never forget the sound of Joseph's mother crying as he was laid in the ground that cold February day. Placed in a grave only a mile from the house where he grew up, it could be seen from the pasture high above a hill where their horses grazed.

"Why do we do this?!" came shouts in my mind. "Why do we take these unnecessary risks for the sake of fun, or a thrill?" Now I was asking the very questions my family had been asking me after I had taken my fall just months before. It began making sense that these things are not worth it when they cause so much suffering to our loved ones. I was determined not to do the same thing. Joseph and I had discussions on this exact thing, and how self-ish it could all be. I remember him saying if he were to die, he would much rather go doing what he loved, than waiting till he was old and fat, dying of heart disease or worse, or to live in fear, never having lived life to its fullest or daring to take risks in pursuit of a dream. What good is it to dream, to live, if never to be challenged or face our fears and take a risk? This is not to say that everyone should run off to battle or take up extreme sports. This idea is also true in our relationships and faith in God. It involves risk to go beyond the ordinary and that is exactly how Joseph lived. Risk is less about our faith than it is God's faithfulness.

Deadpoint Reflections

For great is your love, reaching to the heavens; your faithfulness reaches to the skies (Psalm 57:10).

Whatever you can do, or dream you can, begin it. Boldness has genius, power, and magic in it.[2]
                                                    — W. H. Murray

Crux: Loss. One of the few guarantees we have in life is that it will end. Where and when, we do not know, but death in this life is certain. The crux is coming to peace with this inevitable and unavoidable conclusion for ourselves and for those we love. Losing a friend or a family member for most of us will present some of the hardest and most emotional times of our lives. The more sudden and unexpectedly a life comes to an end, often the more difficult it is to accept, and the younger and healthier the person, the greater the question of why. As we age, we come to expect the certainty of uncertainties as our bodies begin to break down, making us more susceptible to illness and injury. But regardless of our age, one question stands out for us all: What happens when the light goes out?

Hold: Hope. Gradually, like a wound that heals, peace will set in, life will go on, and the acceptance of another's passing will be like the wound that leaves a scar. The grieving process must take place or the wound will be like a picked scab and never heal. The memories will remain as the scar is evidence to, but the pain will fade away. We can believe whatever we like about death and whether or not there is life after it, but true peace does not come from what I believe, it comes from God. I know God has a plan and that plan gives me hope in the midst of death's grip when it unjustly and inexplicably grasps people like my friend's ten-month-old baby, or another person falling asleep at the wheel and crossing the median to claim the sweet young life of a local nurse. I like to think that God is populating heaven with babies, toddlers, children, and people of all ages, so that it has some variety that makes it perfect, like He says it will be. I don't quite know exactly how that will look, but I have hope in His plan and that is what I hold on to.

Anchor: "For God so loved the world that he gave his one and only Son, that whoever believes in him shall not perish but have eternal life" (John 3:16). If we cannot take God at His word and anchor ourselves in this hope, then our faith is in vain. As Thoreau said, "Most men lead lives of quiet desperation because they never truly live." It would seem that to live life fully is a choice, as is living your life for what is eternal.

Endnotes
1. Henry David Thoreau, *Walden* (Boston, MA: Ticknor and Fields, 1854), chapter 2.
2. W.H. Murray, *The Scottish Himalayan Expedition* (London: J.M. Dent & Sons, Ltd., 1951).

A Giant Step of Faith

[Khumbu Icefall]

Everest

NOTABLE EVEREST FACTS

NAMED AFTER: Sir George Everest, the British surveyor-general of India

LOCATION: Latitude 27° 59' N,.Longitude 86° 56' E

HIGHEST CAUSE OF DEATH: Avalanches; about a (2:1) ratio over falls

COUNTRY WITH MOST DEATHS: Nepal with 46

MOST DANGEROUS AREA: Khumbu Ice Fall with 19 deaths

CORPSES ON EVEREST: About 140

Notes:

- January 2001: The NFB team is making final preparations for the Everest climb, including the final team roster.

*Now faith is being sure of what we hope for and
certain of what we do not see.*
— Hebrews 11:1

*The mountaineer returns to his hills because he
remembers always that he has forgotten so much.*[1]
— Goeffrey Winthrop Young

It would be only six weeks before the team left for Everest, and I was now as unsure as ever if I wanted to be a part of this climb and did not want to turn to my family or friends for advice, as I knew that they most certainly would advise against it. I turned to God and began to pray. I would exercise my faith and lean on Him for the answers, knowing full well that He would certainly make it clear to me I was not to be a part of this climb, and for good reason.

Unstable emotionally after Joseph's death, still poor and lacking funding, we were all uncertain if it was going to materialize. Also, a serious lack of training, and of course my poor health and the risk of getting HAPE again weighed heavily on me. I was somewhat terrified about going, thinking of the events of the last year, terrified of letting my team down; terrified to tell my family I was even considering it. No problem. As I prayed, I knew it would be easy because God would close all of these doors for me as I tried to proceed if it was not of His will. My first prayer was to seek an answer regarding my health. I had not yet fully overcome my illness and figured this may be the easiest way out. I made an appointment with a top pulmonologist in Boulder, Colorado, knowing that he had probably seen numerous people who have had HAPE and/or viral pneumonia and could advise me better than anyone.

I had also been able to contact noted high altitude physician Peter Hacket, who had conducted years of leading research on the topic of pulmonary edema. And just to cover my bases in affirmation, I had a conversation with Dr. Gipe from Bozeman, Montana, my friend and teammate on Ama Dablam. My appointment with the pulmonologist went well; too well. He said, "Your x-rays look good, and as long as you're careful, I don't see any reason why you shouldn't go." This was not what I wanted to hear!

This was one of the few times in my life when I actually wanted a doctor to tell me I had a major medical complication. The only other time would be back in grade school when I just wanted to miss school. "C'mon doc, just this once, tell me I'm sick!" Really, I was just afraid.

Dr. Hacket said the same thing, that if the x-rays looked good and I was willing to go up again, why not? Then Steve said that I would have to make the decision, and at some point just go up high. I was beginning to see that I wanted someone else to make the decision for me.

Okay, my next out: money. I will pray about the funding, as we still need tons of money to pull this off. Conversationally, I would pray to God that "without proper funding this certainly won't happen, and I am sure that if it does not come in then You want us to wait, and maybe even want to put together a different team, one without me on it." Shortly after my conversation I got a call from Erik telling me that the National Federation of the Blind stepped in with a gift of $250,000, and Allegra allergy medication gave a significant amount of money for a documentary to be made of the climb. "Nuts!" The trip which was to be unaffordable for me was now paid for, and money could no longer be an excuse. I would ask myself, "What is God trying to tell me?"

The sponsorship was both great and scary because we now had the money, but who said anything about a film crew? Why can't we just go as *us*, the core team? We don't need to make this into a circus, let's just focus on the climbing. My fears were abated when I found out it would be Charlie Mace, a veteran of K2 and the south face of Aconcagua, and Michael Brown, already an Everest veteran and quality film maker. Still, it didn't seem right to add in another distracting element that could affect our ability to make rational decisions. I went along with it as I had no choice in the matter, being lucky I thought to even still have a shot at this. "I know; I've got it! I will let the team ultimately decide my fate. This will be an easy way out and I know they will be justified in saying they don't want me back."

It was during our team retreat in Marble, Colorado, when I would ask this question of my team, just after we had pushed each other off different ropes course objectives. Most people get on a ropes course and the objective is to cross from A to B without falling. This team, of course, had to make it into a "chase and destroy" mission where we would chase each other around and try to knock each other off the course. Needless to say, there was no facilitator and we had free reign over the Outward Bound facility for the weekend. When things had calmed down, I posed the question to the group. I asked if anyone thought my situation should keep me home, that I shouldn't climb. Not one team member thought I might be a hindrance. Gulp! was my second thought, while my first was a warm fuzzy feeling that I was a part of a great team that truly cared for its members.

I was certain that Erik just went along with this because he didn't want to speak up in front of everyone and be the only opposition since he invited me to be a part of this in the first place. I figured I would ask him that same question again in private, find out what he thought, because he would most assuredly say that he would prefer it if I stayed home. After all, he wouldn't want another gimp leading him to the top of the world. I will never forget his answer. He said, "Being blind, people have always made judgments about me and what I can and can't do, and I'm not about to do the same thing to you. You need to decide for yourself."

Oh come on man, just this once make a judgment, I would reply in my mind. It seemed as though I couldn't pray my way out of this one.

Was Everest somehow my Nineveh? Maybe I was reading too much into the whole thing. Maybe I just needed to lighten up and go already. But instead, I came back with this answer: "Erik, I don't know if I am strong enough to get to the top, but I know I am strong enough to help you get there." I said if pulmonary edema comes back at Base Camp, then that will be my summit and I will be glad to have helped you get there. Maybe it is Camp One, or even Camp Two, but I will take it one step at a time, just like you, and we'll see how far we get.

People often ask, "What did you do to train for Everest?" as if I had gotten on some big program and hired a personal trainer, beginning some outrageous fitness routine. Maybe in the back of their minds they think that I will say, "Well, I did what all Everest climbers do; I went to Siberia for nine months of Rocky IV training, carried 300-pound logs through four feet of snow, over ten miles of mountainous terrain, in sub-zero temperatures with a plastic bag over my head to simulate the thin air, all while hairless, muscle-bound trainers punched me in the stomach and called me names." The reality looks more like a healthy diet of ice cream and protein smoothies.

I was working at the time as a full-time ski instructor at Beaver Creek, often working in the adaptive program with people of various abilities and disabilities. This kept my legs strong and my body from getting too used to the comfort of being inside. Beyond that, I would snowshoe and skin up the mountain sometimes with a heavy load on my back. Skinning is when you place an adhesive strip on the bottom of your ski that allows you to slide in one direction, and when pressure is placed upon the ski, little synthetic hairs stand up like the hackles on a dog's back to keep you from sliding backward. The originals were made of sealskin, thus the name "skins." I would skin up in the mornings or after a day on the slopes, sometimes going straight up the ski runs, which is when people inevitably ski down beside you and say something extremely creative like, "Hey, you're going the wrong way!" Or my favorite, "Hey, bud, it's easier going the other way!"

"Ha ha!" I'd reply, and then as they would stop, not to be polite, but to gawk, I would keep climbing upward, knowing that they couldn't go back up, and thereby, I avoided another awkward conversation. Most of the guys stay fit by doing what they love: skiing, climbing, biking, hiking, and the list goes on. I don't think a single one of the guys had to get on the Rocky IV program except for maybe Sherman Bull. Sherman had been on five previous Himalayan expeditions, and reached Everest's south summit on two occasions (first with his son, Brad, in 1995). Everest remained an elusive goal. He has run seven marathons (best time 2:52) and an ultra-marathon. Sherm is a surgeon from Connecticut, who at the time was 64 years old. His son, and favorite climbing partner, Brad, was on our team because he was a friend of P. V., the team leader, and because he was a strong climber with a great head and a calm demeanor who had summited Everest once before in 1995. Sherm had been on Everest four times prior, but had yet to summit. On his third attempt, he fell and broke his back 1,500 feet above Camp Four. Brad helped lead the rescue of his dad. Even though Sherman was now 64, and an inch shorter due to his accident, he wanted to come back to try one more time with his son.

I remember P. V. asking the team if his friend Sherman could be a part of our climb, and everyone seemed excited due to his experience as a climber, his specific Everest experience, and his medical knowledge. We did, however, have our doubts as to his health and fitness at the time. Sherm's strategy was to hire a personal trainer that would put him through the ringer. This guy had Sherman carrying him up hills, dragging tires behind him as he ran, pulling loaded 747s with a rope in his teeth. Well, maybe not that last one, but close. It was the next best thing to going to Siberia with Rocky Balboa, and it worked. Sherm was in great shape and was now on the team, along with the rest of the cast of characters I introduced earlier.

With the team set and the money in, it was time to go. I was at home going over the gear, and the gear list, again and again to make sure I hadn't forgotten anything critical, like my CD player and extra batteries, or my pillow with tropical fish on it. As a team we gathered at P. V.'s house and went through the truckloads of gear that would accompany us on the journey. The last thing to do was say goodbye to friends and family. This was not the easiest thing to do. It was difficult to originally break the news of climbing Everest to my family, and when I did, I made my mom cry. They were indeed concerned, but supportive. More than anything, I think they knew there was no talking me out of it. Most climbers tend to be a little hardheaded.

My friends at home were very supportive and even threw a party for me. I was able to give away some extra goodies from our sponsors that I couldn't use, and did this by way of an Everest trivia game. The ones who could answer questions right would get the gear, with questions like: How tall is it? What country is it located in? Who is it named after; last name only? It was a great time and one friend gave me a small travel Bible with encouraging words written in it from all the others. Then, I was given a string of colorful prayer flags that had Scripture and the prayers of my friends written on them. This, I could hang from my tent instead of the traditional prayer flags of Nepal, which have unknown writings to an unknown god. One of my favorite Scriptures was written on this line of flags: *Trust in the LORD with all your heart and lean not on your own understanding; in all your ways acknowledge him, and he will make your paths straight* (Proverbs 3:5–6).

March 23, 2001, Day 1 — Bags packed, off to the airport, and now on our way across the ocean 12 time zones away, once again to Kathmandu, Nepal. As we would fly through San Francisco, Japan, Bangkok, and finally, Kathmandu, I was amazed to see peaks off the coast of Alaska, Mt. Fuji in Japan, and then finally the mother of them all: Everest. This time when we landed we would have enough equipment, it would seem, to put three expeditions on the mountain.

We were a large team, and with all of the communications equipment, laptops, satellite phones, handheld radios, batteries, solar panels, power converters, not yet including the film crew and all of their gear, it was a site to behold at the airport as we amassed a huge pile, then set off for the first challenge of our climb: customs. Thirteen of us were lined up with 26 carts piled high with about five duffels each. I think the customs agent either thought he had won the jackpot, or he would be there for a couple days sorting out our stuff. Thankfully, P. V. had a talk with him using the Jedi mind trick, and before we knew it, we were heading out the door.

We asked, "P. V., what did you say to the guy?"

"He asked me what we had, and I said we were a blind expedition and we needed a lot of sticks, ya' know, trekking poles." He replied.

Again our Sherpa buddies were there to greet us — Kami Tenzing and a few of his gang. The buses were loaded, and we were glad to get to the Marshyangdi Hotel for some good rest after the two days of travel. We made another visit to Swayambhunath, the "Monkey Temple," where again I would abstain from spinning the prayer wheels or doing anything that might interfere with my faith and honoring God. It is not something I made a big deal of, as I didn't want my teammates getting superstitious on me, but something I did quietly, out of respect to the Lord. "Do not make idols or set up an image or a sacred stone for yourselves, and do not place a carved stone in your land to bow down before it. I am the LORD your God" (Leviticus 26:1). I would try hard to refrain each time the opportunity presented itself, and it would remain a struggle throughout the climb, as there are so many ceremonies and opportunities that require participation.

One of the funniest of these moments was during our team's visit to the Rimpache lama in Katmandu to receive his blessing. We would visit the temple site and then enter into a large dimly lit room, sit quietly (or as quietly as our team ever could) on the floor, and wait for the Rimpache. A bit of a roly poly, jolly looking guy, he arrived with a couple of other monks and a number of scarves called *katas*. After a bit of discussion as to the nature of our visit and our climb, he would invite us up one by one to receive the scarf and a blessing. He would say something in his quiet voice with a heavy Nepalese accent, as you would imagine a high lama would sound: "Ah, you are going to climb Sagarmatha." This is what the Nepalese call Everest, a name that means mother goddess of the earth. We would nod, give a quiet yes, receive the scarf, and then the next person would kneel.

When it was Erik's turn, he came up with his white cane, awkwardly caught the lama's hand for a hand shake, at which time the lama looked around and in a surprised tone with a higher pitch to his voice said, "Him, too?!" Stunned and amazed, he wasn't quite sure if we were serious so he added, "To the top?" We said yes, and I am sure he began to pray to his gods. I received a scarf like everyone else, and continued praying to God.

Now we were back to the other side of the city to reorganize our stacks of gear. We redistributed the supplies into piles of batteries and electronics, food, snacks, and high mountain meals, tents, stoves, ropes, and then we put these in bags according to which camp they were to go. Organizing an expedition of this size takes an unbelievable amount of time, planning, and preparation, and it would have been nearly impossible without somebody like P. V. In some ways he has skills most men don't have, and that is to multi-task like a woman. He can be on the phone talking oil and gas with someone in Russia, while e-mailing details to the team about Everest, and carrying on a conversation with someone else in the same room about his missing finger, and still make fewer mistakes than I would if I were to do just one of those tasks. If you ever meet him and he tells you a crocodile took his finger, don't believe it. He lost it to a "skillsaw-dile."

Organizing the gear and the expedition came easy for him, but trying to do the same with the team, he would tell us, is "like herding cats." When you get a bunch of climbers together, with all of their different egos, personalities, testosterone, ambitions, and put them in front of the world's tallest mountain, you are bound to get some interesting results, and P. V. had his work cut out for him trying to keep us focused.

Now fully prepared, we took an old Russian-made helicopter into Lukla, as the old dirt landing strip was being paved and planes were not being used. There was no doubt now that we were on our way and there was no turning back. We had the whole team together, along with all the people coming along to trek in with us to wish us well, which included some family members, friends, acquaintances, and two more blind trekkers: Maurice Peret from Baltimore, Maryland, and Dan Rossi from Pittsburg, Pennsylvania. Maurice would be coming along on behalf of the National Federation of the Blind, to send dispatches back home via the sat phone, on the blind perspective of this trek and climb, while Dan would be out to gain some more experience for some future goals of his own. Maurice, Dan, and Erik called themselves the three blind mice, and we jokingly referred to them as alternates for Erik should he fall into a crevasse. This may seem cruel to joke in such a way, but it sure makes a long trek more fun for us all when we are able to laugh at each other and ourselves. We said someone needs to pick up the flag should Erik fall, and be ready to represent the blind people of the world.

With Maurice not really having any experience hiking on rugged mountainous terrain, and Dan not being in nearly the shape that Erik was in, there was quite a discrepancy as to the trail abilities of the three, and no real discrepancy in the degree of blindness. All were totally blind, no light, no shadows, nothing. But the way it appeared is that one was blinder than the others. Erik didn't appear, at least to the Sherpas, to be blind at all. After a few days on the trail some of the Sherpas began to have their doubts as to whether or not Erik was really blind because he would be so far ahead, would not stumble, and had an uncanny knack for knowing where things, people, and animals were along the trail.

Dan, and more so Maurice, would occasionally slide off the edge of the trail, need more frequent breaks, and basically appear to be more convincingly blind. Erik's ability was due to his years of experience in the mountains, but the Sherpas saw it more as a hoax and began to try to catch us in the act of pulling off a big lie. So as we would hike, Erik might feel a brush of wind pass his face, and hear the crinkle of a mountain jacket as an arm passed inches from his face, an obvious attempt by someone to get him to flinch. This happened more than a few times, and eventually started to cause a division among the team. As we saw it, the Sherpas are a part of our team and we a part of theirs. It would need to be one big team with a central focus, and this "issue" was beginning to split us apart. If not dealt with, it would certainly affect our progress and ability to work together on the mountain. Erik, tired of this, called for a meeting with the Sherpas and a few others. He said, "I know there are some doubts as to my blindness and whether or not I can actually see. I want to prove that I am indeed blind." The response was less than enthusiastic, and the looks that were on the disbelieving Sherpa faces said, "How you gonna do that?!" Imagine a night high in the Himalayas with the wind blowing lightly against the walls of a tent, illuminated softly by the light of a small lantern. Imagine you are seated at the table about to hear a story of how a young man lost his sight. Get ready for the tears. "Okay, Erik, you're on. Tell your story."

Now, stick your index finger inside your mouth and press it against the inside of your cheek, close your mouth tight around it. Sliding your finger forward and out of your lips, pop your finger out quickly. If you got a nice popping sound when you did it, that's what the Sherpas heard as Erik took out his prosthetic eyes right in front of them. Not quite, but it paints a better picture of what happened. He then took his eyes in his hands and looked around the tent.

"Please do not do that again, we believe you!" was the response spoken in a heavy Nepalese accent and a slightly disgusted tone by our Sherpa friends as they bent over in disgust at the table. Some sat silent, mouths open, as the rest of us ran. This moment, funny as it seems, was a pivotal moment in the climb as it served to unite us, not only with a little laughter and a good story, but to put us all on the task of having a common goal we could rally behind, not being held back by disbelief. Next thing we knew, Sherpas were coming up to Erik to take his arm and aid him, as well as trying to take his pack from him.

A few days into the trip and we had arrived at Namche Bazaar, the hub of high Himalayan trading. I strolled in through the heavy rains with Maurice Peret this day, and could not wait to get inside and warm myself by a nice smoky yak dung fire and a hot cup of *ducha* — milk tea. Our "waterproof" gear had left us nice and soggy as we climbed the trail into Namche, where we would take a rest day and have time to check out the open-air market, which would take place.

Traders would come from all of the surrounding valleys and villages of Nepal and Tibet with loads of goods carried on their heads and backs, hoping to get some cash, and barter for other things they needed. This was a local market and Westerners didn't really play much of a role in the economy of this place, at least not directly. Westerners have played a major role in the shaping of the Khumbu Valley and the modernization of it.

With all of the expeditions and trekkers that flow through this majestic terrain, the money trail has followed, and so have the services offered, especially in Namche, where it is easy to find some good coffee, doughnuts, and Internet cafes. It was great to be able to check in with family and give a progress report of our trek. After observing the market, getting some rest, and sending my e-mails, I went for a walk to stretch the legs and spend some time in prayer. I was blessed by the sight of six ibex standing above me on a rock outcrop — beautiful, strong, and graceful. They looked so much like they belonged in this rugged place, such a contrast to us as we moved slowly, blindly, gasping for air as the elevation increased. Yet, even in our awkwardness with all of our shortcomings, we would be able to climb to heights the ibex would never reach; separated by desire, teamwork, soul, spirit, and innovations. In the same way, all of us were impressed by the courage of these three blind men attempting this 30-plus mile trek to 18,000 feet and Base Camp over rugged and sometimes (at least for them) dangerous terrain.

Lest one get too proud of this accomplishment, there is always a moment which comes at an inopportune time in just the wrong place, which serves as that slice of humble pie or perhaps even the whole pie. This moment came for Dan just after his morning cup of coffee in Namche, at our comfortable teahouse, which still had a bathroom outside and a deep pit for a receptacle. Being truly independent, Dan would take his white cane to the restroom, as his sturdier trekking poles were not necessary. But as the floors with a hole in the center (no seat) are not always clean and can even have a layer of frost on them in the early morning, (I am trying to defend him here) Dan set his cane on an angle, in the corner leaning against the wall, and as he lowered into position, the cane lost its position, and like an arrow heading for a bull's-eye, shot into the muddy pit of despair and wretchedness.

Had this been a trekking pole with its sharper tip, it may not have lost its grip, but the white cane is designed to gently roll over the ground with its rounded hard plastic tip. Of course, being blind he would have a terrible time retrieving his faithful, previously white friend from the hole. I could just envision him lying on his belly, squirming over the slick floor reaching, without a hope of making contact with the cane, as his beard might graze and collect a few leftovers from the last visitor. He came back to the breakfast area a bit disoriented without his cane, hoping no one would notice, and of course, not wanting to mention what had just happened. He was certain he would leave it behind, but he would need it later on the trip, especially as he traveled home.

I asked, "Dan, where is your cane?"

"Oh, you don't want to know," he replied. "It fell into the toilet hole outside and I am not sure I want it back. I don't think it is retrievable anyway."

"Aw, Dan, don't give up. Let me at least go look to see what the damage is." He agreed, and I went outside to survey the possibility of retrieval. I caught a glimpse of it wedged into the corner, miraculously standing upright. Lacking the proper tools to make the grab, I went up to some of our Sherpas merely to ask (yes, I had no intention of enlisting their aid) if they had access to any kind of a tool shed or someplace I could maybe find what I needed, but my intentions and descriptions of what I needed and for what purpose got lost in translation, and before I could say, "who flung pooh," they were on it. Sooner than I could blink, the cane was retrieved and cleaned. These people are amazing, selfless, generous, and kind. They also have a job to do and want to do it as best they can. Dan was pleased to have his cane back, though as you could imagine, had mixed feelings about using it.

The day of rest would help us acclimate, especially those on the team coming from sea level, and would allow us to move on up higher to the site of our next night's stay, the Tengboche Monastery. This was a wonderfully beautiful site perched atop a steep mountainside, yet still in an amphitheater of icy high peaks. Home to perhaps as many as 100 monks, it is a remote, cold, but colorful dwelling full of the sounds of Buddhist chanting. They dress in deep burgundy-colored robes with bits of orange, all have short buzzed hair, and the ages of these monks ranges from very young to that of the mountains themselves.

It is here that a lama from the monastery would come, and as is custom with all expeditions, wish us well on the journey by wrapping our necks in a kata scarf, which by now I had already collected close to half a dozen. Next he would tie around our necks a piece of string called a *sundi*. This is typically left on until it wears out and falls off. I know that some of my team, years later, would still be wearing it. I, on the other hand, am not superstitious and wanted to honor God, while being careful not to offend the giver, so I waited until Base Camp a few days later and cut it off. I know in my heart, and wanted God to know, that my trust is not in a string, a ritual, or a blessing given by men, but that my trust, as I climb, is in Him, and this was a simple way to demonstrate that in a place so unforgiving.

Many in the mountains cling to good luck charms, blessings, and rituals for these reasons: fears are greater, the danger is higher, and the nerves get more rattled, so it is easy to understand how a person would embrace whatever they are given. Psalm 135:15–18 says, "The idols of the nations are silver and gold, made by the hands of men. They have mouths, but cannot speak, eyes, but they cannot see; they have ears, but cannot hear, nor is there breath in their mouths. Those who make them will be like them, and so will all who trust in them." It is easy to see how people are so drawn to the Buddhism of the mountains; attractive with its peaceful setting and peaceful monks withdrawn from the world and its materialistic ways. They sit in their colored robes, in a painted room, reading and chanting all day, sitting up off the floor on a small platform covered with pillows, giving them the higher seat over the visitors and to reflect their position as monks.

The pious living in and of itself is somewhat attractive, but what really draws people is the manner in which the monks and people of the Khumbu live — quiet, peaceful lives, treating others with kindness, compassion, and humility, as well as, generosity that often comes from an annual income of less than our weekly grocery bill. Imagine a wealthy foreigner visiting a poor part of the States and being asked to come sit and dine at someone's table with no ulterior motives. For that matter, imagine inviting a stranger to dine at your own table. It is the exception, not the norm.

There is no doubt that we in the West have a lot to learn from the people high in the mountains of Nepal. (Still not to say they are all so saintly; corruption exists wherever there are people.) We would do well to lose some of the material trappings of our lives, to lose our obsession with what the "beautiful people" are up to, and the distractions of the latest electronic gizmo that robs us of time spent in real communication with the people by our side, instead of the ones in our ears through blue tooth devices.

Living like these people in the mountains can lead us to believe that we can wrap our hands and minds around our destiny, that we can have more control over the outcome and our circumstances, but it is a world out of control and I know too well that real peace does not come from within me or any action of mine, but from the Prince of Peace and His free grace gift. *For to us a child is born, to us a son is given, and the government will be on his shoulders. And he will be called Wonderful Counselor, Mighty God, Everlasting Father, Prince of Peace* (Isaiah 9:6). So what I see are wonderful people trying so hard to earn that which is free, being motivated by fear of consequence and the spirit of the mountain, which must be pleased like a fire that consumes, not cool water that forgives (a spirit indeed, but not a deity).

Now there was a light frost, a little snow, as we prepared for our departure for higher ground. We were getting to a more significant altitude, easy to tell by the ratio of breaths to steps and by the fact that we would, at this point, see some attrition on the team of trekkers, and as well, surprisingly, our climbing Sherpas. The first was a girlfriend of Michael O'Donell. She was beginning to show signs of cerebral edema at just 14,000 feet. She had a splitting headache accompanied by some slurred speech and disorientation. Two Sherpas were able to carry her miles out to the airstrip in a basket they carried on their backs, with a strap that passed from the basket over their foreheads and back to the other side. She checked into the hospital in Kathmandu, and in her condition, had a difficult time getting a flight back home, but eventually did. Her recovery was not fast, and I believe was complicated by some other medical issues.

The second took place as we headed up to Phariche, and involved one of our climbing Sherpas, who had been to Everest's summit five times. He collapsed on the trail as if having a seizure, but certain details about the way it happened led our doc to believe it could be more serious than the Sherpas wanted us to believe. Making this climb and the financial rewards it would offer was not something he wanted to miss out on, and the risk was something he was willing to assume, but not us. We sent him down to be evaluated, and then to recover at home. I am not sure if he was ever able to resume his climbing career.

These series of rescues got me thinking about our climb and how things might go down if I was climbing with Erik and got into some sort of trouble — for example, if my pulmonary edema revisited as the two of us were on the Lhotse face at 23,000 feet. So as we trekked upward through the high meadows, me in front ringing the bell, directing my friend's path with commands of "left, right, chicken heads, ankle buster, big step up, ditch, up and over." I asked, "Erik, what if I get into trouble this time out and it is up to you to rescue me?"

He replied with a chuckle, letting me know he was kidding, "You're the bell boy. Your job is to ring the bell. Are you ringing the bell, boy? The only thing that needs to work on you is your bell-ringing hands, and if they are working we'll keep going. But if your hands freeze and can no longer ring the bell, that's just too bad for you. I'll drop ya right there until someone else comes along who can ring the bell!"

Not exactly the kind of sweet words I had heard before the trip, the kind that make you tear up like those TV commercials for cotton. This time we were eight days into the trek and all of the sweet cotton comments were far behind us. Anything like that was going to have to be saved for a special moment on the summit, or perhaps some other moment of truth that might still lie ahead.

He was joking, of course, but a bit miffed by his comments I took advantage of the freshest pile of yak dung I could find and somehow was able to ring that bell directly over the spot I wanted his foot to hit. "Oops, I'm sorry, Big E, that squishy stuff you just stepped in was not mud, well at least not the dirt and water kind of mud." The best part of this kind of revenge would come later when I would see him in his tent with his shoes off and placed on top of his pillow or his clean clothes. Being the nice guy I am, I would say, "Hey, you got a ton of crap on the bottom of your shoe, you might wanna scrape it off."

The light-hearted moments on the trail for almost every climber and trekker who passes this way come briefly to an end as all must pass by a place of memory, places dedicated to all who have been above and not come down. Rock memorials, known as *chortens*, had been erected to the likes of people such as the guides of the infamous 1996 tragedy, Rob Hall and Scott Fisher, and to others, including Sherpas who have died on the mountain. I did not know them personally, but some on my team did. For us all, but for them especially, it was a sobering reminder of what can happen even to the best and most experienced. This is true in climbing, business, marriage, and life.

As the elevation increased, so did my desire to climb, but not without constant worry of what might unfold with the next step. Making this easier was the fact that I would need to take the focus off myself and place it on one of the three blind members of our team, allowing me to worry less about my own fears and more about their well-being. It would be in these moments of guiding I would try to put myself in another's shoes, at times even close my eyes in an attempt to better understand what this Himalayan landscape would be like if light never hit its slopes, ridges, and valleys. How would I want it described to me? Looking at it this way was a great test for my vocabulary and my ability to notice details, then creatively make them come alive. I would take an arm of my sightless companion and point it to the sky making a near vertical reach that would point to the mountaintops. Even in Colorado, reaching like this will rarely get the arm above one's chin, but in the Himalayas it is a near-vertical reach that shows one the drama of these mountains. I would then take that hand and make a map of the surroundings as we move the arm in and out and up and down over glaciers, ridges, lakes, river valleys, and up again on waterfalls and icefalls, cresting a new sense of perspective and admiration for this place.

It was up to me to make the most of my eyes and enjoyment of this place, translating it for someone else, communicating my findings so this other person could have a richer experience, and even then, it is limited to my interpretation. It surprised me the things noticed by them that I would often miss. An example would be the mani stones — piles of stone tablets inscribed by monks in a very ornate alphabet over the centuries, extending for hundreds of yards at a time. I would often run my own fingers over these in wonder of the time it took and the process involved and for what purpose. I could then run my blind friend's hand over them, knowing that had I not stopped to take it in, it would be just one more thing he would have missed on this trip.

Surprisingly, these things might even be pointed out to me in the same way when a blind trekker might ask, "What is my cane hitting here on the right," or "What is this rocky outcrop above us?" Knowing it was there by the sound waves bouncing back to them, I would look and find that it hid another ornate inscription, which I had missed, reminding me that even though I can see, my eyes are not always open to everything.

April 5, Day 14 — Over a week into the trek, I was beginning to get antsy to reach Base Camp. We had seen the mountain, but now we wanted to touch it and get going on this climb. I was curious to see how I would do at the higher elevations since I had not been back to these heights since my accident. Just for fun, I made a game with myself that I mentioned to no one else, wanting to be the first team member to Base Camp. In a way it pushed me to walk faster, clear my head, and prove to myself that I was acclimating well, giving me a bit of confidence going into the icefall. I won my own silly game.

One by one, the rest of the team began to arrive, and then it was Erik who strolled in facing off against a yak on a slick pond of ice. His dad and brothers were with him at this moment, and remarkably his dad, Ed, had made it even though he had just had his hip replaced. If there is one thing this family has it is resolve. They are a tenacious bunch that won't let too many circumstances deter them from reaching their goals. Also coming into Base Camp some days later was Pasquale's quadriplegic son, Adam. Adam had been injured in high school when wrestling with a friend who did a pile-driver maneuver on him, and now he has only regained partial use of his arms.

What made this trip risky for him is that his body cannot regulate its own temperature, so the cold nights at 18,000 feet could be troublesome. To get to Base Camp, Adam hired three porters to carry him the 35-mile distance using a basket and tumpline to get him there. As his trek began, he saw his porters did not even have shoes. He bought them each shoes and I know tipped them rather well, too. Upon arrival he gave each climbing member a patch with a wheelchair on it that said, "Team Gimp." Every day we would see people wandering into Base Camp overcoming their own obstacles, but with this team we really saw extraordinary feats of will nearly every day, and this was just Base Camp. It certainly fired us up even more to climb.

Inasmuch as these things fired us up, other situations were cause for concern, and we were hoping not to see a pattern develop that would affect our success. If you are superstitious, like the Sherpas tend to be, a pattern like this could keep you off of the mountain. But for us, it helped us see what our team was made of and the heart it had. During the trek, we saw one of our climbing Sherpas, who was a five-time summiter of Everest, evacuated for a seizure disorder; one of our trekkers evacuated for cerebral edema; another helicoptered out for interminable epistaxis, which was finally slowed down with the creative use of a tampon by physician assistant Jeff Evans; yet another, Chris Morris's dad, evacuated due to a heart condition, which caught him by surprise even though he had only recently given up smoking. The team's response to each situation was thoughtful, methodic, and one of genuine concern until there was resolution. This instilled in me a greater degree of trust knowing that if it were me again, this team could be counted on.

Just days after arrival at Base Camp, the Easter holiday was upon us, and a few decided it would be cool to host an Easter service in our dining tent for any who might want to come, including the Sherpas. Brad Bull, Reba Bull, and I read Scripture that morning and shared some time in prayer with what ended up being maybe seven or eight total team members and sadly to me, no Sherpas. I read from Isaiah 53:5–12, which prophesied the life of Jesus:

> *But he was pierced for our transgressions, he was crushed for our iniquities; the punishment that brought us peace was upon him, and by his wounds we are healed. We all, like sheep, have gone astray, each of us has turned to his own way; and the LORD has laid on him the iniquity of us all. He was oppressed and afflicted, yet he did not open his mouth; he was led like a lamb to the slaughter, and as a sheep before her shearers is silent, so he did not open his mouth. By oppression and judgment he was taken away. And who can speak of his descendants? For he was cut off from the land of the living; for the transgression of my people he was stricken. He was assigned a grave with the wicked, and with the rich in his death, though he had done no violence, nor was any deceit in his*

mouth. . . . by his knowledge my righteous servant will justify many, and he will bear their iniquities. . . . For he bore the sin of many, and made intercession for the transgressors.

After the readings, I closed with this prayer: "Dear God, give us the wisdom and the patience to climb this awesome mountain and come home safely to our loved ones. Help us to make good decisions, to take care of one another, and to leave this mountain with our friendships strengthened. And we know, God, that a prayer is not just a wish list, so if standing on top is not to be, give us the wisdom to understand Your great plan for us and the courage to carry it through."

I understand why the Sherpas didn't come. For the same reason, I wasn't too excited about the upcoming Puja ceremony the Sherpas were hosting, which involves making offerings of propitiation and supplication to the mountain spirit by a lama from the region. Juniper would be burned continually from the day the ceremonial chorten was made until the climb was finished. The ritual of the puja would include throwing barley flour into the air and offering incense, snacks, candies, coke, whiskey, and beer to Buddha and the mountain spirits to "appease" them, allowing the team, as they believe, to have safe passage.

Typically, each member of the team will also place their personal climbing effects against the chorten to be blessed by the lama by his placing of some sticky, damp flour upon each item such as crampons, helmets, and ice axes. This ceremony was really difficult for me to take part in, which I did to the least degree, and stood more as an observer than a participant. When a teammate asked me if I had placed my gear "over there," I said yes because over there to me could have meant my tent, which is where it was, but I did not place it against the chorten on purpose. Again, my intent in all of this was to honor God and show my faith is not in ritual, Buddha, superstition, or even just good luck, but rather in Him alone.

In a like manner, I also cut off all of the little blessing sundi strings I had been given along the way, which were also meant to provide luck, because I never wanted to lean on a crutch of superstition, or even let a thought pass through my head that at some point might validate what I had been given. These items I received with respect in honor of the giver, as I believe it was indeed a kind gesture, but when it came to climbing the mountain I just wanted to be real, and clean before God. *Those who cling to worthless idols forfeit the grace that could be theirs* (Jonah 2:8).

When the lama offered each team member a film canister full of uncooked rice to open in a moment of fear, and take a pinch of rice and toss it, I again declined. I did find it humorous when some others took it, then at certain ladder crossings in the icefall would actually use some — and in one instance, all that was left — to quell the fear that resided in us all.

The next few days were used for rest, to acclimate, and to sort equipment and food before establishing Camp One at 20,000 feet. We had an entire 10 by 15 foot tent dedicated to food and team gear. It took a lot to get this organized and it was hard not to eat a lot of the tasty snacks prematurely we had bought for higher on the mountain.

April 8, Day 17 — For this first trip up to Camp One, everyone would need to carry some personal gear to leave high on the mountain for the weeks to come, as well as, what was needed for the day. Erik would miss most of this first climb to make the drop. He would go only part way up the icefall and avoid going all the way until we were ready to spend the night. When that day came, I served as his guide, along with Luis Benitez. Leaving before the sun came up, we had a better chance of passing through the icefall safely while it was still frozen. Unfortunately, this day would be one of the longest of the expedition and would cause us to not only fear the melting ice falling all around us, but to doubt our chances for success in reaching the summit.

With 19 teams making an attempt on Everest, it became imperative that one reliable route be set for all to use through the icefall. If not, there would be 19 unreliable routes to plague us. The job of establishing one solid route would be done by the "ice doctors;" two Sherpas paid a fee from each team to secure that one route. If not for these two brave Sherpas, the task would be left up to each individual team, and petty crimes would undoubtedly arise as ladders and ropes would be stolen and people would get protective of their routes.

To ensure that this was all done properly and each team was on the same page in terms of getting things done, we hosted an international team leaders meeting in our dining tent. This meeting, to me, was reminiscent of the bar scene in the original *Star Wars* movie. There was one of every kind of creature in our tent that night — people from all different continents, speaking different languages, some with teeth and some without, some with fingers and some without, some with moral and ethical principles and some without. So began the climbing game, with teams jockeying for position and looking out for themselves, trying to get out of doing work or getting pinned behind less experienced teams. Through all of this, we did find a couple of other teams that could be trusted, and especially some good individuals with whom we would share equipment, ideas, and even DVDs to watch while at Base Camp.

To leave Base Camp and begin climbing meant to circle the chorten in a counterclockwise direction for good luck, for the superstitious. I would crack up as I saw people doing this from all the different teams, including my own, but I just couldn't bring myself to participate in this ritual even if it meant letting those in front of me make a circle and then falling in behind once again.

April 11, Day 20 — This was our first ascent with a blind man through the icefall, and was harrowing, so I can understand why certain people would become superstitious. Giving perhaps far too much detail to Erik as he would climb was exhausting at this elevation. Maybe it was nerves stemming from our first trip through together, but it was hard not to point out every hole, bump, crack, step, and block of ice, knowing that some of these could be hiding a bigger danger beneath. There is really no time to heal a twisted knee, so one misstep could end the climb. Along the trail we had become an efficient pair, and now were relearning our communication methods, trying to do the minimum amount of speaking required, to allow for more breaths.

Before we knew it we had come to the first ladder crossing in the icefall; a series of seven of the cheapest recycled ladders money could buy or yak dung could barter. It was comforting to know that at least they were tied together with the thinnest, cheapest cord that could be found in the back alleys of a Chinese market. Michael Brown crossed first with his large HD camera to set up the nervous shot of Erik crossing. I went after, and soon there was a mix of team members on either side watching to see what would happen when Erik would take his first step onto the first of these seven ladders. This was something we had practiced at home but there is no substitute for a true icy abyss at 19,000 feet spanned by something that swings in the breeze giving "Elvis leg" (rapid gyrations of the leg) to any who cross in fear.

Pasquale on the far end gave Erik instructions, while Brad Bull on the near end held a pair of ropes tight like a handrail, giving Erik confidence in his first step. Though he was clipped in and surrounded by a strong team, he still had to make those steps himself. Wondering if it was better to crawl across, he asked nervously if the lines were tight. "So these lines will be tight? You guys will keep them tight? Cause if I fall I will just dangle in space." Then, with the steel points of his crampons threatening to trip him up, he stepped forward onto this bridge, which was neither level nor flat. The ladder angled upward while at the same time it leaned to the left. It would bow in the middle and sway as climbers walked across.

Moving forward one rung at a time, a climber with a large foot can put the front points of his crampons right over one rung while those at the back slip nicely over the rung under the heel. This worked well for Erik and his size 12 hooves, but even so, he would make us all nervous when he would dab around feeling for the ladder with his feet trying to figure out how exactly to place each step. One could wonder if it would be scarier to cross this deep, icy obstacle with the ability to see what is beneath, or blinded, not knowing how far you have to fall. I'm just glad I could see the other side.

After a six-minute bout on this swaying ladder, and encouragement and instructions from each of his teammates, Erik made it across, breathing a heavy sigh of relief, but this was just the beginning of the icefall. Michael was able to capture this on video; truly a stunning scene. It would be hard work for him and the Sherpas as they would carry that heavy camera ahead of the group, continually trying to get good shots.

Throughout the day we would cross what seemed to be 50 such ladders. Some short, some long, some steep, some flat, but all questionable. On the crossing of one of these ladders I pulled hard on a rope which had been secured with an ice screw on the far side, but as the sun hit the steel screw, warming it, and thereby loosening it from the ice, the screw came zinging out at me like a like a missile in a dodge ball match, nearly hitting me in the face. I couldn't help but think about what would have happened if I had fallen onto that rope with my full body weight. The rope may as well have not even been there. From this point on, I treated every anchor as suspect and did my best to simply balance on the ladders instead of leaning too heavily upon the ropes.

It was slow going and the team members who were ahead of us were wondering what was going on, and if we would make it to Camp One before nightfall. We were doing our best, getting tired of the questions from the others and frustrated in this long day, knowing on our own we had been able to make it to Camp One in just a few hours.

It would take us 13 hours to get to our destination; Brad Bull would wait to help Luis and me guide Erik through the last bit. Then, when we were just 30 minutes from Camp One, Erik and Luis miscommunicated, and I, being the third in line, also failed to help Erik adjust to the crevasse that was running in line with the trail. This is simple if you can see it, because all that needs to be done is to sidestep the crevasse, taking it in stride and continuing on.

Tired from the climb, we relied on habit, when what we really needed to do was tell Erik to stop, take one big sidestep left, another large step forward, then proceed. Instead, our alignment was off, our communication slow, and Erik stepped right into the crevasse. As he fell, Luis turned back in an attempt to catch him, but instead ended up catching Erik's nose on the handle of his trekking pole, giving Erik a bloody nose and a more rugged appearance. The crevasse merely acted to trip him up. He didn't fall all the way in. However, if the snow bridge was weak and he'd fallen sideways, I suppose he could have been swallowed up a little bit. This was a tough blow after an exhausting day when morale was low anyway, as we started to question this pace and the feasibility of continuing with the climb.

A night's rest, some hot tea, and a hot meal boosted morale, but the question would remain until our next trip through the icefall as to whether this would go or not. Normally, this climb will take four to five hours for a sighted person on the first try, but for us it took over 13, an unacceptable pace, and a number that would need to change in order for us to be successful. The night at 20,000 feet served us well in terms of acclimatization, caching gear high on the mountain, and giving us perspective on what would need to be done in order to improve not only our speed but our chances for success. Needless to say, the trip down went much faster and the thicker air elevated our spirits. We took a couple of days to rest, work on our oxygen systems, and wait for a clear window of weather before making our second trip up the icefall.

April 18, Day 27 — This time we knew what to expect and a little fresh snow was covering some of the uneven terrain of the now more-traveled ice fall, and so the route became a little simpler for us all, especially for Erik. We made it through the vertical maze of ice, slots, walls, and falling frozen houses in just under 10 hours. Still slow, but a huge improvement. We thought that if we could continue to improve upon this time and technique our chances would increase accordingly.

Erik and two guides stayed at Camp One while the rest of us continued on up to Camp Two. This for me was a new altitude record at 22,000 feet, and a huge relief with still no sign of any respiratory issues. Maybe, just maybe, my lungs were going to be okay. I gave thanks to the Great Physician; no, not Steve Gipe, though he is pretty great himself. The next day Erik climbed up to Camp Two to join us and as a team we were now all together, relatively high. It appeared we had solved one piece of the puzzle.

Deadpoint Reflections

Call to me and I will answer you and tell you great and unsearchable things you do not know. — Jeremiah 33:3

For us the mountains had been a natural field of activity where, playing on the frontiers of life and death, we had found the freedom for which we were blindly groping and which was as necessary to us as bread.[2] — Maurice Herzog Annapurna

 Crux: Having confidence in things not seen. I don't know where, but somewhere along the way so many of us lose the faith we had as children. Perhaps it is the reality of having been let down over the years when expectations of people and God were not met. I remember a time a few years ago when I reached down to pick something up off the floor, turning away from the bunk bed which held my four-year-old niece Katie on the upper level. Standing back up and turning toward the bed I was caught off guard when I found her airborne, arms stretched open wide, and zinging at me in the superman position, not doubting for a second that I would catch her. Had I paused to pick up a second toy or to tie my shoe, the event would have had an unhappy ending. As it was, I caught her as my heart raced quickly to 120 BPM. Most of us struggle to exhibit this kind of faith in anyone, or anything, and never risk a dive off the top bunk, so to speak. The faith my niece had in me and my ability to catch her had been learned over time as we developed a relationship through play and time together. She knew I had the strength to carry her and in this relationship, whether I was watching or not, she knew she could trust me. She then quickly figured as long as I was in the room, I would be able to catch her.

 Hold: Faith that is expectant. Is faith in God merely a fire insurance policy? Just like with my niece, it is trust that is built on relationship over time, which leads to understanding when faith can be exercised and certain outcomes can be expected.

It would be wrong to march out and expect God to give us whatever we want all the time, which would look like a spoiled child demanding to have all the toys in a toy store. I see expectant faith the way that a young girl was recently rescued from a Florida swamp. She had been missing for days, and experienced search crews had failed to find even a clue to her whereabouts. A skilled civilian outdoorsman heard the voice of God tell him to go seek her out. Without hesitation or question as to where the voice came from, he used his skills and knowledge of the swamp to go directly to her, giving the Lord the credit for guiding him right to the spot where she was stuck. He left his house fully expecting God to use him to find this little girl; hours after he left he had found her.

 Anchor: *And without faith it is impossible to please God, because anyone who comes to him must believe that he exists and that he rewards those who earnestly seek him* (Hebrews 11:6).

Endnotes
1. Goeffrey Winthrop Young, *Mountains with a Difference* (London: Eyre Spottiswood, Ltd., 1951).
2. Maurtice Herzog, *Annapurna* (UK: Johnathan Cape; New York: Random House, 1997), p. 246.

When Everest Isn't Enough

[Mount Elbrus[1]] [Mount Cook[2]]

ELEVATION: Mount Elbrus: 18,510 feet
Mount Cook: 12,316 feet

HOW LONG TO CLIMB: Mount Elbrus: One week, or can be done in one day if acclimated
Mount Cook: One day from glacier camp if acclimated; as many as three to four days

HOW MANY IN THE TEAM: Mount Elbrus: A team of 18
Mount Cook: Two in my team

RATING: Mount Elbrus: F
Mount Cook: AD+; YDS 5.5

BEST TO CLIMB DURING: Mount Elbrus: Late May through August
Mount Cook: November to February

ALSO KNOWN AS: Mount Elbrus: *Mingi Taw* means "Eternal mountain," *Koushha Makhue* means "Mountain of happiness" or "Mountain of light" in Turkic
Mount Cook: *Aoraki* means "Cloud piercer" in the Māori language

Notes:

With the team safely at rest at Camp Two, I want to leave Everest until Chapter 8 to share a bit about the passion of climbing and of mountains and of some of the distant places this passion has taken me. Most people climb the Seven Summits having Everest as their last — it was my first.

But one thing I do: Forgetting what is behind and straining toward what is ahead, I press on toward the goal to win the prize for which God has called me heavenward in Christ Jesus.
— Philippians 3:13–14

You've climbed the highest mountain in the world. What's left? It's all downhill from there. You've got to set your sights on something higher than Everest.[1]
— Willi Unsoeld

The high that one gets standing on top of the world lasts a few months, maybe even a year. What follows for most is the big question: "What's next?" Climbers who have stood on Everest commonly struggle with depression once the goal has been met. Often it is the symbol of a lifetime of hard work, training, saving financially, planning, and finally executing that long sought-after goal that stood on the horizon as merely a dream, perhaps even unthinkable. Now one day awakened, back from the dream, reality sets in — back to the grind, only this time without the goal, the object of desire and longing.

What could possibly fill that void in a climber's life? A return trip? Rekindle the magic and do it again! For some it may be that, for others that one summit was the prize and all they wanted was that moment, that one photo, a trophy, and their climbing career is over as quickly as it began. This person sells the boots, crampons, tent, sleeping bag, and goes back to a cozy urban existence, satisfied at having conquered, disinterested in further discomfort in the mountains. What they miss perhaps is the true soul and spirit of why we climb. The passion was for the object and what that object might do for them, for their ego; passion not for the journey, nor the camaraderie born of adversity, but for that summit which may become "just an empty cup" as Lightning McQueen says in the movie *Cars*.

What it really comes down to is passion. I never experienced the post-Everest depression largely because God gave me a passion for His creation of which I feel privileged to be able to explore. I tend not to see these summits as booty that I am able to loot and plunder; rather, each is an adventure with a story to be discovered, even if it is "just the same old local peak." The day will be different, the people, the weather, the way I feel, the view, and the route, or maybe it will be the exact same and it will be that sense of familiarity that brings comfort like an old friend.

Locally, there is a rock climb I like to go and visit each spring. I know it well, and even know all the moves that I need to make to get to the top. Along the way I know where each piece of gear needs to go and exactly which piece of gear will fit into which slot, so as to best protect me should I fall. I know just where to sit so I can look up while belaying my friend without getting a crick in my neck, and I truly enjoy the conversation as we walk down the rail-road tracks to get to the steep climb that brings us to the base of the familiar, orange, lichen-covered cliffs. Because of the climb, we have become friends, and because we are friends, we enjoy the climb. I can assuredly say that there are some people who look at Everest in this very way. The mountain itself has become more friend than foe, more familiar than foreign.

Perhaps in a way this small crag near my home could present itself to some as great a challenge as Mount Everest; that same sense of adventure, ty-ing into the rope and standing far enough off the ground to know that if you fell without the rope attached to your waist it could be your last time feeling the wind wash over your face. I try to live with the perspective that no matter how large or small, common or not, some grand journey awaits me each day and I have to look forward to whatever summit I may gain, even if it is setting a new speed record for a diaper change.

For success, we need to seek the extraordinary, but learn to find joy in the ordinary. It may sound like an aim-low strategy, but what I am trying to understand and apply in my life is I can't walk only on mountaintops. Life is lived in the valleys, and for moments we are able to reach the heights and look out. But these places are inhospitable for the long term. No, go crazy, plan the biggest and baddest thing you can imagine — just don't expect it to fulfill you completely. We need and should have goals, plans, and dreams; we should also seek joy in the journey, the valleys, and the normal. I want to fol-low the passion God has given me and I want to be true to the desires He has put on my heart. I also need to understand that this applies to my family and my work as well. Priorities and balance, with the joy coming from knowing God. "So, God, what's next?"

An adventure is only an inconvenience rightly considered. An in-convenience is only an adventure wrongly considered.[2]
— G.K. Chesterton

"In the middle of the night my ski guide, Eric Alexander, fell on the icy slopes as we climbed. I heard him slipping by me. I had no choice but to act quickly. Even though I can't see, I was able to hear where he was sliding by me and lunged out in a desperate jump — saving him from a horrendous fall." These were the words spoken by blind climber and skier, Erik Weihenmayer, at the end of our last adventure together in Australia, as we finished Erik's quest to be the first blind man to climb the highest peak on each continent.

September 2002 — We began our ski training the year before in preparation for our next objective, which would be to ski off the top of the last two of the Seven Summits. Erik's tone was a little less bold and a lot more nervous the morning of our first ski adventure together: "Hey, Eric, are you ready for this? " he asked.

"Yes I am, are you? You seem nervous. Why would you be nervous? After all, I got you down from the top of the world in one piece. Don't you think I can get you down Vail Mountain?"

"Yeah, but skiing is different — are you sure you know how to do this?"

"E, I've been skiing my whole life and guiding blind skiers for a number of years; trust me a little."

Erik grabs my arm as we get in line for his ability plus ski pass; something that alludes to him having just a little something more special than all the other skiers. Not a disability pass or a handi-capable pass, this one implies ability and then some to make him feel good about himself. As he grabs my arm he says, "Did I just grab your ski pole or is that your puny arm!"

I reply, "Don't forget who your guide is today; best you watch your mouth, boy."

"Right, no picking on the guide till the day is over," he says.

Erik Weihenmayer and I were beginning to get ready for our next adventure together: we were heading off to climb the highest peak in Europe: Mt. Elbrus at 18,500 feet. Most people can't believe it when they hear of a blind climber, but what really gets them is to hear that we want to ski off of this icy summit in southern Russia. In order to pull this off, we need to train for a number of days in all kinds of conditions to prepare for what we might encounter ten time zones away. We need to develop timing, turns, and trust.

We got on the chairlift for our first run together, and as we rode I was barraged with questions: "What do you say when it's time to get off? What if I need to stop really fast or turn out of the way of something? How will you call turns for me? Are we getting close? Do you know about the two tower out rule?"

Soon we were at the top and nothing I could say would make him believe I knew what I was doing; it was time to just do, and we did. It all went so smoothly that Erik's next comment to me was, "Oh, I guess you do know what you are doing," spoken in a quiet, humbled tone, of course. For the next several months we trained on the slopes of Vail, trying runs like Rasputin's revenge, Riva Ridge, Roger's, and headwall, where Erik proved his athleticism and ability to handle varied conditions; it was time for bigger and better challenges.

One nice thing about skiing with a blind guy is he really has no concept of how severe some ideas are, or just how steep certain slopes are until we are doing it. He can't look over and say, "No way — that's too steep," or, "I can't ski trees." I can say things like, "I know this great little run; it has some trees, but I think you'll really like it." Truth be told, it's a veritable forest with dips and branches sticking out everywhere. I can't pull this trick too often or he'll never trust a thing I say ever again. This time it worked and we headed out for an 18-mile backcountry journey known locally as the Commando Run. One thing that continues to impress me about Erik is his ability to trust and rely on the people around him. I have faith, but certainly have learned a lot from Erik about blind faith, without which he could be a couch potato.

The Commando Run would serve us well as we broke in our new Randonee gear by going up and down numerous times, requiring multiple skin removals and applications. This, I thought would be a challenge for Big E as we dealt with wind and the ever-so-sticky bottoms of the skins. He got the best of them and we headed off into the woods. We cruised up through the four feet of new snow at a rate faster than our descent. As we twisted up and around on Bowman's shortcut, me ringing a bear bell in front as if peppering the trail with sound for Erik to follow, I would occasionally get lost in thought or conversation and forget my friend's visual shortcomings (like not being able to see the tree branches at face level or the occasional snag at ankle level; nothing but black). Just humming right along and then behind me a sudden shout of "Aaarrggh!" or something not fit for print! Really, it would make me feel bad, but I'd be lying if I told you I didn't laugh a little from time to time, or use it as a way to get back at him for his off-color jokes and comments.

Things began to intensify as we headed down through the tight trees, dodging left, right, down, under, and up over obstacles. I lead by ringing my bell, verbally giving directions, and batting my poles together and on trees for direction. And surprisingly, E wouldn't even get mad when I'd say things like, "Go left. Go left!!!" SPLAT! "Oops, I meant right." After hours on the trail we finally made it to Vail's back bowls, and were soon in town enjoying a big fat sandwich and a beer at the Red Lion.

We had just had a great success. I knew that if E could "hang" on the commando route and on the steeper slopes at a resort, he could most likely make it in Russia. We invited a friend/videographer to come join us for a day here and also to come to Russia to put it all on tape. Michael Brown set himself up at the bottom of a nice wide run, perfectly groomed, and not a soul in sight. *This will be a great shot*, I thought to myself. As we got nearer to the camera I thought how cool it would be if Erik skied directly at the camera, turned quickly with a spray for the perfect image. Well I misjudged his turn, and he says he never heard me shout "stop." It was a good shot and is also why Erik now has a scar like Harry Potter on his forehead, as he collided with the cameraman. Erik either suffers from short-term memory loss now, or he has a big heart to forgive people for nearly ruining his ski career (I think it is the latter).

Off to Whistler and then to the summit of Mt. Hood, where we were able to enjoy the wide-open slopes and challenges of whiteout conditions; definitely a case of the blind leading the blind. One last day of June training on Loveland Pass, then Russia, look out!

June 6, 2002 — Two long days of travel brought us to our hotel in the Baksan Valley at the foot of Mt. Elbrus. A place one-half finished or one-half demolished; I had a hard time telling the difference. As I gazed upon the hills and mountains around us, the beauty and magnitude of this region mesmerized me. It was everything that the Alps of Western Europe were and higher. It was rugged, and had glaciated, high peaks offering every type of challenge for mountaineers and skiers alike. From the photos I brought back, however, this appeared to be a bit of a posh trip, staying at hotels and eating foods prepared for us by our Russian cook. What you don't see from our photos are the excruciatingly cold showers and the grumpy floor mom who told us when we were to take showers with a hand signal, showing us the number of fingers she is holding up so that we will know when the water will, or should I say could, be hot. Nothing like a cold day on the mountain followed by a cold shower in a building with no heat. But hey, we are rugged mountaineers, right?

Slowly we filter into the kitchen for our first meal and are excited to try some of the region's epicurean delights. What came next was a nice bowl of borsch. The first time it was good, but after two weeks it began to remind me of the menu at Base Camp on Everest; a menu that never changed. We tried to fatten up for our ascent the following day, and the cheap Russian beer probably helped us do this more than anything. After having spent a couple of days skiing and acclimating, we went for Elbrus. The team was huge. A number of us who had been on the Everest expedition were again here: Michael Brown, Luis Benitez, Chris Morris, Erik and Eric, Didrik Johnk, Kevin Cherilla, and a host of other friends who had been invited to make this a fun trip.

The Russian crew we had with us had never seen such a large team with so much gear. We had a film crew with us and then of course we had all kinds of computer and communications equipment as well. I sometimes think it's not possible to climb a mountain without this stuff any more. The Russians who were with us thought this was crazy, and couldn't understand the necessity. We, on the other hand, saw it as fun and didn't mind the effort, especially when it kept us in close contact with loved ones at home. Day one would bring us up an old tram; it was old, but at least it was poorly maintained (if I am to be perfectly positive in my pessimism). As we departed the terminal in the overloaded cable car, I made the mistake of looking back at the terminal and seeing the support for the tram: a broomstick wedged in below the cable to act as a bushing, and thereby, reduce friction on the cable. What a great time to be blind!

At the top we were greeted by a bit of a storm and shuttled our gear over to "the barrels" — recycled fuel barrels that served as our home for the next couple of days as we acclimated some more. These were quite nice really. No need to worry about the wind or shoveling snow off them. They had heaters, and even lights inside. At this point I was beginning to feel like a very fat American climber. Where are the dangers, the risks, and the hard nights out — the challenges? I suppose the heart of adventure is not always in the challenge itself, but as much in the soul of the people who make up the team and the excitement of doing something new. It doesn't matter that this mountain has been climbed before and even skied before; it never had been by us and never by a blind man, and this was our adventure.

After some more borsch, we made our first foray up the lower slopes of the mountain. We were hit by nearly 60 mph winds and blowing snow. I take back what I said earlier; here began the adventure. Yelling over the wind to my blind friend and making sure to steer him away from the rocks and other dangers of the mountain, we made our way up to 15,000 feet. This was the highest we would get before summit day.

Moving from the Barrels camp to the Priut hut was really not much of a day. A short climb of 3,000 feet and setting up camp left us with a little extra time for some skiing. Here we set up three tents and had a hut available for some of the team. This hut was perched on the edge of a steep hill above the glacier and we were thankful that the construction was so shoddy. Perhaps the most interesting thing here was the "john" and how it was tied down with cables, sealed by a thin particleboard door. When someone would go in, they put themselves in harm's way. There was nowhere to sit and when the person inside assumed the position, all the others on the outside would gather the hardest snowballs they could and bombard the precarious tin structure. This stopped when Kevin, on the inside, received a near-fatal blow that went through the door and hit him in the face. It sure made for some good laughs, and still does today.

It was the typical alpine start: 2:30 a.m., cold and dark. We got up and couldn't see through the snow. Waiting two hours, again we find trying to keep a schedule doesn't work in the mountains; they don't care where you need to be or when, just that they are the boss. At 4:30 the weather finally calmed enough for us to get out and give it a try. Erik, Chris, and I went for the summit together, with the rest of the team up ahead. Slowly we made it up, and as we did, to our surprise, the weather got better. It was never very cold as we pushed up through the snow and fog.

It seemed as though Erik was struggling a little this day, and after spending the entire winter training for this, I couldn't understand why. We made our way up over the steep, icy section and then over the final crest, at which time we saw the entire team waiting for us in the form of a gauntlet line. As we went for the summit, we passed through the line and each person smacked Erik on the back, letting him have first crack at the summit. This kind of camaraderie made my eyes well up with tears. There is something about achieving a goal as a team, at which time, the entire team gives back the success to an individual which makes one feel all warm and fuzzy, no matter how cold it may be.

For a few moments we stood on top and reveled. We were able to make contact with family back home and share the moment with loved ones ten hours away. Eager as I was to make the summit, I absolutely could not wait to ski down. I quickly clicked into my skis and said, "It's time to ski!"

Erik looked my way and said in a tired drawl, still panting as he ate an energy bar, "Ya know I really don't feel like skiing. I think I'll just walk down." If someone is incapable or unable, I am the first one to support the idea of stopping; guess that is just the ski patrolman in me. But Erik was just not in the mood, so it seemed. I understand he was a little tired, but we had just spent the last six months getting ready for this moment, hours of time on the phone, making deals, organizing, preparing, skiing together, coordinating, planning, and now he didn't want to ski! I got so mad that steam started coming out of my ears.

I went over to him and gently said, "Oh, you're gonna ski! We didn't go through all of this so you could be the first blind guy to *think* about skiing off the top: no, you actually gotta do it."

Henry Ford said, "You can't build a reputation on what you are going to do."[3]

He buckled up and skied off the top with me. We had the longest run of our lives; 9,500 vertical feet of descent. It was a blast. There were conditions ranging from crust to powder to blue glacial ice to knee-deep slush. I would ski behind him calling out his turns, a process where the shape of his turn is determined by the length of time I hold the word in a shout: "Tuuuurrrrrnnn aaa rriiiggghhhtt!" would be a long right turn; "Turn a left!" would be a short left turn.

When it got steep and narrow, the calls would become quick, and so would our turns, much like a dance. Normally soft spoken, Erik preferred that I really shout if there was ever anything of concern for him. "STOP!" was preferred to "Stop," and "CLIFF!" was another important one. A remarkable lesson I have learned in our time skiing together is about this thing called forgiveness; usually after using "stop, cliff" instead of really getting after it with "STOP! CLIFF!" This was certainly a good challenge for a tired, blind guy and his merciless friend.

As we neared the bottom, we again came into whiteout conditions. I could see generally where we should go, but could not see the terrain, so I used Erik and his bright red jacket skiing in front of me to let me know where the drops would be; again a case of the blind leading the blind. When he would suddenly drop I knew there was a big roller coming. This was fun, especially when he was interviewed on the *Today Show*, telling the world that he got us off the mountain that day; kind of like Rudolph guiding Santa's sleigh.

When we got down, Erik turned to me with a big ole grin and said, "Do ya wanna go back up? That was possibly the best run I have ever had." Erik later thanked me for making him click into his skis that day, and as much as I kid him, I have to thank my friend for helping me to realize many dreams and see the possibilities in all things. He gave it his best effort. We made it off the mountain unharmed, and even more impressive is we made it down the tram unharmed. One of our Russian friends said to me, in his thick Russian accent, "I did not know invalid could ski like this."

Erik having overheard this turned and said, "Yeah, but he does pretty good, doesn't he!"

A celebration at the dacha of former President Brezhnev awaited us at the bottom, and after the team put away a few cocktails, a new plan had been formulated to paraglide off Australia's highest summit: the final chapter of Erik's quest to be the first blind man to scale the Seven Summits.

Only a few months later we were skiing again — this time upside-down, as we were in the Southern Hemisphere. We had followed through with a trip to Thredbo, Australia, for what was supposed to be a "cakewalk" of a summit. We thought that flying off it would make this tour a little more special, so we enrolled in a paragliding school, gaining enough experience to attempt a flight from Australia's highest peak. We brought all our gear down, only to be denied the opportunity to fly by the rain and the wind.

When the skies finally cleared enough, the runs were left frozen hard like the Lhotse face of Everest; just in time for an early morning summit bid. We left at 4 a.m. so we could get good sunrise pictures near the summit of this peak. As we climbed, one of our team members fell when his skins lost their purchase on the icy slope, sending him spinning 500 feet to the bottom of the slope, nearly hitting the trees. Laughing in relief as we heard him yell from below, "I'm okay, boss!" another skier went down, this time right in front of me. I couldn't move out of the way fast enough, and before I knew it, I was riding down the mountain on the world's blindest man. I set my edges and we came to a stop.

Breathing a sigh of relief, I heard a shout in an irritated tone, as if to say I had caused the problem: "Get off me!" I should have been the one upset, having just been knocked to the icy ground, yet able to stop us from the same 500-foot slide that Kevin had just taken. I replied, "Oh, I'm sorry you knocked me down and I saved your life. Next time I will be more careful and get out of your way and let you slide to the bottom, too." We made it up the hill, and as the sun came up, so did the clouds and the winds. I pulled out my compass to get a bearing on where the true summit might be hiding, and we all headed into the 65 mph winds and whiteout. After a bit of guesswork/teamwork we stood on top of that icy summit at 8:30 a.m., making this a momentous occasion in mountaineering's history: the first blind person to climb to the top of each continent's highest peak.

Mike Brown froze his hands trying to film the event as the rest of us sipped on champagne and cheered the moment. It was a brief, windy celebration followed by a swift ski down to a wonderful breakfast at the resort. That is my kind of mountaineering. A roo steak for dinner (kangaroo tastes a lot like beef), a couple days at the beach, and soon we were home planning our next trip to Mt. Cook, New Zealand: a peak that *Climbing Magazine* calls the most difficult peak in the area known as Australasia.

The trip ended with a great time at Brighton Beach, and Erik, on Australian television telling the world how he had saved my life when he fell and was sliding down the treacherous icy slopes in the dark. He did this with a straight face, which is why I write the following sarcastic comment: "I am thankful for his ability to hone in on sounds like a bat, and the courage it took to risk his life for mine (sarcasm), as well as, his ability to get the facts mixed up."

In alpine climbing, it seldom matters if a climber can see or not because so much of it is done in the dark before the sun rises. This is called an alpine start. Just like the climb in Australia began in the dark, so too did the ascent of New Zealand's highest peak, Mt. Cook. There are the Seven Summits, and then there is what has been termed the Super Seven: the hardest peak on each continent, which is not always the highest. Mt. Cook made the list. After some paragliding around Queenstown, the two of us left our hut high on the flanks of Mt. Cook at 10:30 p.m.

The three feet of new snow had all avalanched off our route and it was now safe to climb, providing perfect conditions. For most of the approach we used our snowshoes in what was the early part of their summer, approaching Christmas. The beginning of the climb went smoothly, but as we neared the top and the sun began to hit us, we knew we needed to hurry. To speed up this process up, we simul-climbed with a rope between us. The tension of the rope provided Erik with much-needed direction, and we climbed without anchors between us. This meant if the blind guy made a mistake and slipped, or fell, and pulled on the rope, he would pull me down with him. It was only a couple of thousand icy feet down to the rocks and ice of the glacier below, so I wasn't worried at all; I was terrified. I was terrified, not because he was blind, but because my climbing partner had chosen to forego his quality steel crampons and ice axe, and instead brought only his aluminum crampons and ice axe for this climb. They were barely able to penetrate the ice, as they are so light and soft.

The sweat was beading up on my forehead as much from fear as it was from the sun. I knew that every swing of my axe and every kick of my steel-cramponed feet was critical. If he fell, it would be my axe that would save us both. I stuck every swing like planting a tree. I meant it, and I kept the rope tight. If any slack were to work its way into the system, it would only add momentum to the fall of his 180-pound body pulling me from my purchase on the slope.

Once we reached the shoulder of the mountain, the climb and the stress were long from gone. We scaled the vertical rock bands to get to the knife-edged summit ridge. This ridge reminded me of the ridge on Everest, only steeper. Adding to the sense of height and place was the fact that we could see the ocean from this 12,000-foot summit. It was as airy a perch as can be imagined, but now I was not only looking out for where I was going, I had to manage the rope behind me, as well as, my partner's steps. If only I had two more eyes in the back of my head, or even just one! I sunk in the shaft of my ice axe with every step, and as Erik neared the summit I gave him a belay using my deeply rooted ice axe. The view was as dramatic as any I had ever seen, and so was the descent. Hours of post-holing up to our waists through the deep new snow and warm glacier below brought us back to the hut at 10:30 p.m., 24 hours later, utterly exhausted. This effort, being just the two of us, tired me more than the climb of Everest, and I couldn't imagine how Erik felt.

The flight home took us through Auckland, where we were able to hop off the plane for a short visit with Sir Edmund Hillary and his wife, Lady June. At the airport I bought his new book which had just been released and made sure I got change in the form of two crisp new $5 NZ bills, because his face was gracing the front side of the bill. If the opportunity presented itself I was going to ask him to sign them. I am not normally a fan and really don't collect signatures, but this was different, somehow bigger and more meaningful than just celebrity, it was inspiration; he was a pioneer.

We talked of mountains and their people and the work he did for them both. We shared briefly our thoughts on the summit and then posed for a picture, where I was able to stand with one of my friends and two of my heroes, both pioneers. As much as we kid, I am thankful to God for the opportunities we have in the mountains together. I am thankful for the friendship we share, which is built upon trust, respect, and a willingness to try what the world tells us is crazy. Giving others the courage to get out and try to break down some of the barriers in their own lives is not something we set out to do, but comes as a great result of what we have been able to do. Each time I go out I am again encouraged to take a chance today on something I have been dreaming of all of my yesterdays.

Deadpoint Reflections

All men dream, but not equally. Those who dream by night, in the dusty recesses of their minds, awake in the day to find that it was vanity. But the dreamers of the day are dangerous men, for they may act on their dreams with open eyes to make it reality.[4] — T.E. Lawrence

Crux: Trust. It should come naturally in marriage, in church, and in support groups, but it doesn't. Most of us at some time or another have been burned by words, actions, and misdeeds of others, and we live guarded lives, never allowing others to have a secure position of trust. When we close this door, we miss out on the fullness of what relationships are meant to be. There is an easy-to-grasp climbing analogy of trust where the lead climber must rely on the steady hand of his belayer and have trust in him and also in the rope that keeps him connected to the rock, should the climber fall. This can be likened to the kind of trust we need to have in marriage or in work, but in a way this trust in climbing is easier because the rope is generally solidly anchored.

So how strong is the trust when the rope is taken away and mistakes are even more serious? Skiing with someone who is blind is like climbing without that rope, and trust really becomes a major factor in the relationship. It really boils down to words: precision in vocalizing exactly what needs to be communicated at just the right moment without a second chance. Most of us in a way similar to these examples have been dropped by our belayers or driven into a tree by our ski guide — we have had trust betrayed. It is with words that we typically blow it. In skiing, that would be saying turn left when I mean right, in life, it usually means just keep your mouth shut, think, think some more, then speak. We come away with an attitude of "In me I trust. I'll get it done in my time, my way, on my own." I have been guilty of this kind of thinking and it reminds me of the Frank Sinatra song, "My Way." To me, that is a sad, lonely, and somewhat desperate song.

Hold: Attentiveness. Be trustworthy. Let your actions match your word, and keep your word. Simple. The fastest way to lose a friend is to be a hypocrite, to gossip about that friend, or even people within your circle. I know because I have made this mistake. I have known some gossips, and yes, they can be friends, but I never let them in close, and I never give them any more information than what I think of the weather forecast. A friendship like this can never go too deep. But there is a certain core of friends that I have observed who never divulge information about others, not even under the guise of "prayer." These are people I can trust and do trust with matters of the heart. This is my wife, and just a small select group of others. A gossip will never earn my trust or my close friendship.

Anchor: The Word. We can take God at His Word. It is what He has given us. If we don't trust this, the Bible, then what is the point of having faith? To meet women at church? For some that is exactly it. "Trust in the LORD with all of your heart and lean not on your own understanding; in all of your ways acknowledge him, and he will make your paths straight" (Proverbs 3:5–6). If you only trust God as far as you can throw Him, you don't trust at all. You have got to trust Him as far as He can throw you. If we approach trust in the Lord like we do human relationships, that is to say with a piece of our heart leaning on our own understanding, we will fail. Maybe you can only give a piece at a time; that is okay, but be determined to give it all. Later, you will gain it all.

Endnotes
1. Thomas Hornbein, *Everest: The West Ridge* (San Francisco, CA: Sierra Club-Ballantine Books, 1966).
2. http://quotationsbook.com/quote/944.
3. William S. Walsh, *International Encyclopedia of Prose and Poetical Quotations* (Philadelphia, PA: Winston, 1951).
4. T.E. Lawrence, *Seven Pillars of Wisdom* (Herfordshire, UK: Wordsworth Editions, 1997).

2Xtreme Dream

[Pisco]

View of Kusum Kanguru at 20,889 feet as trek begins.

Bridge along Khumbu trek.

A team member on the shoulder of Island Peak, also known as Imjatse. Pumori is on top left and Everest is back right.

Ama Dablam means "Mother's jewel box" and refers to the glacier hanging near the top as like a charm on a necklace. The mountain has ridges which look like the outstretched arms of a welcoming mother. This climb would serve as a warmup to Everest for our team.

Ama Dablam Base Camp.

Erik Weihenmayer ascends high on the peak.

Camp One, Ama Dablam 19,000 feet; the site of my fall. Photo Brad Bull.

Climbing the south west ridge of Ama Dablam between Camps One and Two. This is slow and agonizing terrain for a blind person.

This is the Yellow Tower. The spot where the climbers are standing became nicknamed "Abject Terror" due to the fact that a fall from here would be 2,000 feet or so. Rope is used on this last big obstacle before Camp Two at 20,000 feet. Reading the rock like braille, this terrain is easier for a blind man than the boulder fields lower on the mountain.

With a 2,000 foot drop, this is high exposure! Climber is on Ama Dablam's Yellow Tower.

Luis Benitez on the Yellow Tower. Ama Dablam.

Home sweet home. One week here, and Erik wouldn't even grant me the courtesy of sleeping on the left.

Chris Morris descending in full conditions on Ama Dablam.

Descending on O₂ with Dr. Steve .

Eric in Gamow bag.

The author deals with high altitude pulmonary edema suffered after a 150 foot fall. With an 0₂ saturation of 45% it was imperative to breathe oxygen, descend to a lower elevation, and eventually be flown out of the mountains to a hospital in Kathmandu. First Thessalonians 4:17 says that we are to pray continually. Being in a position like this makes that easy.

Joseph Chonko: 1972-2001
Plans: "To make a difference in the
world around me." My good friend
and climbing partner died two months
before the Everest climb.

Joseph's caribiner kept me linked to
the rope as I climbed the fixed lines of
Everest.

Our Everest Team:

Back row: Eric Alexander, Luis Benitez, Dr. Steve Gipe

Standing: Didrik Johnck, Pasquale Scatturo, Erik Weihenmayer, Chris Morris, Jeff Evans, Kevin Cherilla, Sherman Bull

Front row: Michael Brown, Charlie Mace, Brad Bull, Mike O'Donnell

Others: Maurice Peret, Reba Bull, Kim Morris, Zac German, Jason Dimmig, Johnathon McDonaugh.

Chhiring Sona Sherpa carries Adam Scaturro, quadriplegic, to Everest Base Camp.

Mt. Everest Base Camp: 17,800 feet.

Climbers circle a chorten as they arrive back in Everest Base Camp.

Base Camp after a spring snow. Photo by Steve Gipe.

View from Base Camp of the Khumbu icefall, Nuptse to the right, Lhotse center, and Everest left.

This became known as the "Jesus" ladder. It was the first word out of my teammate's mouth when he stepped on it. He then said, "If you don't believe, step on this thing and you're gonna start."

The icefall is a place that rattles a climber's nerves. The ice indiscriminately calves off, shifts, breaks and rolls down the slope to swallow anything or anyone in its path. Blocks as big as houses can fall without a moment's notice. Many people die here. Pictured is Jeff Evans at "the lunch spot."

Mike O'Donnell and Chris Morris rest at Camp One after ascending the icefall.

Mt. Everest is on the left and Lhotse, the 4th highest mountain in the world, is on the right.

Camp Two (next page) - 22,000 feet, and the icy 45+ degree Lhotse face. The climb will continue up the Lhotse face to Camp Three, over the Yellow Band and then on to the Geneva Spur (seen rising up at the left). Often times this day of climbing above Camp Three is combined with the summit day giving climbers only a few hours of rest at Camp Four at 26,000 feet, limiting a person's time and exposure to the "Death Zone."

Erik and Brad Bull arrive at Camp Three 24,000 feet. Camp Two in the Western CWM is below near the strip of black rocks. It is at this point that sleeping becomes more difficult as the tents become more cramped, the food tastes worse, and the cold, thin air robs climbers of valuable air.

The Yellow Band seen here above Camp Three. A fallen climber makes it back to camp after a fall from Lhotse. Most climbers begin to use oxygen on this day, some will even start with a low flow the night before, as they sleep.

This is the view from Camp Four looking up the route to the South Summit. We would leave at 9:00 p.m. to hopefully return to camp before the typical afternoon storms would roll in. The route goes up the faint line in the center of the photograph, up onto the shoulder at the right (the Balcony), then continues to the South Summit at 28,500 feet.

Sherpas from another expedition prepare loads for the descent after their summit attempt. Cho Oyu, the 6th highest mountain at 26,901 feet is in the distance.

Jeff Evans sucking down O's in the tent at Camp Four. All of us trying to push out the voices of doubt, as well as the thoughts of those who had just died higher up on the mountain.

Luis bundled up ready to leave the South Col and Camp Four at 9:20 p.m.

Only a few hours after the departure for the summit, team leader Pasquale Scaturro selflessly turned back. I believe true leaders are visionaries that take action and back up decisions with character when it matters most. With his feet beginning to freeze and his energy level dropping, Pasquale would have risked not only his own life, but the lives of others had he continued.

Luis Benitez near the South Summit of Everest just before sunrise at 27,800 feet.

Sunrise behind Makalu, the world's fifth highest peak at 27,762 feet, on the Nepal Tibet border. By 4:30 in the morning we were higher than that point. Kangchenjunga, the world's 3rd highest mountain sits in the orange glow of the sunrise I will never forget.

Beyond the Hillary Step (pictured here in shadows) it is just a few hundred feet more to the summit. Many have seen this part of the climb as a very formidable obstacle, which it most certainly was in the the early years of Everest's climbing history.

Erik Weihenmayer following Luis up the Hillary step. Ang Pasang in back.

The top of the world! Five world records were set: first blind man; oldest man (Sherman Bull 64); largest team (19); first American father / son (Sherman and Brad Bull); largest camera to the summit (25 pound HD camera carried by two Sherpas and Michael Brown).
Clockwise from left: Michael Brown, Eric Alexander, Luis Benitez, Erik Weihenmayer, Ang Pasang Sherpa.

Self portrait near Everest's summit, 29,035 feet.

Makalu as seen from Camp Four. Kachenjunga is in the distance - the world's fifth and third highest mountains respectively. Charles Mace Collection.

A storm closes in during our descent the following day. The team gathers on the Geneva Spur after Camp Four is taken down.

Jeff Evans descends the upper Lhotse face en route to Camp Three which is packed up and jettisoned down the face by the Sherpas. More fatalities typically occur on the way down the mountain as climbers lose focus in an exhausted or euphoric state. We were fortunate to have no lasting injuries or fatalities on our team.

The arrival back at Base Camp is a better feeling than that of standing on the summit. Friends greet the team with hugs and drink. It is what I refer to as the ex-lax effect - a sweet release of weeks of pent up anxiety. Charles Moore Collection.

The team received an invitation to the White House, and a meeting in the Oval Office with President George W. Bush. I am the one on the right.

Kami Tenzing, Eric Alexander,
Charles Mace (left)

Erik, Ellen,
and Emma
Weihenmayer
(above)

Eric Alexander, Sir Edmund Hillary,
Erik Weihenmayer (left)

Ice Doctors

Dr. Steve Gipe

Everest Base Camp

Phurba Botc Shcrpa

Pemba Gyaljen Sherpa

Ang Pasang Sherpa

Chuldim Nuru Sherpa

Some of the faces of those that made it all possible.

Pemba Chote Sherpa

Ang Sona Sherpa

Chombi Sherpa

Ang Pasang Sherpa

Ang Kami Sherpa (bottom right)

Tenzing Sherpa

Lhakpa Tsering Sherpa

Mingma Sherpa

Pasang Sherpa

Yak Brown

Yak Black

Kancha Sherpa

ELEVATION: 18,871 feet

HOW LONG TO CLIMB: Approximately two weeks;
plan for time to sight see and acclimate

HOW MANY IN THE TEAM: Six on our team

RATING: PD

BEST TO CLIMB DURING: June to August;
Peruvian winter

ALSO KNOWN AS: Pisco means "bird" in Quechua

Notes:
Three of the six made the summit of
this peak in Peru which is often used
to acclimate for other climbs.

Do you not know that in a race all the runners run, but only one gets the prize? Run in such a way as to get the prize. — 1 Corinthians 9:24

There is, in man, an essential paradox. On the one hand he seeks all the ways and means to make his life comfortable, safe, and certain; but, on the other, he knows intuitively that only by taking risks and facing up to uncertainty is he going to stretch himself, and arrive at that moment of truth when he can see more of the unknown around him.[1]

— Doug Scott

I have to admit that sometimes when the phone rings, I don't jump up out of my seat and run to answer. When the number is unrecognized and from a distant area code, I often think it is someone asking for money or demanding my services for free. I guess I should have a more positive approach to the noisy device like, "Hey, that could be my new best friend calling," or maybe, "This is an opportunity I won't want to miss," or even, "Buddy the Elf. What's your favorite color?"

However, once in a while I do get that call that does change my course and challenges me to take giant leaps out of my comfort zone, which is again why I don't run to the phone but approach it with trepidation, wonder, and fear, sometimes picking it up with sweaty palms touching it as though it is a hot potato. It was shortly after I had returned from Australia that I received this call: "Hey, Eric. This is John Davis."

"Hey, John, how are you?" I said, and immediately asked myself, *Who is John Davis and what does he want? Did I pay my taxes last year?*

"I am a counselor in Denver and got your name from a colleague here who knows your mother. Anyway, I went to high school with Erik Weihenmayer and have heard a lot about what you guys have done, and I know you were responsible for getting him up Everest. I got your number and thought I would introduce myself, and also ask you about possibly doing a Denali trip for some of my guys." As in *Jerry McGuire* when Renee Zellweger said, "You had me at hello," I must admit John had me at "Denali."

I said, "John, you certainly have my interest, but tell me more about you, and more about your guys, and why Denali?" He proceeded to tell me about the non-profit called 2Xtreme he had started for teen boys who have undergone extensive counseling for violence, drug addiction, alcoholism, and other types of behavioral issues. When the guys in his program reach a point, usually in their junior year of high school, they must be able to commit a year to the following seven criteria:

1. Help design and follow a therapy plan
2. Have no negative police contact
3. Stay clean from drugs and alcohol (we drug test our youth)
4. Maintain a part-time job
5. Participate in a community service program
6. Resolve conflicts at home
7. Maintain good grades

They must also comply with "house rules" while demonstrating a positive attitude, and if so, they are rewarded with what John calls the 2Xtreme dream. Those who have succeeded for the year will, at the end of their senior year, be able to choose a dream adventure trip anywhere in the world and the foundation, along with certain sponsors, will pay for it. The boys will contribute some of their own funds toward this as well and the result could well be a life-changing experience. After I heard John's description of a past trip to Kilimanjaro and I had a few moments to think about it, I said, "Why not? Well, let's at least meet and determine the feasibility of this since none of these guys are climbers, and besides, we need to get to know each other a little bit anyway."

We set up a preliminary meeting after which we then set up an early winter ascent of Buyer's Peak near Fraser, Colorado. This would be a long day on snowshoes, skis, snowboards, and would give me an idea where the guys were physically, mentally, and experientially. We had only six months to prepare, and with each of them being so busy we would only be able to get out a handful of days together, and I wouldn't have any way to keep them accountable to a training program. Denali is a high, cold, and intense place where people die each year, and I wasn't taking it lightly. When I saw the equipment they had, and how one or two had a little bit of a draggy butt syndrome, I thought it would take more than six months to get them ready. I was not prepared to drag anyone up Denali; they needed to have the desire inside, because it is harder than they think, and is much more than just a cool idea.

I told John after that first long day out when we did not reach the top of Buyer's, or even get above timberline, that we may need to reconsider our "dream." "Let's give it one more outing, but be thinking of something else that they may accept as an alternative plan," I said. The second outing was a day of ice climbing at Lincoln Falls with a winter overnight at 11,000 feet. I knew right away that Denali was not going to happen. Maybe it was the untied tennis shoes hanging loosely off their feet, or maybe it was the oversized

$5 Aviator glasses that got me thinking this way, but definitely the baggy mesh basketball shorts flown at half-mast with boxers coming out the top convinced me that we needed a new plan.

It was late December in Colorado and we were at 11,000 feet. I had sent out a gear list, knowing these guys had lived here a lifetime and are avid skiers and snowboarders, so I could deduce that they would at least have warm long johns, fleece, and Gore-Tex clothing, but it was nowhere to be seen. "Okay, guys, pack up and let's get going. Hope those shorts keep you warm!" Well, when we got over to the falls, the warm clothes did come out and I discovered that these guys were truly likeable, they just didn't have any experience at this. I cut them slack when it came to organizing and climbing, but not when it came to attitude.

There was Nelson, Peter, and Dude, as he liked to be called, a fan of *The Big Lebowski*. Nelson was tall and physical and had a very kind nature, and buried deep down inside he truly had a heart of gold. My thoughts about him were it was just hard for him to let that show and be who he truly was. Perhaps he was allowing himself to be who others wanted him to be, or even who he thought he should be, and this was guiding him more than his heart.

Peter immediately stood out to me as the most physical, most interested, and most dedicated to not only this trip, but to getting his life turned around. A great guy, likeable, and easy to be with, I wondered how he got into this program because he seemed so well adjusted.

Now, Dude's a slow-talking, slow-moving guy I think would have had more fun and more desire if we were to put on a soccer camp for the little kids of a distant, poor community. Dude was a standout soccer player for his school, yet every time we went out for a climb his knees seemed to bother him. I took him at his word and hoped it wouldn't be an issue for him or become an excuse. Though I liked all three guys, I really seemed to enjoy Peter's enthusiasm and abilities. He was really excited about the trip, training, and really took it seriously. I think Peter would have not only been ready for Denali, but would have excelled on that climb. This trip, however, had to meet the needs of all three and the timetable we had for training.

I wanted to go somewhere rich in culture and geography that would still provide each person a feeling of accomplishment while going for their dream. We had basically the month of June to work with, which would really only allow us to choose among a few places on the globe. The one that stood out to me was the high Andes of Peru and the Cordillera Blanca. The climate here was a little warmer and more forgiving, the peaks as high as Denali, and the culture fascinating.

After speaking with John and our other leader, Rich Collins, who would join us later in the training program, we decided that this would be a perfect option to present to the guys. The guys agreed that they were not ready for Denali and this change to the dream actually seemed every bit as cool. The peaks we would attempt would first be Pisco at 18,500 feet, to help us acclimate, and then across the valley would be Chopicalqui at 20,300 feet, and about the same elevation as Denali. Costs would be about the same and gear less expensive, so we were on our way.

From these outings, I immediately took a liking to John. He was a good leader and had a kind and compassionate heart, while at the same time, standing firm and running a tight ship, with the program holding these young men accountable. He cares for each of his guys and truly wants each one of them to succeed. At the forefront was John's enthusiasm for positive life change in these young men that really made me want to be a contributor to his program. John is a tall, handsome, athletic guy that many might find intimidating, but he wears his heart on his sleeve, almost to a fault. Most of the young men who are in need of John's program have lacked a father figure, and I know that for a lot of them John takes this place and loves them while pushing them to expect more from themselves. John has authored a book, *Extreme Pursuit*, and if anyone is having troubles with their teenage son, I highly recommend it.

Rich worked as a ski patrolman on Vail Mountain, just like I had done years earlier. Rich shared something with both me and John that really united us very quickly into a tight brotherhood: faith in Jesus. It is amazing to me how having this as the core of a bond can unite certain ones of us in mere minutes, making us feel as though we have known each other a lifetime. It doesn't quite work like this with all Christians, but with a certain few like John and Rich it was amazing, and we would lean on this faith and each other throughout our journey. While John does not proselytize in his work place or even get preachy with his kids, his values and character are evidence of his faith. When asked, he will share; when provoked, he will pray.

Nelson attended church regularly, but that didn't always serve to keep him out of trouble, and I can attest it didn't for me, either. I know that inside all of us is a bad boy image and/or act that wants to let itself out. I can say that only by the grace of God was I able to sometimes contain my urges, and sometimes I wasn't. I guess in this way I could identify with these three young men. I knew that I had strong Christian mentors growing up, and these men gave me a positive role model to follow early in my life, all while encouraging me in my faith. I wanted to be like them, I still do, and I wanted to be that person for these guys.

Peter and Dude, perhaps more out of respect for the leaders and our faith, went with the flow on this because every time we met, we would pray as a team for safety and guidance. No one was forced to be a part of this, but they always patiently went along with it, and I think even came to enjoy what was almost a ritual each day, the ceremony of gathering and unifying in purpose, or perhaps just the humility it required when taking on the unknown. It did always provide for us a platform to begin communications as to how we were feeling, what was going on at home, what concerns there may be, and a way to unload when we just needed to unload. In this way, our prayers were never forced but always present.

Rich had just gotten off work and skied over to join us for one of our final training days. We had hiked up Vail Mountain earlier in the day and were now again at 11,000 feet, digging in to Ptarmigan cornice, building a nice, cozy snow cave where we would have dinner and sleep, and the following day ski to the bottom and off for home. This was actually a blast and showed me that the guys were coming along in their efforts, beginning to take this more seriously.

One last training day in May, high off Loveland Pass with another overnight stay testing our systems, and learning to set up our tents in high winds would serve us well. We spent a long, cold day hiking over to Grizzly Peak. We learned how to stop a fall on steep snow with a self-arrest using an ice-axe; carried heavy loads at high altitude; and finally looked as though we had our equipment mastered. It appeared as though we were ready for Peru. After a team 10k run in the Bolder Boulder, we packed up and headed off.

June 16, 2003 — Everything went smoothly, even perfectly, until we got to the heights of Ciudad Huaraz. We hiked, rock climbed, acclimated, and did everything we should have done, by the book. The one mistake we made was we ate. Was it the guinea pig? Was it the Alpaca steak? It definitely was not the Coca tea or any of the vegetables, because John, the only vegetarian on the team, was the only one to not get sick. Nelson was the first to go down: fever, shakes, vomiting, diarrhea, weakness, cold sweats, hot flashes, and desires to go home. Getting sick like this in a foreign country is like a right of passage. It makes you a man, or that's what I told Nelson anyway, in hopes he would get up and go with us the next day on our scheduled departure for the trailhead.

The next day Nelson arose like the bright sun itself. We loaded up and all hopped in the back of a small pickup truck headed into Huascaran National Park. The only thing missing from our ride in this old truck, with the static-filled FM Peruvian tunes, was a few chickens to ride on top. A right turn at the town of Yungay (pronounced young guy), and I began to feel like an old guy. The blood began to drain from my head, the air suddenly felt cold all around me, my stomach felt like it was floating inside me and now wanted out; a burn took over deeper inside, and soon there was that familiar flash feeling you get just before you know something is about to explode.

I don't remember if it was John or me who hit the roof of the truck, but someone said, "You don't look so good."

"I don't feel so good," I said. "We need to stop." Two hard bangs on the roof, a sudden stop, a quick exit, a romp down the embankment, and then that ever so important decision: Which way do I lean? Which end first? The bomb went off big. I don't know if there has ever been a time in my life when I have felt worse, and yes, that includes having pulmonary edema.

Turning around, wiping my mouth with my sleeve to remove the fragments of some foreign beast that had made its way back up and out into the wild, I saw the truck was empty and the woods were full of similar activity from Rich, Dude, and Peter. I was the trigger, the catalyst for the ensuing party, the pukers joining me as if to genuflect before the giant peak of Huascaran itself. We climbed back in, signed in at the park entrance, and then met our little mule friends and driver at the trailhead.

Looking back, this was perhaps one of the worst decisions I have ever made in the mountains. We should have stayed and rested at least one, if not two days, before going higher. Nelson was only just now better, I was sick and dehydrated, Dude was sick, but felt like moving on, and as a team we just needed rest. I also believe this move would have allowed us to reassess our goals and would have changed the outcome of the entire trip for the better. Instead I opted to tough it out, no big deal, I can climb through it, and I'm a big, strong climber guy. I didn't want to appear gutless, even though at this rate is what I was becoming.

As we began to climb, so did my stomach. This trail had a hundred switchbacks and I think I left a piece of me on every one of them. It got so bad I could not continue and had to set up camp well below our destination. Rich went on with the team, and John stayed with me, wiping up my mess, feeding me, and watching me shiver with fever even inside all my warm down.

Richard was a small but reliable pack mule, and he became my best friend the next day as he carried all my gear on his back up to our Base Camp, asking for nothing more than some open pasture on which to feed. This became a bit of joke since he shared a name with one of our leaders who was somewhat of an understudy of John. We did rest a little at Base Camp. We got to see some beautiful guanacos and also realized that we didn't buy the "easy" rice, but instead bought the slow cook variety, which at 13,000 feet robs you of all your time and fuel. Oh, well. Soon we were on our way up in the darkness.

Climbers get used to an "alpine start," meaning you begin the climb before the sun peeks over the horizon. Things are frozen and the world we tread upon is safer for it. The morning started in blizzard-like conditions, but since we were just traversing the moraine, we pressed on, hoping they would clear. Somehow in that storm we missed our turn, and it must have been the constant movement of our headlamps that clued someone at a higher camp to the fact we were off course. We saw them attempting Morse code by flashing lamps at us and soon realized we needed to go back. Not because we were brilliant with Morse code, but because our trail abruptly ended. Soon we found it, and the next thing we knew the sun was rising, the air was still, and we were on the glacier, tied together and moving higher. It was a glorious morning after all, and a little patience was paying off. Dude, due to his nagging knees had decided to stay back at Base Camp and did not join us for the climb.

Peter was going strong, but Nelson was beginning to get a distressing headache. He guzzled some more water and pushed on. In fact, on this day I truly admired Nelson — not because he was trying to tough it out, but because really for the first time I saw his heart in what he was doing, in what we were doing. He was part of the team and he really wanted success for us all. It was terrific to see this transformation and to see him extend his heart out onto his sleeve a little bit.

Desire and passion are such key components for reaching any goal. Complacency will stop you dead in your tracks every time, and I believe Dude fell victim to this mindset, or perhaps the recipe had a dash of fear mixed in as well. The headache concerned us and we continually checked in with Nelson, perhaps to the point of annoyance. Part of the reason for this is Nelson is not a wimp and was showing such resolve that should there be a real concern for an altitude illness, we really didn't want to press on.

Five hundred feet from the summit we stood together on the flats of the glacier, just before the summit slopes with the majestic peak of Artesonraju (the mountain used in the opening of Paramount Pictures productions), and had a heart to heart. Nelson said it had gotten so severe and was bothering him so much he could not continue. It saddened us all because the effort he had put in on this day was really extraordinary, and as a team we knew he could have the prize of the summit. We didn't push. I decided I would go down. Nelson tied in to the other end of my rope, we hugged the others, wished them well, and were on our way. We maintained radio contact with the others, and even Dude at Base Camp, to let each other know our whereabouts and movements.

As I reached the col with Nelson, somewhere around 17,000 feet, I noticed my nose was running, and it wouldn't stop. I wiped it and moved on. I blew it and kept going. Then I looked at my bandana and my sleeve and they were covered in blood. I had been so severely dehydrated it caused a blood vessel in my sinuses to rupture. The bleeding went on and on. I used a snow pack, blocked it up, drank a ton of water, and even used my stove to melt more ice into drinkable water, all the while making a huge red stain on the side of the mountain.

Nelson started to worry, and I wanted it to stop before moving on. I don't know how much blood a person can lose in an hour from a nose bleed, but I am sure it is a lot and that it is not good, especially at high altitude. Finally, though feeling lightheaded, we were able to continue our descent, slow as it was. It was good to see Dude, and about the time we did I got a call on the radio asking what had been slaughtered in the col. I said I had a bloody nose and it was all good now. John was upset I hadn't told him sooner. I really had just wanted to make sure no one else turned around so as many people as possible, especially Peter, could make the summit.

The next day we headed down and by this point had pretty much decided "Chopi," the peak across the valley we had targeted for our second climb, was not an option. Dude said his knees were bad; Nelson didn't want a repeat of the headache; I needed some recovery time; and John was thinking the beach sounded pretty good. We decided that the 2Xtreme dream can be as flexible as our dreams often are and need to be, determining that a dream is a living thing, which can change and is dynamic, not static. Why not move with it, taking advantage of our time, our youth, and desire to see the world and the beauty that it offers. Don't quit, don't give up, flex, go with the change. That said, it was easy to drop the mountains and plan for a surf adventure. My disappointment would be in myself. I should have set up the team for success by choosing one simple goal that could be achievable by all with enough time to make it happen even if we had been laid out with food poisoning. Perhaps my dream for them was too big, more of a goal for myself than for novice climbers.

I could not help but feel a little responsible for not getting the whole group up to that first summit. What it became was a perfect learning experience for us all. Desire can't be given and leadership will have its failures. I can say we have all grown as a result, but perhaps even more from the events that followed. Dude ran down the trail and was the first to the trailhead. Hmm, how are those knees, anyway? They certainly seemed strong when a soccer game broke out in Huaraz. I was disappointed that he didn't even try.

The waves in Trujillo were perfect, the climate hospitable, and the food more reliable. I think to some degree we were all glad to be here in the sun and the surf; yep, this was the dream. The "dudes" rented surfboards and wet suits, while we sat at a second story café eating and watching. Soon we planned to head up to the site of the *Endless Summer* movie's perfect wave. The dream just kept getting better.

"Hey, John, have you seen Peter? He went out into the waves over here a while ago and I haven't seen him in a long time; just these other surfers," I said, concerned for where he had gone.

John replied, "No, no idea, have not seen him. I was watching these other two try to get out into the surf."

Then Rich burst out: "There he is. Oh, no, what's wrong . . . he just collapsed!" We all jumped up, ran down the stairs and across the street onto the beach, sprinting to Peter who had collapsed onto the sand in dramatic fashion. When we got to him we tried to get him to talk, but he was groggy and disoriented.

One look at his surfboard told us that something really bad had happened. The fin was broken off and the board itself was cracked in half. I'm not a surfer, but I'm just guessing that if someone whacked me over the head with a surfboard, it would take quite a hit for it to break. That kind of blow could give a major concussion or even a broken neck. Immediately, we assumed this about Peter, and since he was a sturdy guy who was now severely disoriented we knew it could be bad.

The ambulance would be too long coming all the way from Trujillo to Juanchaco, while the hospital was just minutes away. Instead, we called a taxi, immobilized Peter on his surf board with tape and whatever other tie-downs we could find, just like it were a true backboard. We left Nelson and Dude behind while we rushed Peter to the hospital.

He got x-rays which showed no cervical spine breaks, and pressed the doc as we thought we were getting the runaround for fear of our not paying. Satisfied with a second opinion, and Peter in a neck brace, we left only to find the guys who had been sober for a year had used this moment of near tragedy to turn to booze for a little comfort or relaxation.

The dream was over. Nelson and Dude were sent home, though Nelson ran at the airport, stating that an 18-year-old need not be subject to these decisions. Dude went home with John and Rich, while I took Peter, neck brace and all, to discover the archaeology of Trujillo and later Machu Pichu. My last memory of Peter, after we had seen the lost city and climbed it's highest point, was of him running to catch the last train out of town that day, which would get us to the last plane and take us home. Running like a stiff board, with the neck brace still on, he lunged for what was now a nearly moving train. I chased him, laughing the whole way, not believing the moment we were in.

The trip home was uneventful, and we hoped Nelson was doing okay. The drama that unfolded from Peter's accident, the boys' decision to drink, and Nelson's decision to abort the flight home while in John's "custody" at the airport, challenged us all to dig deep for understanding and forgiveness. The boys were by no means inebriated and, as they stated, they were even of legal drinking age in Peru. But the fact remained they had broken one of the rules of the program that clearly stated no substances whatsoever, legal or not; these were the rules.

Assessing this as a leader, perhaps one problem was we did not have a communicated consequence set in place for this occurring on the trip; we just did not think it would happen after a full year, and with us nearby. We took it away from them on the fly while away, and that alone was what made it so difficult.

I learned several great lessons from this experience: One, you must set a more reasonable and attainable objective with enough time to allow everyone to accomplish it. Two, you must clearly communicate consequences of broken program rules even though the activity may be legal. Third, it is good to keep young guys busy every minute, especially on a foreign trip, which is a lesson I wouldn't fully understand until a later trip to Peru. Free time, especially unsupervised, equals free trouble. Yes, trust needs to be a part of it, but good sense and good planning can eliminate a lot of issues. This trip would not be my last to Peru; in fact, I would return on two separate occasions with unlikely groups of trekkers as an advisor for a program called Leading the Way.

A few short weeks after returning from Peru I decided to put together a climb of a "14er" in Colorado called Pyramid Peak. It is steep, challenging, and is exactly the kind of thing that is fun to do with some of your best friends, and your 61-year-old mother. During the planning process, while at an outdoor concert series in Vail, I saw Amy Malmsten sitting with my good friends, Rick and Julie Haller, who were planning to go on this climb. Amy is a cute, blonde girl I had seen two years earlier at one of my presentations, and had now gotten to know just a little. As I talked with our friend Wendy, I thought, why not ask Amy to join us; the more the merrier. Amy said yes, and I got excited, looking forward to a great climb the following week.

The week got shorter and so did the list of people going. The final list was Eric, Amy, and Mom. The plan had been to go to Aspen, have dinner, then camp near the peak for our climb the next day so we could eliminate driving it all in one day. The plan remained the same, and I feared it might get awkward. It now looked like a date with Amy, and Mom would be along for the ride.

I had no worries about my mom getting up the peak. She has done well on over 40 of these peaks in Colorado, and I knew she could get up this one. Amy was athletic, and I hoped the steeper sections wouldn't scare her off since this was still a little new to her, even though she was a Colorado native. The drive was fine, dinner was fine, and even letting Amy and Mom tent together while I slept outside in my bivy sac was a smooth non-event. Amy was strong on the climb, was not afraid of the mountain goats beside the trail, and was unflappable as I made stormy wind noises for her on one particularly exposed, narrow ridge. What impressed me most was she was even able to glissade, or glide on her feet, over the snowy sections as we made our way down off our successful summit.

The conversation came easy, she was quick to laugh, and her big, beautiful, bright blue eyes seemed to sparkle as brightly as Maroon Lake itself there at the base of the peak. I guess I had fallen for her, and the way she knew this was I came over to her house every day for the next two weeks. I had no cable TV, she did, and the Tour de France was on. It was my perfect excuse.

Amy continued to impress me with her skiing ability, her love for others, and mostly her love for the Lord. Amy knew Jesus, and this was not just evident in the way she talked, but in her heart and who she was in character. She kinda had it all, I must say, and I had to decide if I wanted all of that (which was very good), or the life of a single mountain traveler, always off in some distant land, stuffed inside of a tent with flatulent climbing partners (not always what it is cracked up to be). I chose the former; a climbing partner to rope up with me through all of life's good times and bad times, one who stands beside me and encourages me in all I do, and most importantly in my faith, challenging me to be more like Jesus.

One year after our climb of Pyramid Peak, I nervously hiked up the North Trail in Vail. I found a tree overlooking the valley from a prominent point on the edge of a rock outcropping, giving me a view of Mount of the Holy Cross, and just behind it another tree with a branch just the perfect size to carve something from. Hearing the screech of a hawk in the distant air, I proceeded to carve from that branch a ring, using the knife that had summited Everest with me.

While painting a room in the Beaver Creek Chapel for my future father-in-law, I got up the nerve to ask him for Amy's hand. He gave me a short story of why he thought it was a good match, and finally said yes. Wow! Now I am committed. When Amy had recovered enough from recent knee surgery, I took her out to a favorite climbing spot down the railroad tracks below the town of Redcliff. I tied her into a rope at the base of a climb and set up my camera from above before we started on our climb. I was going to propose and capture the whole moment on camera. The thought then occurred to me, *What if she can't get to the top; I'll blow it*. I tore down the rig and belayed her from below.

She made it to the top, but when I lowered her I stopped her just before she could touch her feet to the ground and held her there. From my pocket, I pulled the wooden ring and asked her about climbing, and trust, and marriage, and she said, "Yes!" with a laugh and a tear. On our way out I asked her if she knew I was going to do this, and she replied, "Maybe. I kinda wondered why you prayed for courage today before we did this little rock climb. That seemed a little odd to me, cause the guy has climbed Everest; why does he need courage?"

Deadpoint Reflections

May the God who gives endurance and encouragement give you a spirit of unity among yourselves as you follow Christ Jesus, so that with one heart and mouth you may glorify the God and Father of our Lord Jesus Christ. — Romans 15:5–6

 Crux: Choices. We sometimes get caught in a downward spiral of poor choices. It might be that second, third, or fifth scoop of ice cream, that next beer, the decision to push on for the summit in spite of the building dark clouds, or the seemingly innocent flirtation that makes a spouse jealous, and the choice to let one little lie turn into a stream of bigger ones. It seems at first so benign, but eventually will develop into a cancer that can wreck our families and our lives.

Hold: Develop the discipline to look ahead and see the consequences of each decision, and the fortitude to care enough to carry the right decision through. We must deny ourselves in our selfish desires in order to make the right decision. "I'm already fat and there is nothing I can do about it so why not have a fourth plate of pasta." "I can drive after four beers, so a fifth probably won't matter too much, besides it is a short drive home." Start with one choice at a time, look ahead, see the results and work backward, making this a habit and developing consistency and accountability. Make a plan. If my weakness is ice cream, I shouldn't keep it in the house, and if that is not enough, avoid that aisle at the supermarket or invite someone to help. Knowing the right choice is often easy, it is selecting it that is difficult.

Anchor: Integrity. Don't focus on the wrong behavior and choices to avoid, instead focus on the direction that will steer you away from it. Don't focus on the ice cream, focus on the fruit. Don't focus on the crowd that gets you in trouble, focus on those you wish to emulate for their character and integrity. *Finally, brothers, whatever is true, whatever is noble, whatever is right, whatever is pure, whatever is lovely, whatever is admirable — if anything is excellent or praiseworthy — think about such things* (Philippians 4:8).

Endnotes

1. *Voices from the Summit* (Washington, DC: Adventure Press, National Geographic, in association with the Banff Centre for Mountain Culture, 2000).

Blind Kids Discover a Lost City

Inca Trail to Machu Pichu

ELEVATION: 7,970 feet, high point of trail 15,000 feet

HOW LONG TO CLIMB: One week

HOW MANY IN THE TEAM: A total of 19

RATING: Class 2; YDS

BEST TO CLIMB DURING: June to September

ALSO KNOWN AS: Name means "Old mountain" in Quechua

Notes:

Blind and sighted students made this journey possible through partnership. www.youTube.com/highersummits

We live by faith, not by sight. — 2 Corinthians 5:7

If your actions inspire others to dream more,
learn more, do more, and become more, you are a
leader.[1]   — John Quincy Adams

Three years ago, a cute girl named Amy called to see how my first trip to Peru went. This time Amy, as my wife, sent me back to Peru, with 19 high school kids and a blind chaperone.

July 9, 2006 — I helped facilitate this Leading the Way trip along with Erik Weihenmayer and Colorado based non-profit Global Explorers. The focus would be a 35-mile trek for blind teens and sighted peers along what is called the Super-Inca trail, ending at Machu Pichu. The students applied for these trips, with teacher recommendations, and were then critically selected based on academic and other criteria. What we ended up with was a team of nine blind and nine sighted kids coming together for a unique and extraordinary journey.

Why bother? Why bother to go to Machu Pichu and visit an ancient Inca site when you can't even see a bit of it? Add to that a trek of 35 miles, two mountain passes of 15,000 feet, some serious gastro-intestinal dysfunction, and you really have the makings of a nonsensical, stumbling adventure. When people, curious to know my summer plans, find out I was partnering with a group of blind teens to retrace a portion of the Inca Trail, the above was the question I was most often asked.

I must admit at first when I hear this I think: *Man, you are right. It will be slow, difficult navigating all the rough terrain for days on end, passing by sights which are surely a sweet discovery for my eyes and will only fall short of whatever expectations a blind person might have. Seemingly endless chatter on the trail, making up new names for every size rock one could step on, being sure to let the person I am guiding know this could twist an ankle and end the trip. Then the countless probing jabs of a trekking pole in my ankle, finding the perfect slot between my shoe and bone, and sometimes even drawing blood.* Hitting the trail with a blind trekking partner will not be easy, but it will certainly be rewarding.

Hearing the words of one of the students before the trip was enough to motivate me to offer all I could. "I don't want to go on the Super Inca Trail workshop for my own benefit, I want to stand as a stepping stone for other blind individuals," said Terry Garrett of Fort Lupton, Colorado. Alysha

Jeans, another blind participant said, "To me [leadership] is always showing a smile, being there when I am needed, respecting others, demonstrating responsibility, and setting an example by my own actions. Being a leader can be both a struggle and a joy, but it is always a learning experience."

The purpose of this trip was not only to discover an ancient civilization, but to discover the very thing that must have had made this civilization great and served to form the foundation of these structures as much as any stone has: things like leadership, discipline, teamwork, friendship, perseverance, hard work, selflessness, and vision, sighted or not. Could it somehow be misunderstood the purpose of this trip was to show the world what blind and sighted kids are capable of? I think the purpose was not to show the world, but to show the kids they have a place in this world and can do anything they want to if they just reach out to get it. If you are still asking why bother, then read on. Perhaps this unlikely bunch of student leaders stumbling through the Andes of Peru can teach all of us a lesson on what it is to lead the way.

Machu Pichu in the Quechua language means "old mountain." It is the name of the mountain sitting high above the ancient city that carries the same name. It will be our destination, not our high point or summit, but certainly the goal for six days on the trail. An attraction for tourists all around the globe, people come to see Machu Pichu for its stunning architecture and vistas, and some to find a sort of spiritual meaning, claiming there is a "magical vibration," and walking barefoot on the land will offer healing or spiritual benefits.

For us it is not so much what we will see, but what we might accomplish along the way. To travel internationally with 18 high school students might in itself seem a worthy goal, especially when the destination is an impoverished country such as Peru. With nine of our students being either blind or visually impaired, they had never done much significant hiking. Numerous students had never even camped, and most had never been out of the United States.

The climb to the top of Everest with Erik Weihenmayer opened my eyes to what is possible, and I can have extremely high expectations for people at times, so when I was first asked to do this trip I did not hesitate to say yes. I knew there was a way and I knew it would be possible, especially with the right people, who had the right attitudes and the right training, as well as, support from home, the ability to raise money and, and, and. . . . I started to work backward from the big picture to see a few more of the obstacles we had facing us.

One of the biggest obstacles, I thought, would be keeping 18 people who were 18 years old and under motivated for six days of hiking with no showers and no flushing toilets, and the most terrible thing of all: no iPods! It was April 2006 in Estes Park, Colorado, that my concerns were put to rest when

I met the group in person for the first time. I strolled into the meeting room and most of them were carrying on as if they had been friends for life, though they had just met. After two days of discussion and training on how to function on the trail, mostly for the blind students, it was apparent we would be ready for any obstacle that might come our way.

Erik and I worked closely with the staff of Global Explorers putting this trip together, making sure the students had all they would need to continue preparing on their own after the weekend together. We showed everyone how to navigate by using sounds and trekking poles, we made a human obstacle course that all had to complete with a blindfold using only verbal communication, and then we did a hike of a few miles through snow, mud, and manure to ensure their commitment to the trek. In this short time we did have concerns about a few members of the team and whether or not these people would be able to make it. With extra training and the help of this special team, we put our concerns to rest and figured we would just have to see how it might all play out.

The time had come. I checked my bags in and proceeded to the gate in Denver where I would meet Terry Garrett, AKA "Lupton", as he was affectionately called for his hometown, a small town on the eastern plains of Colorado. There his church got together to help him fundraise for this trek in the Andes. I met Terry, his mother, and a reporter from the *Greeley Tribune* at the gate. Somehow if you are blind, you can sweet-talk security into letting your "posse" come to the gate with you; I dare anyone else to try this without a boarding pass. Maybe it was nerves, or perhaps just the fact he knew he would be sitting for a long time, but Lupton couldn't sit still, so he walked laps around the A concourse until it was time to board. As we said farewell, I asked mom if she was nervous and she said, "No, I just close my eyes." How appropriate.

The gang was all there in Houston, Texas, or so we thought. One had a graduation ceremony to attend and would meet us in Cusco, while the other simply overslept and missed his flight out of Bozeman, Montana. Max Lowe is the son of well-known American alpinists Alex Lowe (who died in an avalanche on Shishapangma). Max, too, would meet us in Cusco, a day or so late. It was a nice six-plus hour flight, but what made it so super was the cake served to us by one of our own, "Red Hot" Ryan Charleston. Making and selling cakes was just one way Ryan raised enough money to go on this trip to Peru.

We arrived with all our bags, were whisked to a hotel for a wonderful hour and a half of sleep, then up and on to Cusco. Arriving in Cusco was fun because at first no one wanted to admit 10,500 feet felt any different than sea level, but as soon as we began to walk around the city and visit some of the ruins, I could see and hear the effects of the high altitude. Andrew Johnson described it by saying, "My first sensation was this is not so hard; 30 minutes later I was panting like a dog and chugging water like a Clydesdale."

The first site we saw after being introduced to our Peruvian guide, Julio, was one of the "most special and important Inca sites" we would see. It was called Saqsaywaman (sounds like *sexy woman*). Soon every site would become the "most special and important" one, though this one was known by the Incas as the "house of the sun," and was crafted from huge sculpted boulders of limestone precisely stacked upon each other and formed by ancients using basic tools, the re-creation of which would challenge even today's best masons with modern tools. The students were able to run their hands along the stones, seams, and walls, feeling them like Braille blocks and looking as though they were about to begin a rock climb, searching for that first hold to get them off of the ground.

Two more days of touring brought us to the Pisaq market deep in the Sacred Valley, the steep stairs and terraces of Ollantaytombo, and the intriguing deep pit of concentric circles, called Moray. The visit to the rural market gave everyone a chance to make a purchase of authentic Peruvian goods to bring on the trail, as well as, home. It was not every day, if ever, that these Peruvian peddlers got to see blind kids touching everything they had laid out on their tables.

The Alpaca items were especially popular as they were so soft to the touch, making sweaters the number one sellers, and keeping students warm on the trail. The pan flutes were also a big hit, giving us numerous headaches and functioning as annoying alarm clocks along the way. Perhaps the funniest sight was watching the students barter in an English-Spanish mix with Quechua-speaking natives who might walk away to get another item, a calculator, or just escape the awkward conversation altogether, and the students then continuing to barter to an empty tent. Later, the worker would return with renewed strength and vigor to seal the deal.

The terraced rings of Moray provided access down into a perfectly round crater, with the feel of a giant amphitheater. Access was only possible by a steep hike down to the rim followed by a climb down stairs nearly imperceptible from a distance, that would allow a person to float down on the 12 by 12 inch steps of stone to the following terrace, in a series of nearly 20 terraces, ten feet below one another.

Each of these was definitely a step of faith, even for those of us who could see perfectly well, and forced more than a few people to use hands, knees, stomachs, and whatever means possible to get down without a fall. The cameras were definitely rolling here to catch this action in hopes too, of getting a little carnage. No one did fall, but many were challenged, and everyone experienced something unlike anything we had seen or touched before; this was only just the beginning.

The last visit before our departure was to a local salt mine described by Didrik Johnk (of my Everest team fame), as the "salt mines of Mordor." It seemed a fitting name given its high evaporative pools, cascading their way down 800 feet of the mountainside in a labyrinth of yellow and gold-colored waterways with white crusty salt covering the tops and edges. The workers would effortlessly move along the spines and hills, collecting salt from the dry pools and diverting the flow of water from one project to the next. It was hard work and it showed in the rough appearance of these men who labored here under the intense sun of these high mountains. From a distance, this mine looked like a snow-covered hillside and an impossible place to work, and certainly an impossible trail system for a blind person. We did manage to survive the perilous journey down through it to arrive at a lovely green campsite. The narrow trails of this descent and the student's abilities to handle them showed us, though we may be slow, we were ready for the Super Inca Trail.

These first couple days would serve not only to help us acclimate, but also to see the ability levels of our blind trekkers and their sighted leaders. This gave us an opportunity to help everyone hone their skills before ending up in trouble on some remote part of the Inca trail. Even though we had horses along for support, nobody wanted to be the person who needed one.

Right away, on the first day of our trek, the ruins of an ancient lookout post high on the side of a clear ridge would serve as the stunning backdrop for our lunch and dining pleasure. It was no wonder this site, called Qosqoq Awarina, on the Watuq'Asa Pass had been chosen for this purpose, as it was teetering thousands of feet above the junction of two valleys critical to passage through this rugged countryside. A person, or group of people, would be easily spotted miles away in any direction.

As we stumbled into our campsite, the cool of the evening was upon us. Tired and tested, camp was established on the soccer field of a settlement called Chilipahua. Here we would do a community service project for the small local school and deliver some gifts we had brought from home. One student gave away key chains, though I don't believe these people had keys to anything in particular, though perhaps, they would be useful in other ways, while other students delivered soccer balls, pumps, and Frisbees. The soccer balls were a hit and soon a game of keepaway, usually with a blind student in the middle of a circle, ensued. With the ball wrapped in a plastic bag, just enough sound could be detected and traced, as with sonar, to actually make this a fair game.

Soon the kids from the village came out, along with our caballeros, and we had a full-fledged soccer game. We promptly got our butts whooped by the agile and well-acclimated Peruvians. The community service project set up for us by the wishes of the local people, was to purchase supplies and paint the school inside and out. Thankfully, it would be one color, and thankfully, it was a one-room schoolhouse. Sadly, the locals did not know the painters would be blind.

Peruvians, Americans, sighted and blind, young and old, we all joined in together, and in a matter of hours had a crisp new blue coat of paint on the walls, windows, and bodies, too. This school was important to the people, and they were proud of it. It was the only school around for miles and some kids would walk three hours one way each day just to come and study here. Those same kids awakened us with laughter in the morning as they played outside our tents, inviting this group of strange strangers to come and interact with them.

The kids knew this was to be a special day since a lamb had been slaughtered that night as we slept in our tents, giving many cause for alarm, as well as nightmares. It was offered to us the next day in a ceremony known as a *Pancha Manca;* as thanks for the gifts we had given. The town gathered as the lamb was cooked in the ground with hot stones and covered by dirt and straw. We stood together in the center square, participating in a ceremony with songs and games, and wrapping up the time spent here taking turns singing each country's respective national anthem, one group to the other. Very ceremonious, a little funny, but somehow a meaningful conveyance of gratitude and pride for what we had accomplished in deed and relationship.

The days that followed presented the usual: altitude illness, gastrointestinal issues, joint pains, inside jokes formed over dinner time, riddles and games, and accents of the porters who would say things like "hod waddy" when they offered hot water. Along one of the steeper sections of the trail I noticed one of the students who was leading his blind partner had put his attention fully on the scenery and completely forgotten about the responsibility of leading his blind counterpart step by step on the precarious, loose, and gravelly edge, hundreds of feet above the creek's raging torrent below.

With camera to eye, eye to peak, and mind to clouds, this teen leader had forced Terry to fend for himself. *If a blind man leads a blind man, both will fall into a pit* (Matthew 15:14). Terry did not know this slope was off camber, and that loose rocks on top would send him for a ride he would never forget. It was just like walking on a pitched roof as a bucket of marbles was released from above. It was the right time to be in the right place as I was able to grab Terry by the hair on his neck and pull him back up onto the trail.

Nearly oblivious to the potential outcome, I assured Terry that I had just saved his life or maybe a broken bone anyway, certainly a major annoyance at the very least. I had hit it off with Terry immediately and am convinced it was because we shared a common faith. Not only was Terry a Christian, he was tough, strong-willed, and capable. I saw so much potential in him I invited him to climb a Colorado "14er" with me when we got home, in winter.

In contrast to the skills and wit that Terry possessed was an older student, Paul. Not nearly the physical type that so many of the others on this trip were, Paul also struggled to fit in with the group socially. I applaud this group, and especially some of the young girls, for being able to leave their comfort zones to be with the person day after day who was the most demanding. We had traversed our highest passes, hiked our longest days, managed to push on through illness, blindness, doubt, and pain. What was remarkable was this group was truly becoming a team, and this team was finding joy in every day's journey.

The destination was important, but each day's focus was about moving beyond what obstacles were present before us. This was a biblical principle coming to life where Jesus says in Matthew 6:25, *Do not worry about your life, what you will eat or drink; or about your body, what you will wear. Is not life more important than food, and the body more important than clothes?* We were learning to do just that — enjoy life one day at a time without worrying about whether or not we would get there. If there is a group that should worry, it is a group of blind teens hiking at high altitude through the high Andes with teen guides, but here they were, doing this one step at a time, a lot of laughs along the way, lending a hand to each other, and leading the way for others to follow.

Before coming back down to the trails more heavily used by tourists, we saw a few last remote ruins and then were challenged by the students to go as fast as we could. A blind train was formed with one sighted leader, trekking poles jutting out all over, probing for objects that tried to upset their balance and knock them off their feet. Hands were placed on packs, from pack to pack to pack, and if the one in front was to fall it would have been one messy pileup with maybe even a few prosthetic eyes rolling down the trail. That would be one way to keep your eyes out ahead and watch where you are going. The blind train would blow by other unsuspecting tourists who had no idea how badly this group wanted a cold Coca-Cola and would trample anyone to get it.

Hot showers awaited us this night in camp, as did the amazing blind card tricks of Andrew Johnson, who, though quarantined from all others, could still call out the color of every card he placed against his forehead when asked. Having distributed an entire deck, to this day I still do not know how he called the color of each card. I know there was a system, but I'm stumped.

From here it was one last day; one in which I would again barely keep a blind student on the narrow, now densely rain forested trail.

Climbing steeply upward toward the Sun Gate and following the narrow traversing ledges, a fall from some of these places, one small misstep, could potentially lead someone to the grave. Having not known each other for long, these students really did form a deep sense of trust with each other, one that I hope they will remember and use to forge future relationships. Today was my day to be with Paul and see to it that no permanent damage would befall him. One trick I would employ with Paul was to use my trekking poles like rails for him to grab onto, provided the terrain was smooth enough.

A lifetime of being blind had left Paul without some of the agility and balance that seemed to come more naturally to some of the other students who had sight for at least a small part of their lives. Some of the others were only partially blind and could skip along quite well without assistance, need-ing just a silhouette to follow. We moved slowly up and over the blocky stairs and rugged high terrain, some of the stairs slick, covered with moss, Paul was fatigued from a week of hard work and only one short pony ride. With only hours remaining at the end of this epic journey, the city and our final goal, Machu Pichu was waiting.

I believe now, more than the excitement of discovering this place was the excitement of finishing, finding rest, a smooth sidewalk, and a flat street to walk down. The desire now was to pull out the familiar white cane and put away, maybe forever, the Leki trekking poles that were sometimes friend and at others a dreaded foe. Paul's foot lost its purchase as he went down on his side, sliding over the precipice into the forested abyss. I worried that I might lose him forever. I could see his feet swinging in the air below him as he tried futilely to step on something that just wasn't there.

One thing Paul had learned to employ was his kung fu death grip. Good thing I had mine going as well, because he held that pole so firmly nothing was going to shake him. *I was eyes to the blind and feet to the lame* (Job 29:15), but not at every turn. Paul regained his composure, and although we were the last to arrive, the entire team was waiting at the Sun Gate. It was a testament to their character that they did not proceed, but rather waited to celebrate as one unit who had strived together for this goal, worked through adversity, and overcome fears to celebrate the moment with some whoops and hollers.

Sharing the view and the horizon with the now familiar grasp of a hand, a slow moving wave rolling up and down together describing what lies ahead, and what we stand upon. The golden sun was ready to set as we stood revel-ing in the moment, one that was perhaps better than finding the "lost" city itself. For the sighted students, this moment signified our arrival at our goal. The descent to Machu Pichu for them would be quick and easy, and their excitement continued to build as they took in the scenery and the sunset. They attempted to convey a sense of their elation through words to their blind counterparts, and did the best they could.

For the blind students, this moment at the Sun Gate was the summit. The arduous journey was over; the warmth of the sun's rays hit their faces as it cast its approval upon them. Fear and apprehension now only covered the trail behind them and in its place was a sense of pride and the joy of completing the task. The completion of the task was a bigger prize than the visit to this city, which is more visually stunning than it is anything else. For those who could see the city for what it was, more joy was derived from the destination perhaps than from the journey. But for all it stood out as a high point, a summit, the culmination of a goal reached in good style by an unlikely team of underdogs bent on shattering perceptions of blindness, maybe even some of their own.

Our tour of Machu Pichu lasted but a few hours. A place where I feel I could have easily spent a week inside was soon given up for the comforts of the familiar waiting for us in town below. Even though the blind students were granted special permission to touch what is off limits, they soon would have their fill. I suppose the rugged steep steps of the city and the artistry of the stonework could only be appreciated so much with the tactile sense. How many rocks can a hand touch before a meticulously carved ancient symbol of a lost civilization becomes just another rock.

Looking back on our time in Peru, there are indeed some special memories. I think of the obstacles overcome, the boundaries that were stretched, perspectives and perceptions that were shifted, the courage it took to find the faith to step out into the unknown and trust. There was Clayton, blind since birth, who never was allowed outside his home, not even to check the mail. His eyes were opened. Terry wanted to be the first blind man in space, and now has an internship with NASA. The summit was obvious in the beginning — it was Machu Pichu. In the end, our true summit was crested in the journey of everyday, in the bonds that were formed, in the future which now had its door opened wider to the new goals set before us with a new perspective of what may be possible.

One by one, I could hear the rattle of the little white canes gathering around me. Like a little gang who had experienced the first taste of something sweet, they mounted an assault on my seat in the train. Pinned against the window there was nowhere to run. The questions came firing out like machine gun rounds: "What can we do next? Where can we go? Are you gonna do Kili? Will you take us there? How much harder is that than this? Do you think we could do it? How much would it cost?" The questioning only lasted a couple of weeks before I gave in and said, "Yes. I will take you to climb Kilimanjaro! Now quit hitting me with those canes!"

Deadpoint Reflections

Life is either a daring adventure or nothing.[2]   — Helen Keller

Crux: Perception. Countless people prejudged our Everest team and especially Erik Weihenmayer. It was hard to hear their uninvited comments stream in from all over the globe, especially when they did not know this team or this blind man personally. These comments ticked me off. Even worse, I got mad at these people for something I have been just as guilty of doing myself: making a judgment based on a perception of my own rather than on evidence and truth. I have judged people before meeting them, cars before driving them, restaurants before tasting their food (sometimes this is just wisdom), cities before visiting them, and cultures before engaging them. I even judged these blind kids before we hit the Inca trail. The crux here is to let people show who they are and what they are capable of before putting a label on them. Recently, I had the opportunity to spend some quality time with someone from my church. This person usually had an unhappy look on his face and would come and go rather quickly. I got the feeling he was arrogant, and self-absorbed, and even looking down on people in general. I had these feelings even though I had never had a conversation with him that lasted longer than a handshake. After our circumstantially forced time together I learned this guy had a great sense of humor, was easy going, his heart for kids was very big, and his heart for the Lord even bigger still. This is a mistake I have made numerous times, and I wonder how many great friendships, opportunities, and experiences I have missed out on because of a wrongly formed perception.

Hold: Take a risk to get to know someone a little better. Take a risk to put your beliefs to the fire and see if they remain standing in truth. Take a risk to believe in someone and their dream and stand by them in it. Turn criticism into fuel for the fire if you are wrongly perceived.

Anchor: Want a better perception of yourself and of others? Understand that you are made in the image of God. *God created man in his own image, in the image of God he created him; male and female he created them. God blessed them and said to them, 'Be fruitful and increase in number; fill the earth and subdue it. Rule over the fish of the sea and the birds of the air and over every living creature that moves on the ground.' Then God said, 'I give you every seed-bearing plant on the face of the whole earth and every tree that has fruit with seed in it. They will be yours for food.*

And to all the beasts of the earth and all the birds of the air and all the creatures that move on the ground — everything that has the breath of life in it — I give every green plant for food.' And it was so. God saw all that he had made, and it was very good (Genesis 1:27–31).

Not only did God create us in His own image, He gave us responsibility and work to do. Now if you want to feel good about yourself take into account that He paused, took a look at His creation, and said it was better than bad — it was good, very good even. He liked how He made us. Being made in His image, He has also told us that all things are possible: *I can do everything through him who gives me strength* (Philippians 4:13). Jesus . . . said, *With man this is impossible, but not with God; all things are possible with God* (Mark 10:27). If I perceive an obstacle to be too great, myself too lacking, or someone else too <u>fill in the blank here</u>, I need to anchor myself and realize that I am probably the one who needs a shift of perspective.

Endnotes
1. www.govleaders.org/quotes6.
2. Jane Sutcliff, *Helen Keller* (Minneapolis, MN: Lerner Publications, 2009), p. 40.

Blind Broken not Beaten

Kilimanjaro[1]

Aconcagua[2]

Denali[3]

ELEVATION:
Kilimanjaro: 19,340 feet
Aconcagua: 22,841 feet
Denali: 20,320 feet

HOW LONG TO CLIMB:
Kilimanjaro: Four to eight days
Aconcagua: Two to three weeks
Denali: 12 days, though typically three weeks

HOW MANY IN THE TEAM:
Kilimanjaro: Four blind students with leaders
Aconcagua: Two Americans
Denali: Two members

RATING:
Kilimanjaro: F; Class 2
Aconcagua: AD
Denali: AD

BEST TO CLIMB DURING:
Kilimanjaro: Can be climbed year round though fall is recommended
Aconcagua: November to February South American summer
Denali: May through July

ALSO KNOWN AS:
Kilimanjaro: Name most likely means "White mountain" *Uhuru* means "Freedom" in Swahili
Aconcagua: Name means either "Comes from the other side" in Arauca or "Stone Sentinel" in Quechua
Denali: Name means "The high one" in Athabaskan Mount McKinley named after the 25th President, William McKinley

THE SUMMIT

O God . . . lead me to the rock that is higher than I.
— Psalm 61:1–2

Why is it everyone who comes to Africa has to write a book about it?[1]   —Ernest Hemingway

*H*akuna Matata. Jambo. Pole', pole'. I had seen the Disney movie *The Lion King* years ago and was surprised that when I went to Africa these were real words in Swahili. *Hakuna Matata* really does mean "no worries," *jambo* hello, and *pole'* means slow. (I went on an African safari along with a trip to the "Roof of Africa," Mt. Kilimanjaro is the highest peak on this continent and my fourth of the Seven Summits.) Climbing it had long been a dream since I was a boy watching Mutual of Omaha videos with Marlin Perkins. The first of many opportunities to climb this mountain came when Everest Base Camp manager, Kevin Cherilla, organized a climb for the students of his school and needed some help while on the mountain. I obliged his offer and invited my 62-year-old mother, as well as a new friend of mine who was an old friend of Joseph — Skip Jeffries from Pennsylvania. The next thing you know we were on our way to Africa.

March 2004 — We cruised along the Machame route known for its long, meandering nature, scenic vistas, and steep Baranca wall. This team was amazing. There were a few who had dietary issues along the way, but the attitudes were amazing and the fortitude of spirit uncommon for a group as diverse as this in age and background. There were father-daughter, mother-daughter, and mother-son teams on the trail, and in spite of the lack of experience of many, the joy could not be taken away.

The "14ers" at home were a great way to train for a climb of Kilimanjaro and I had done a number of them with my mom, but this climb would be extra special and require a far greater effort than any of those. My mom had never camped for more than one night, never been above 14,000 feet, and with the elevation being 19,340 feet here, I had to keep not only her, but many of the group from thinking too much about it. We needed to just go slow, drink plenty of water, eat everything we could, and take it one day at a time. Next thing you know, we would be there.

The Baranca wall, an 800-foot obstacle of steep and winding rock, was a formidable obstacle, but not our biggest. The biggest would come on summit day when those who felt sick would need to turn back in the middle of the night, others would need to leave camp at 15,000 feet for lower elevations in order to feel better, and the rest would climb up into high winds and near whiteout conditions. Staying near the back of the pack, I ensured that all those who went down were well enough to do so with the aid of an African porter or guide. We had employed the services of Masai Giraffe Safaris, which provided us with great attention and wonderful, trustworthy guides.

All of this took time, and the distance had grown great between me and the group at the front, which included my mother. I was imagining her standing on top, having done this trip at my urging, and then not being able to be there with me because I was too far back. Fueled by emotion and the thought of not being able to summit with my mom, let alone anyone else on the team, I revved it into high gear and almost began to jog up at 18,600 feet. This was tiring, especially going into the wind, but I eventually caught up and was able to stand on the summit with my mom.

Others of the team had already begun the descent, and what became apparent right away to me was exactly how miraculous the Everest climb was, when we had so few turn back. Here we were on much lower Kilimanjaro with a similar sized team, taking our time, and yet nearly half had to turn back. To stand on this summit with these kids and my mom, many who had asthma, was nothing short of glorious. This time it was Skip's turn to leave a photo of Joseph on top of the continent. This allowed us to share many great moments we had enjoyed with our friend, and drew us closer as friends as well.

The peak was a priceless memory, and almost as special was finding the vines of the trees really can support a person's weight, and therefore swinging like Tarzan is totally possible. My first ride was a rush through the leaves of the forest as the monkeys above looked on in disgust. The second was higher and farther, and the third was my mom's turn. The safari lived up to my expectations as elephants walked by our Toyota Landcruiser brushing up against its side, baboons scurried across the road in front of us, and lions could be seen sleeping in the tree branches above our car.

Truly unlike anything else anywhere on the planet was this expansive landscape, teeming with wildlife that was free to roam and migrate from place to place, through fearing predators and poachers; this was not a petting zoo. For many in Africa, this means a person might encounter a lion, giraffe, elephant, or leopard in their backyard on any given day.

On the edge of the Ngorongoro crater we stopped by a Masai village, authentic yes, but heavily visited. They had their handicrafts for sale and drove a hard bargain with any tourist that stopped by. I tried to trade my Benchmade knife to one of them for his Masai spear, and after attempting to shave his bare cheeks with it, he decided it was not worth it. The dollar value of the knife was far greater than that of the spear, yet he didn't see the practicality in a four-inch knife blade.

While trying to make my trade, I turned around to ask my mom something only to find that she was already out dancing with the women of the tribe who were dressed in their bright ornamental colors and large, disc-like necklaces. Hospitality ran through the village by way of invitations into the cow dung huts, seats offered on the cowhide beds, and then into the stick schoolhouse where we were offered a cup of tea that Mom nearly drank. I told her if she drank this tea, though it was kind of them to offer, she would likely see her stomach on the floor of the bathroom that night.

These excursions are what truly make any trip abroad special; summits are good and worthy, but to get to know a little about the people and the culture is indeed what will make the experience more memorable. Such was the case with white cane-carrying kids from the Leading the Way expedition, who talked me into a Kilimanjaro climb of their own three years after my first Kili climb.

June 2007 — We visited AIDS patients in a hospital near Moshi and we spent time with children from the Moshi School for the Blind. We learned about the local ecology and sustainable living, and even had the privilege of being treated to presentations and songs from students of a different school, including the African yell of an albino black girl that made me shiver. To send us on our way up the mountain we exchanged gifts and received tokens of well wishes for our climb. We were treated to meals and honored like dignitaries. To go with the intention of serving is a great thing, but it is hard to actually do so as the people of the Tanzanian countryside are proud and don't want to be outdone. For them, accepting a gift does not come easy, and charity, though needed, is not always wanted.

Here in Africa more than in Peru, people were shocked, stunned, inspired, and impressed that any blind person would try to pull off something like climbing this high, icy peak, and they would always be supportive, cheering these kids on; that was not always the case back home. This time the climb would ascend the Marangu route, also known as the Coca Cola route due to the fact it is the easiest way up the mountain and has refreshments available, for a price, at each of its camps. The route has established huts and really no tent camping to speak of.

We had guys in one hut and girls in the other, and at one camp had to put a guy in the girls' hut. He was blind, so it didn't seem to matter much. We all smelled anyway, never changed clothes, and could have been happy sharing one giant room as would be the case at the final high shelter. Privacy on a trip like this comes in small doses and usually only when you are alone on the trail or alone on the pot.

This time around we had just the fast students from the year before, and winding our way up the mountain, acclimating, and overcoming the trials and tribulations of the trail was becoming second nature. Before we knew it, we had reached our high camp and were poised for the summit attempt; a perfect time to get sick. It wasn't the vomiting I minded, but the shivering and fever that I had along with it. It was not enough to completely wipe me out of contention for the summit, but it did take away a bit of my enthusiasm.

As we headed out that night for our final push to the Roof of Africa, two of the students needed to turn back. I knew it wasn't right to send them back alone on this mountain, especially to a hut shared by strangers from all around the world. Since our other leader, Casey, was going strong, and had all the necessary skills and judgment, I sent her on to the top with the blind students, while I went back to be with those who were not feeling so well. This was probably for the better anyway. I was able to apply lessons learned from the past: don't be the hero, don't push so hard when sick and dehydrated. Stepping back at times opens the door wider for someone else to succeed and increases the joy in their experience.

Four blind students summited Kilimanjaro; I did not, and I was happy. That was my summit; I did what was right. Not really realizing it, I had now climbed four of the Seven Summits, and had been able to lead a person with a disability to the top of each in a unique way. Three more summits remained, and having just been married, I wasn't sure how to get this done.

Enter j. Jay is a peculiar feller. I have known "j," as he prefers, since college, when I was a resident assistant on his floor at the University of Denver. James Whorton and I became friends quickly, sharing common interests like climbing and cycling, as well as, a quick wit and a faith in Jesus. Later we would become roommates, spend hours jamming on the guitar together, and playing the game of sneak up on and tackle the roommate as he studies for an exam.

J became like a brother to me and stood beside me when I married Amy. We've shared a lot of amazing experiences, like summiting Mt. Rainier via the Liberty Ridge on the 4th of July, followed by a slow ascent of the Exum direct on the Grand Teton, where I had to kick him to wake him up when he fell asleep at the belay, technical routes on Longs Peak, Spearhead, and many others. We even made a 14,000 mile, three-month motorcycle tour of North America after college.

I want everyone to have a friend like j: loyal, trustworthy, goofy as the day is long, a brother in Christ who is always there. The potential is there to take a friend like this for granted, until the one day you think you might lose him. Still not over the death of my friend Joseph, I got the news from my friend Dennis on February 23 of 2002 about the 100 Acre Wood Rally race in Missouri that j was participating in with co-driver Matt Deye.

The *Dusty Times* stated what happened was "the most serious event of the day. It occurred when J. B. Whorton and Matt Deye's PGT Mazda 323 GTX smashed into a tree on Stage 10. The two were airlifted to a nearby hospital. As the night drew long, the organizers and stewards conferred and eventually the organizers wisely decided to cancel the remaining two stages of the race." The guy builds bikes, works on dragsters, now on airliners, and in his spare time builds rally race cars. This is the type of racing where participants fly through the back roads of different townships like the Duke boys running from sheriff Roscoe. In this race, j was driving fast around a gravel-covered corner when his tires lost grip with the road, causing the heavily fortified car to hurl through the air into a nearby tree.

Entering that turn is j's last memory of that weekend and nearly the last one of his life. He thinks he had brake issues, while a competitor said he just couldn't manage the turn, stating j was a "wild driver." The car was totaled. Matt sustained broken ribs and a concussion and j, who has no recollection, suffered a concussion and a major fracture of C2, then got out of the wreckage to help his co-driver from the car. The pair was airlifted to a nearby hospital where they put j straight into surgery. He was lucky to be alive; he had C2 fused to C3. His break was called a "hangman's fracture," and was similar to the break that left Christopher Reeve quadriplegic. Death can be instant, usually occurring from suffocation when the nerves are damaged.

The large displacement in his neck showed that one little bit more of stretch would have been all that was required to end his life or leave him a vegetable. Now he is still a little bit of a vegetable. They took a piece of his hip and put it in his neck. The private and secret prayer that j would say every day as he got on his motorcycle or in his rally car was, "Lord, keep me safe from injury, accident, or paralyzation, and thank You for this day, amen." The recovery has taken years and he still complains of stiffness and pain. I think it is just an excuse he uses to get me to do the leading on some of our harder climbs.

February and May 2005 — The dream we'd had since college was to climb Denali in Alaska or some other great peak in the world. When he had healed enough we put the plan in motion to climb 22,841-foot Cerro Aconcagua in Argentina followed by an ascent of Denali that same spring. This would be a total of just over a month away from home that first year of my marriage. Knowing what this meant to both j and me, Amy was gracious and supportive of the effort. It would be summits five and six on what was becoming my goal of the Seven Summits.

The trend was to take someone with a disability to the summit of each, and I saw this as no different. It is debatable, I suppose, that j was not truly or permanently disabled. The way I see it is that my friend got up from what could have been his deathbed, he came within a millimeter of losing the use of all of his limbs, his spine had been fused, and praise the Lord he can walk. Many would call it quits there, but j wanted to continue to pursue his passion, yet was unsure if he would be able to carry the heavy loads these peaks required. I wanted to help him, and I wasn't about to lose him as a climbing partner. Together we made a plan, train hard all winter long, then fly south.

The Stone Sentinel stands alone as the highest mountain in the world outside of the Himalayas. If it were placed in the midst of those giants it would however disappear among them and would not be the sought-after climb that it is. At 22,841 feet, Aconcagua is almost 9,000 feet higher than any peak in Colorado, and our route would go up the center of the north face on the Polish Direct. We would have a rope and all the technical gear this climb would require and, with just one tent, the load that the mules had to carry was a little lighter than some. A three-day walk up the trail of the Vacas Valley delivered us to the comforts of the 13,000-foot Base Camp.

Along the way we ran into more than one party, including a professionally guided team, that tried to dissuade us from going up the Polish Direct saying it was way out of condition, and to not even bother bringing our gear up with us. Surely this was information to be considered, but we thought let's go ahead and bring our gear up to the foot of it and if we need to, we will leave it there, not at the bottom based on hearsay. Besides, if it looks good, then we are way out of luck without it. One of the tricks of mountaineering is learning who to listen to and when.

The "last cowboy of Argentina" was not one of those people you would want to get information from. I call him this because of the way he rode that mule into our camp the day before we arrived at Base Camp. His stories could be heard 100 yards away and it appeared as though he had just come down out of the mountains driving the last, meanest, orneriest, wildest herd of donkeys the West had ever seen, and he wanted everyone to know it. They had forded deep, icy mountain rivers, pushed against hammering winds, and ridden more miles than was possible to count. Immediately I said to j, "Don't even look at him," as the guy continued to cast his voice out in all directions not really speaking to anyone in particular, but rather addressing the camp as a whole. We lay inside our tent and I even curled up as if this would make me harder to see. I wanted no part of the conversation. Slowly the voice got louder, closer, more focused in one direction, until it was right over our tent. "Just pretend we're not in here, shhhh!" I said to j.

"You boys going up the mountain!?" He blurted out in a big Texas-style obnoxious way. I looked at j; he stared at me.

I shook my head no, he said, "yep." That was it. For the next 30 minutes we got educated about this and all other mountains, about donkeys, about rivers, about altitude and the dangers of these places, and on and on and on.

Then he asked the big question: "So what kind of experience you boys got anyway?"

I again looked at j, he looked at me. I shook my head no and added a "Don't you dare!" look. He said, "Everest."

"Crap, j, really, c'mon!" Round two was sure to start, the stories of how he climbed Mole hill when he was a boy and yada yada. Instead I guess he figured he had been one upped and shut up.

"J, that was genius! I forgive you," I said.

Other than the climber who was airlifted out for frostbite, and the arrest of the president of the Argentine Alpine club for stealing a pair of mittens (maybe not mutually exclusive events), our arrival at Base Camp and climb to Camp Two was uneventful. We met the usual Polish guy, a group of friendly Swedes, a Seven Summits film crew, and a host of others. Even here at Base Camp people were still saying not to bother with the Polish Direct route, it was in bad shape, so we were stunned upon our arrival at Camp Two to find that, at the base at least, it was perfect.

The snow was hard and dense like Styrofoam, not too icy, not too soft; no chance of avalanches, and the climbing would be secure and fast. It could not have been better, it was optimal, and it wasn't bad — it was BAAD! I think what happens sometimes in these situations is that people want to feel better about the decisions they have made — the choice to maybe even let fear be their guide, to convince themselves there was a good reason to go the easier way. Our food hung side by side with our dirty socks inside the tent as we made final preparations and acclimated for our final big day.

With an early start, j was extremely strong and even eager to get going, not something I had seen in him even on our motorcycle journey. This showed me how good he felt and how excited he was for this summit. Maybe it was to get to a personal high point, or maybe it was his getting over his recent low point, but he was inspired. The crampons crunched over the frozen snow in the dark of night and side by side we marched up the initial slopes of the mountain. This was like the old days. I had my buddy back and we were gonna make an adventure out of this, summit or not! My climbing partner had overcome; he was back on his feet; spiked and all.

Fifteen hundred feet up we pulled out the rope as we climbed the icy section nicknamed the "bottleneck." The blue ice would lead us up into the meat of the climb and farther into the final obstacle of the rock gully. By far the steepest portion of the climb, it comes at the moment 22,000 feet is reached. Not only is there the struggle to find good footing, there is the struggle to breathe. Technically it is not nearly the climb that the south face is, but people have died on these slopes and it is not the time to let yourself be complacent with altitude or let your guard down with basic safety.

Soon j was up over the sugary top pitch and on to the ridge. I followed only to find him "dropping trou" on the ridge as I approached his "stance." Next thing I knew his pack came rolling down at me. I had to catch it or he would lose his warm layers, gloves, and headlamp, all good things to have for the descent. The remainder of the climb was a few hundred feet of the slowest in my life. I think I needed food, water, rest, and another day to acclimate and rest below. But here we were, in the now. Push on. I was tired, climbing in slow motion, but reaching that summit was incredible.

The summit of the Stone Sentinel was adorned with a cross. I was wearing a baseball hat that said "Calvary." I removed my hat and knelt by the cross, truly thankful to be free this day from injury, accident, and paralysis; to be with my good friend climbing in the presence of our Lord celebrating life, friendship, and adventure.

Every climber has that one meal they look forward to more than any other upon returning from a sustained effort. For me it is, has been, and always will be pizza. I love pizza. Bread, zesty sauce, cheese, meat, and veggies are all welcome to the party. The thing about pizza is no matter where you go in the world, you are safe with pizza. Pizza can't be messed up. It is wonderful and hot, it is round, it is square, it is cut into triangular slices, and it is pizza! We knew in Base Camp we had just enough money with us to buy a pizza apiece. The anticipation after a week of freeze-dried meals was killing me, and now the smell was almost more than I could bear. "Contain yourself," I would say. "Patience!"

Then as if delivered by an angel straight from heaven out of the golden clouds, blessed by the Lord himself, it was delivered. The beautiful disc (cue the choir and horns) sat before me with . . . uh oh . . . what the . . . (stop the choir, zip it with the horns) . . . how could this be . . . it is a fallen world indeed . . . the devil himself is roaming camp and he just RUINED MY PIZZA! There is good on this earth and there is evil. There is a God in heaven and there is Lucifer loosed on earth. I'll never understand it as long as I live why the Lord allowed Satan to touch my pizza.

As much as I like pizza, there is one food item that can bring even that mighty staple to its knees and ruin just about any dish that it touches. Its taste can permeate most things, and to put it on a pizza is a culinary disaster equivalent to wearing stripes with plaid — never do it. This pizza had eggs — yes, the unborn, boiled chicken fetus. "Why!!" The menu wasn't even in Spanish, and even if it was, I know *huevos* when I see them. When ordering a pizza, how often do you say, "Hold the eggs?" Never. What on earth possessed these people to do such a thing to a harmless pizza? I had yet to barf on this trip, but maybe this was my chance. Having spent my last *denaro* on this thing I wasn't about to waste it; besides, I needed the energy for tomorrow's 28-mile hike out. I scraped it clean and inspected it under the microscope in an effort to resuscitate my dinner.

Just as quickly as we ran down the 28 miles off the mountain, in the blink of an eye we were once again jammed into a small tent on the glaciers of Alaska's Mt. McKinley. To the native Athabaskans and to most people it is now called Denali, like it was originally, which means "the high one." It is enormous — taking your breath away upon first viewing it. The mountain stands tall above everything else with the mountains around it appearing to lap up against it like little waves hitting a lighthouse.

With this climb I was able to get my church involved and made it a prayer summit, where for the entire length of time I would be on the mountain, the church would pray for the needs of the community and the people in the church. I would again wear my Calvary hat as I climbed to be reminded that I, too, was committed in prayer to this effort and offering up these needs to God. We had cards printed with specific things to pray for each day of the expedition as we would journey, taking steps of faith together to climb the mountain, or if God would choose, to flat-out move the mountains of trouble and doubt from many of our lives.

We progressed steadily up this mountain, determined to climb it "alpine style," meaning we would not shuttle loads but carry with us all we needed to each camp, moving upward the whole time, never back. The usual caches were made in case we had to wait out lengthy storms, and for a day we thought we might be in the midst of a good one, when the weather never cleared. We moved upward with camps at 8,000, 11,000, 14,000, and finally 17,000 feet. We went up with skis mostly and were especially grateful for them when it made the descent fly by.

This trip went quickly, a total of 12 days with the weather cooperating nearly every day but two of the entire adventure. In late May, there were a lot of people on the mountain and with that comes a lot of tension from different personalities, fears, nationalities, and intentions. These differences would escalate into fights and it seemed the higher we got, the worse people were. In fact, at one spot while waiting to clip in to some fixed lines at 16,000 feet, a few guides, the ones who are supposed to be professional, got into quarrels like little school kids fighting over a place in line for the playground:

"I was here first!"

"NO, I was!"

"Well you went over there to talk to that guy."

"But I was just there for a second!"

"More like ten seconds!"

"Long enough to lose your place!"

I really thought at the end they were going to kill each other. I looked up the hill at the line of people waiting for the ropes and looked back at j. He nodded, and we set off up the snow-covered rocks around the side of all this chaos. It wasn't hard climbing and it certainly beat being around old grumpy-pants climbers. This move saved us an hour of waiting, and spared us the agony and drama of the CCC: Crotchety Climber Club.

Really, it was just one more day of balmy 20 below weather with high winds at 17,000 feet when we left our tent and the security it offered, making a slow and steady pace to the summit, where the sky dawned clear and blue and stayed that way until we were through. The biggest adjustment to Alaskan climbing is that the sun never quite goes down this time of year, so the usual alpine start is less necessary, and a headlamp not necessary at all, save digging for food crumbs in the bottom of the pack.

This summit would come to signify our solidarity as a body of believers, turning our focus higher, not to "the high one," but to the Highest One: hosanna in the highest. The beauty of skiing down the Kahiltna Glacier in an almost eternal twilight of color was unforgettable. My attention turned to our flight out, off the glacier and to my wife, whose flight in to meet us was just overhead. I was excited to see her because I felt like the hero coming back from the far reaches of the world to welcome her into my arms. Besides, she would smell so much better than j ever could, even after a thousand showers. As I flew out of the mountains she flew into them, asking her stewardess if Denali could be seen from the plane. Having asked the pilot, the stewardess returned with an answer and said, "No, I'm sorry we can't see Denali, but if you look out the other side of the plane you can see McKinley."

Deadpoint Reflections

There are summits everywhere. You just have to know where to look.[2]
— Blind climber Erik Weihenmayer

 Crux: Distraction. There is perhaps no better example of this than the PYT (pretty young thing) in the convertible, cranking her latest Miley Cyrus tunes by way of the iPod remote, eating a messy tofu burger, drinking a soda too big for the cup holder, which is messing up her lipstick that now needs to be repainted on but is in her purse in the backseat under one of the new shopping bags full of clothes only to find that her little purse poodle has messed on it and is now yapping at her from atop the backseat. She follows the GPS but didn't put in the destination before departure and now finds the need to check herself out in the mirror while talking on the phone as a second call comes in only to disrupt the text message she was sending to update her Facebook and other social media sites to alert them of how some idiot was honking his horn at her for failing to signal an unintentional lane change that put her through a sprinkler from which she is now wiping up water with the drive-through napkins that are threatening to blow out of the car and ruin her reputation as an eco-warrior, as she frantically tries to snatch them out of mid-air. Never mind the flip-flop sandal that is stuck under the gas pedal. That's what the other hand is for. Wasn't there a time when just driving itself was enough? In climbing, as in life, we need to keep the main thing the main thing. So many times on so many mountains I have encountered parties backing off a route saying how bad the conditions are. "Don't bother," "Can't do it," or "Go the other way," only to find the conditions could be no more perfect and those who spoke the words were only repeating what they heard from someone, who knew it from somewhere, that someone else had read on the Internet from a posting a year ago in another language. Discerning the difference between a distraction steering you off course and the need for focus on the original objective is the crux here. Many accidents occur in climbing when a distracted belayer fails to watch the leader or even when a lead climber setting up an anchor gets distracted and fails to set up properly.

 Hold: Focus, be intentional. List priorities and then implement a plan to make sure they remain priorities. This is what climbing really boils down to and why I love it so much. Just like the Houston quote in the front of this book states, all distraction fades away and everything boils down to just the simple task at hand.

Anchor: The Summit. The goal, the prize, reward, purpose, reason for the season. Knowing the difference between an authentic piece and a counterfeit — don't study the counterfeits as that distracts from the real thing. Study the true original and anything else will show itself to be a fake. God's Word is truth; study it and don't be distracted by all the other self-help "secrets" out there, including this one. By knowing God's Word, unauthentic words will rise to the surface and show themselves as false. We can become so engrossed in a distraction we think it is the real thing and put all our focus on that. An example would be the "Tree of Knowledge of Good and Evil." God told Adam and Eve to put their focus on anything else but that. Boom! Their focus was on that tree! This is how to stay focused: *Then he said to them all: 'If anyone would come after me, he must deny himself and take up his cross daily and follow me. For whoever wants to save his life will lose it, but whoever loses his life for me will save it'* (Luke 9:23–24).

Endnotes

1. Ernest Hemingway, *Snows of Kilimanjaro* (New York: Scriber, 1964).
2. Erik Weihenmayer, "Blind to Failure," by Karl Taro Greenfeld, June 18, 2001, www.time.com/time/magazine/article/0,9171,129942,00.

Breathing in the Death Zone

["Jesus" Ladder] Everest

NOTABLE EVEREST FIRSTS

FIRST ASCENT: May 29, 1953 by Sir Edmund Hillary, New Zealand and Tenzing Norgay, Nepal

FIRST ASCENT BY A WOMAN: May 16, 1975 by Junko Tabei, Japan

FIRST WINTER ASCENT: Feb. 17, 1980 by L. Cichy and K. Wielicki, Poland

FIRST SOLO ASCENT: Aug. 20, 1980 by Reinhold Messner, Italy

*FIRST BLIND PERSON: May 25, 2001 by Erik Weihenmayer

FIRST FAMILY/YOUNGEST: May 22, 2010 by Jordan Romero, age 13 who stood with dad, Paul, and step mom, Karen, on the summit of Mt. Everest

* Our team

Notes:

Continuing the ascent of Everest, the team is encamped at nearly 22,000 feet in the Western CWM of Everest.

*I lift up my eyes to the hills — where does my
help come from? My help comes from the LORD,
the Maker of heaven and earth. He will not let
your foot slip — he who watches over you will not
slumber; indeed, he who watches over Israel will
neither slumber nor sleep. The LORD watches over
you — the LORD is your shade at your right hand;
the sun will not harm you by day, nor the moon by
night. The LORD will keep you from all harm — he
will watch over your life; the LORD will watch over
your coming and going both now and forevermore.*
— Psalm 121

*Everest is a harsh and hostile immensity. Whoever
challenges it declares war. He must mount his
assault with the skill and ruthlessness of a military
operation. And when the battle ends, the mountain
remains unvanquished. There are no true victors,
only survivors.*[1]   — Barry Bishop

April 19, 2001, Day 28 — Everest again. The goal for us now was to
spend a few days at Camp Two, also known as Advanced Base Camp,
acclimating and preparing to go higher still. We would make day
trips to the base of the Lhotse face and eventually go as high as 24,000 feet to
establish Camp Three in the middle of the Lhotse Face. The face is a 3,000-
foot wall of ice with an average pitch of around 40 degrees, but as steep as 70
in some short sections. As we waited at Camp Two, we would be thankful for
the Sherpas who were there, dedicating themselves to the kitchen detail and
to the maintenance of camp.

Our week here consisted of some wrestling matches, games of spades
and hearts, and me burning the backside of my down suit as I sat too close
to the propane heater we had near the dinner table one evening. The smell
of smoke wafted up, causing me to look around to see what was burning. I
had no idea it was me until one of my teammates said, "Eric, your butt is on
fire!" The first inclination in my mind is to tease and think of a response like,
"All this climbing is finally paying off," but the reality is I was burning up at
22,000 feet. Had it gotten out of control it could have ended my climb, as we
rely so heavily on good gear and the condition of it. Fortunately, it wasn't too
bad and was nothing a little duct tape couldn't fix. Welcome to Camp Two.

Having arrived here ahead of some of the others I was firmly established in my tent awaiting the arrival of the others coming up from Camp One.

It is customary when we would see our heavily loaded teammates coming up the final stretch, we, who were feeling good, would meet them down the trail to relieve them of their load and bring it into camp where they would then be greeted by a hot cup of tea. On this day it was Luis who was coming up the trail, not having a particularly good day physically or emotionally, and he appeared tired from being the team punching bag once again. He always got riled up when picked on, which made him all the more a prime target.

I saw Luis arrive, setting his pack down next to the dining tent. This was my chance to make him feel better and do something nice. As he sipped his tea I snuck down, grabbed his heavy pack, carried it off to his tent on the far side of camp, and then went back to my tent without saying anything. I should have told him what I had done. When he exited the dining tent and found no pack, he exploded. Thinking it was just one more prank, he broke out into a tirade, a verbal onslaught directed to all within earshot. "Where is my pack?! Who the hell hid my pack?! You SOBs! I'm tired of always being the whipping boy!"

Then the gallery would chime in, "Chill out, fat boy, no one hid your pack. You probably just forgot where you put it!" Now everyone was just throwing fuel on the fire to see what would happen. It was this type of interaction that earned Luis the title of "Drama Queen" on our team. It wasn't until a minute later I was able to tell him I had actually tried to do something nice by placing it in his tent. The gesture that was intended to be kind got overlooked and only made a bad day worse for Luis. I guess sometimes we try to do things, not seeking attention or credit, but the wise thing would be to see a situation for what it is and let others in on it, not for the attention, but rather to let them know you care. Lesson learned.

Yes, this climb and story at first look like the perfect Disney after-school program, but the truth is we had our moments, just like families do, brothers and sisters squabble and fight, and parents that sometimes act more like children than the kids. At times we did not get along, want to be together, or especially listen to each other at dinner, but what made us a strong team was the ability to get over it, work through it, and move on toward the bigger goal. As men can do, and women often struggle to do, we could communicate bluntly and truthfully to each other to work out our differences, forgive, and continue to climb.

Five days had been spent up high, losing sleep, weight, and appetite. The daily routine was sleeping until the sun hit the tent, getting up for eggs on toast, a team effort of pouring warm water over each other's hands outside the dining tent, picking up the dirty little frozen soap brick from the slimy bowl, soaping your hands — only to find your wash partner has gone inside and left you all lathered up in the freezing air. No problem, "Blindheimer" (as he is regularly, mistakenly called) is coming down from his tent and needs a little guidance to the tent. He'll give me a rinse in exchange for some sounds. "Hey, E, over here! Go left, forward three steps, and watch out for the tent string riiiiight there. Yep, you got it, no worries, we'll fix it later."

Then it is the usual group meal goings on of chatter, crude jokes, weather speculation, gossip on other teams, and the constant never-ending passing of items back and forth, over and under the table, condiments, silverware, cups, water, and tea drinks. Things never sit still long on the table and they always seem to be at the most inconvenient spot when you want them most, like the bacon bits and BBQ sauce, which make everything taste better. Dining becomes much like its own little sport and there are certain advantages to the seat you select, or disadvantages to the one you get should you arrive late for dinner. Such as the seat by the door of the small tent so that everyone who gets up to leave must go past you, and the freezing air is always beside you. If you get pinned on the other end, you'd better not need to go to the bathroom unless you want to wrestle past all your team. The middle gives good access to all food on the table, is warm, and allows for an exit should you need to; the only drawback is you become the hands for every item that passes from one end of the table to the other. It comes down to your mood that day, and if you can handle being a part of all the conversation and a part of every course of the meal.

Once the sun has set and the hot drinks are no more, it is time for the dreaded crawl into the cold sleeping bag. This is best done while wearing a warm down suit with a Nalgene bottle full of hot water. It becomes a little bit of a personal science as you unzip the suit and slide into the bag, allowing the warmth of your body and the warm water bottle to fill the airspace of the cold nylon sleeping bag. Once warm, the down suit can come off, or if higher up on the mountain, stay on until the climbing begins.

When acclimating, it is good to stay active, but also good to make sure you have some naptime. And since the night does not usually provide climbers with the best sleep, the warmth of the day and the solar heating of the tents make for some prime napping conditions. Contrary to the hyperbole of so many Everest stories, it is not always death-defyingly cold on the mountain, and at times it is so hot it becomes inescapable and miserable. The best thing to do is seek shade in the dining tent or cover your own tent with a sleeping bag so as to shield it from the sun, then strip to your skivvies and wait for some clouds to pass by. It can be so intense up in the thin atmosphere that people have sunburned their tongues while hiking with their mouths open. It's a good idea to climb early in stable and cool conditions and avoid this issue all together.

One nap in the morning and one in the afternoon can usually help to fend off the effects of the previous night's sleep deprivation from altitude and a snoring tentmate. Really, until you become acclimated or even just accustomed to it, the periodic breathing is perhaps the most unnerving thing about sleeping up high. Just as you doze off into dreamland you suddenly feel as though your lungs have shut down and no air is coming in, causing a slight panic and then reawakening. It is the O_2/CO_2 confusion in the body that causes this lapse of breathing, which at times can stop for a whole minute.

Typically, our body is driven to breathe by a buildup of CO_2 in the blood and the need to expel this gas. At high altitude, this buildup is much slower, causing the CO_2 drive to be replaced by a drive for O_2, but with this being an abnormal process, the body times out until it senses the need. This gasp for air then raises the heart rate and makes getting back to sleep even more difficult than before. Usually it is not until re-entry of the thick air of Base Camp near 18,000 feet that one can again sleep soundly.

Camp Two for me was the toughest place to sleep, even more so than Camp Four, maybe because at Camp Four you're so tired and loopy, sleep just happens. Also figuring into the equation is the nausea, and the frequent upset stomach that comes with high altitude eating and sleeping and, worst of all, the 2:00 in the morning bathroom blitz. Hold on until all hope is lost, because it is cold, dark, stinky, and miserable. It requires getting nearly fully geared up just to get some relief. Doing one's business in a plastic bucket lined with a Hefty Steel Sack, covered by a nylon tent, anchored into the ice, was typically the most dreaded time of the day or, heaven forbid, night, and closing the door would be a mistake made only one time. I only write this because it is one of the most frequently asked questions about Mount Everest which I, or probably any climber, get asked, therefore reading it you need not embarrass yourself by asking anyone who has been on the mountain, "How do you go to the bathroom?" When full, the bag is jettisoned into a distant crevasse hopefully not making its way back into the drinking water at Base Camp.

Efforts are now being made around the globe to implement new systems and reduce the impact of human waste. People often have the perception that the trash left behind on the mountain is one of the biggest issues facing Mount Everest, but I contend it is the impact of human waste itself that is a greater danger. The numbers of trekkers, climbers, Sherpas, and yaks that make their way each season up the narrow trail system of the Khumbu valley easily overload the feeble infrastructure, and all but non-existent treatment facilities.

The rushing river seems to do the job "just fine." I would guess out of sight is out of mind, and the roar of the river is a simulation of the flush of the toilet. Many of the teahouses have composting pit toilets, but all too often, the call must be answered on the trail, behind a rock, over a bank, or into the river. It is good to live higher up than in the valley below. I know as time goes on and the number of tourists continues to increase, this issue will be addressed, if not just by the demands and expectations of these visitors.

The climbers are the only visitors allowed past Base Camp, and for the most part, are doing a better and better job of keeping the mountain clean, thanks largely to ethics espoused by many alpine clubs and guiding services, but also by the Nepalese government and the paid garbage removal incentives they have implemented for Sherpas. Always eager to earn a few more rupees, this program has worked well for the Sherpas who then get paid by the kilogram of trash they are able to bring down. This seems great until you are climbing the Lhotse face and see a bag of trash and gear being jettisoned down the 3,000-foot wall of ice only to be retrieved at the bottom. I guess I wouldn't want to carry it down on my back either, and it seemed to be gathered up rather effortlessly at the bottom without hurting any climbers on their way up.

Finally, after a number of days acclimating at Camp Two, which included one short foray up to the base of the Lhotse face, it is time to make a push for Camp Three and, hopefully, some real benefits from its 24,000-foot elevation two-thirds of the way up the face. It would mean an early 4:00 a.m. start with a quick breakfast in all our gear, and then stepping into the dark, all with our headlamps, minus one. It's a time of nervous excitement knowing most of us on this team would achieve an altitude high mark, and the first time with Erik on this new terrain.

April 23, Day 32 — All went well as we approached the face where it became my lead. I was followed by Erik, and he by Brad Bull, as most of the others went on up ahead. Jeff Evans went down early from Camp Two affected by a gastro-intestinal bug.

I know I just said that it can be unbearably hot on the glaciers of this mountain, but the truth remains that overall it is a cold place to be. It is a common question to receive, after climbing this mountain, "Was it cold on Everest?" Most of the time I am gracious in my response, but every once in a while I want to answer the question with a question: "Is rain wet? Is the sky blue?" and it goes on from there.

Yes, it is cold on Everest and while I didn't necessarily ever get cold on the expedition, the temperature would often be below zero, which is compounded for climbers due to the fact the blood thickens and there is less oxygen to burn, making the body cold more easily and quickly. Basically, this can be said about the temperature on Everest: if the sun is up and on you and the wind is calm, it will feel warm. If the sun has set, wind or not, it will be cold. It was only on this early morning that I experienced cold toes. It was cold enough for me to keep an eye on the horizon for that rising sun, as our route was shaded by the great mountain. The slow pace made re-warming difficult and it wasn't until the incline and my heart rate increased, that my toes again felt welcome in my boots.

The face rose steady and steep at first and I was feeling safe since it was still not getting warmed up too much by the sun. Our concern became greater as the sun would warm not only the steel of the ice screws anchoring the ropes, but also the rocks and chunks of ice that sat on the surface waiting for an excuse to jump down at us. The rocks got their chance and gave us their best effort. We kept our pace rapid so as to limit our time here in this bowling alley of debris. Wearing an ascender and a cow's tail (a carabiner attached to a sling to clip ourselves into the rope), we could climb the slope faster on the fixed lines than we could if we were ascending alpine-style (ascending with our own rope that moves up with us).

The climbing Sherpas, along with a few guides from other teams, would establish the route and secure ropes to the icy face ahead of time to facilitate the high volume of climbers on the mountain, and thereby make it safer. Speed is often equal to safety in the mountains. The only bad news was the rope on the face is the cheapest Chinese 8mm rope money can buy, reminding me of the black and yellow "bumble bee" rope used at the ski resorts back home. To make matters more unnerving still, one would never know the integrity of the rope above (e.g. had it been cramponed to death, had a rock hit it, had a screw popped out, was it old or new?) All of this made me sweat even though I was cold, giving me that nice, nauseous feeling that was becoming very familiar on this unpredictable mountain. This feeling affected Mike O'Donnell so much we could always tell if he had left camp ahead of us or not by the certain stains in the snow he left behind from nervousness. That says a lot, because Mike is an outstanding climber who will lead out ice pitches, placing screws at 50-foot intervals with confidence.

Three hours had gone by since we departed Camp Two, and I was feeling horrible. From the day I arrived at Camp Two, I had felt this way. With a heavy load, I left Base Camp, set on getting to Camp Two in less than five hours. The climb is 4,000 feet up through the icefall, ending at 22,000 feet; not a big deal if you climb at lower elevations of 5,000 or even 8,000 feet, or if you're a well-acclimated Sherpa carrying twice the weight in half the time, while making it back in time to serve us lunch; truly humbling. Climbing this mountain does require a person to focus a little heavily on oneself, making it easy to overlook the amazing abilities of others, especially those who make the whole climb possible. I am always grateful for the Sherpas and their humility, and how this certainly forces one to keep his own pride and perceived abilities in check.

An example of speed looks like this: I have climbed Mt. Washington in New Hampshire (3,000 vertical feet) in just over three hours roundtrip from Pinkham Notch Visitor Center, up Huntington ravine and down Tuckerman's; in Colorado, I have made a similar round trip ascent of 14,421 foot Mt. Massive in three and a half hours, starting at an elevation of 10,500 feet — but here on Everest, starting at 18,000, I was pushing myself too hard, too early in the acclimatization process, making it difficult to recover from a four-hour ascent to 22,000 feet. In fact, the entire time my resting heart rate (the number of beats per minute when I awoke in the morning) would not go below 124 bpm. High on the Lhotse face, my heart felt like it was going to explode, and I came to the decision that I didn't want to create a situation for my team that night at Camp Three. So with Erik depending on me, I made the unpopular decision to turn around. I could tell Erik was disappointed; Brad was too easy going to be upset, and could handle rather well just about anything that came his way; but P. V. really lost it. I, of course, didn't hear this over the radio, but was informed later of his reaction.

I, too, was disappointed and wondered how this might play out on summit day as far as who would get called up to be a part of the small squad that would inevitably get to go with Erik; after all, I don't believe any of us thought we would all be making the trip up the last three thousand feet to the summit when that night came. Historically speaking, most expeditions considered it a success if any one or two members are able to make it to the summit. Fear and doubt had plagued me since the year before, and it was trying once more to gain a foothold on me at my highest point.

The decision was the right one, and I knew with the coming week of rest, as we had planned, it would make all the difference. For now, I was content knowing my lungs would not fill with fluid above 23,000 feet. With my head held low, I ashamedly made my way back down to Camp Two, gathered my things, had lunch, and then went down to Base Camp with Steve Gipe.

Steve had earlier weighed the emotions of having a concerned wife and son at home and said, "Pooky and Paul would not approve," when he saw all the falling debris cascading down the Lhotse face like marbles and Superballs loosed from above. It was on my way down, as I knelt by an anchor to move my attachment point around the anchor, that a rock the size of a truck tire came thundering down the face. This is one of the scariest sounds I have ever heard. It begins very deep and very dull. It grows louder and faster, and the delays between the thuds do nothing to add calm or give the belief that the falling object has stopped or disappeared. The delays only mean that the object is now more difficult to spot since it is in the air, blocked by the glare of the sun and the ice.

While being attached to the rope and standing on a steep ice face, there is really nowhere, and no way, to run to avoid these fast-moving, giant, hard objects. Since I was already in the kneeling position, I made perhaps the quickest request of my life to God when I said, "God, please not today!" The rolling rock pounded the ice right beside me and kept going on its way, just as fast as it had arrived. My next thought was of the ropes, knowing that a rock like that would surely sever the ropes if it hit them. I was more than relieved to have made it off of the face in one shaky piece.

Those who did continue on to spend the night at Camp Three had a wonderful sleepless night: windy, cold, nausea, headaches, vomiting, panic attacks, and even talk of giving each other altitude meds in the rear (even though this is not where they normally would be administered). Luis said, "You have not lived until you have had to vomit in a Ziploc bag!" It was good hearing them joke from below at Camp Two, knowing things must not be so bad; at least he didn't vomit on himself.

One month on the mountain and it now feels like home. We have gotten to know it very well and to some degree, this feels like our own little world. It's a lot like how I see the old west, with the teams of climbers really making the rules we all live by, rules which others break, with justice being left to God, revenge, and sometimes the mountain itself. Though we all know this process of acclimatization is necessary, none of us wants to go down after having reached this height. I suppose a person could go on from Camp Three and attempt a summit, but most likely it would be premature.

Research shows that the most successful climbers not only descend to Base Camp, they go even as much as six thousand feet lower than that to fully recover in the fat air of 12–14,000 feet. The body can rebuild, regain its appetite, renew vigor, and after a week climb again — rejuvenated and enthusiastic, having lost the lethargy of altitude like a welfare recipient who just won the lottery; finally able to get off your butt without a fire under it. Knowing the distance up to the summit is equal to, if not less than, that of Base Camp, makes going down a hard pill to swallow. This process of going up and down not only gets a climber's body ready to climb, I think it steels the mind and gets a climber's head in the game as well. This process creates an iron resolve within us perhaps when we feel most like quitting and going home.

With Sherpas staying behind to watch camp, the team would make a half day's journey down to Dengboche at 14,200 feet with just a sleeping bag, water bottle, and other basics, for the sole purpose of getting some R&R. It is now April 28, and upon having made it to Dengboche we drop our packs, have a snack, and out of guilt, as well as, knowledge of the fatigue our blind friend was experiencing, Mike O and I headed 20 minutes back up the hill with a handful of snacks, and that ever-so-delectable cold Sprite, to meet EW and welcome him into town. It was these acts of service that the team would often perform for each other that made us forget about our own pain and gripes, forget about some of the squabbles we might have had and some of the grudges we perhaps had been holding on to. We'd play card games, talk to trekkers, take short hikes, nap, go bouldering on nearby rocks, and enjoy the taste of food just a little bit more. That is, until we stumble into the kitchen horrified to see the cook stoking the fire with yak dung patties, and almost in the same motion kneading the dough for a pizza that would be our dinner. I truly believe an increase in hand washing by both the Nepalis and Western climbers would directly correlate to a decrease in the amount of antibiotics taken for gastro-intestinal illnesses.

Now, back down so low, how easy would it be to say we were close enough; let's just keep going and get home? There would be loved ones, a clean, soft bed, a hot shower, and perhaps best of all, a crispy salad, cold beer, and hot cheesy pizza with grease oozing off the sides and all over your face. The fact remains the prize has not yet been claimed, the task is still at hand, and a job is yet to be done — something we are reminded of over the next days as Erik sits down to a number of interviews with NPR, Brian Williams of NBC, and various others who all want to know how this story is unfolding and will continue to unfold. Down here the sleep is deeper, the belly is fuller, the shower hotter, the stink is gone, and the desire has come back. Just when I thought I couldn't eat another meal next to one of these foul-smelling teammates, who talk with their mouths full and with enough expletives to last a lifetime, I suddenly saw the bigger purpose and it became clear again, once the oxygen reached the brain, as to why I was climbing.

April 27, Day 36 — After a night of cheating at cards by being able to look at blind Erik's hand (a fact made known when someone asked Erik if he had any spades and Jeff responded for him before he could scan the Braille cards, saying, "No, he doesn't"), sleeping all in one large dorm-style bunk room, and getting cleaned up, Erik, Mike, and I headed over to Pheriche the next day to chat with the high altitude docs, who have a clinic set up over the hill to treat ailing trekkers and climbers. At nearly 15,000 feet, this clinic has saved a number of climbers from life-threatening injuries and ailments.

Upon arrival we learn of a short seminar being given on understanding altitude and its effects, so we sit in with a group of trekkers. As the doctor speaks, he passes around a pulse oximeter for everyone to put on and get a reference point for how they are acclimating. Without saying anything about where we have been, we wait our turn, as the others, all eager to share their results, begin to shout out their numbers: "I'm 82," "I'm 79," "Whoa, that's bad," "I'm doing awesome. I'm 84." Then Erik puts it on and in a low tone mumbles, "I'm 94," followed by Mike at 92, and me also at 94. We look at each other and say, "Looks like we are acclimating a little better than these folks, but don't worry, you guys will be okay, I think. Maybe." We were then able to break the straight face and tell them we had already been up to 23,000 feet and to quit panicking because they were doing just great.

The laugh was short-lived, because moments later we received the news that Babu Chiri Sherpa had just died. Our jaws dropped as our mouths hung open in disbelief. Babu, was at the time, the most celebrated climbing Sherpa after Tenzing Norgay. He was climbing the mountain right there along side us. He had shared a meal in our tent with us. Babu had ten Everest summits and seven daughters. He had climbed the mountain faster than anyone in history, spent the night on the summit without oxygen, and was still the most lovable, humble person you would ever want to meet. We were stunned. How could it be possible? No way, not Babu!

This definitely had an impact on our morale and even to a degree, albeit short-lived, our belief in our climb and its success. After all, if someone like Babu could die, so could any one of us, and with Erik it seemed even more likely that we could take a misstep. Those are the kind of thoughts you must clear from your mind, and then refocus on just the next step. It was exactly this, a misstep, which was responsible for the early end to Babu's life. He was roaming the glacier at Camp Two taking pictures by himself when the snow beneath him gave way, revealing a previously hidden crevasse. Immediately he plummeted deeply into the open chasm, maybe 100 feet, dying on impact, only to be retrieved hours later with the help of respected guide, Willie Benegas.

Erik had this to say, when we heard the news that sent all of Nepal into a state of shock: "He was one of Nepal's national heroes who I had the pleasure of meeting on my second trip through the icefall, as he was coming down. He leaned in toward me and I felt his big-barreled chest. His gloved hand patted me on the back. It sounds strange, but I can still feel his hand on my back; warm and confident. Today, I have been fighting to keep my head in a positive space. I have a lot of conflicting thoughts in my head and I'm not sure what to think. I want to make sure this accident doesn't make my friends and family worry more about us. One thing I've learned about our team is that we'll stick together and take care of each other, which gives me just enough courage to head back up there for the final push." We must mourn the loss of a great climber and great man, and then take a step forward because our own lives must keep moving onward.

It is strange to say that though we were deeply saddened by the tragic loss of Babu, and we would resolve to climb in a manner respectful and honoring to his life, somehow in spite of Babu's death, a spring now filled our steps as we easily made it back up to Base Camp, where before we had drug ourselves slowly up into its rarified air. Maybe it was because we knew that at any moment the door could swing wide open for us to make an attempt at the summit. There was a feeling now of really being in the game; that at any moment, if the weather was right and we felt good, it would be off to the summit. The gear was ready, our bodies were ready, our camps established, and now our vision could be more firmly set on the summit, knowing that many of Everest's obstacles had been overcome.

I am constantly impressed by Erik's strength, endurance, and inner determination. He also demonstrates patience like no other climber on the team. As we guide him through obstacles and over narrow bridges, vocally describing how best to navigate the terrain, we often make mistakes. "Hey, Erik, this bridge is ten feet long and one foot wide — go left a little bit . . . oops! No, I meant right, er, no, left was right; I mean correct, go left! GO LEFT!" The blind man scans with his poles, continuing on his way without getting angry about the fact his foot just went into the water and his life was put in jeopardy by an oversight of mine. It would not be the last time, for sure, and it makes me realize just how independent my friend is on this climb, relying more on his senses, balance, and abilities than on anything else.

May 3, Day 42 — Back at Base Camp, we were antsy to get going higher and hopefully finish this long process. More meals together, more tired conversation, and then, the gathering in the big dome tent to watch some more of the same DVDs. Once in a while we would go over to the neighboring camp to see what we could swap to watch on our laptop, which was powered by the sun and surrounded by 20 people in down coats, stocking caps, and sleeping bags. The "theater" would fill with our frosty breath until it was warmed enough by our bodies to keep the fog down.

Even an event like this could only happen with careful planning. There had to be enough juice in the batteries to show an entire video in the cold of Base Camp. If too many people had emailed or surfed the web that day, or even if it had been too cloudy to get a good charge, we would be out of luck. The often-pirated DVD or, even worse, VCD bought in Kathmandu also had to be compatible and not skip. On more than one occasion we would only make it halfway through a movie before we called it a night due to any one of these circumstances being true. But, we were happy with any entertainment at all and a theatrical distraction was the best kind. Cards would get old just like the company we kept, so a movie was a nice escape, just like it is at home.

From May 5 to May 9, the team stayed at Base Camp waiting for a good window. Time was spent eating, sleeping, hiking, writing, vegging, and ice climbing the frozen uplift of the bottom of the Khumbu icefall. This was a fun way to exercise and work off a little of the frustration. Among the frozen pools, ice pillars, rock, and other oddities of the glacier were little mementos of expeditions past and their failures. One of my teammates, on a foray into the ice, found some old equipment that had been ejected from an entry high above, years ago. The gear had been swallowed up and now spit out from the glacier.

The find, that I never went to investigate, was that of a human hand. The bones of a deceased climber had survived the crushing ice and emerged as a sobering reminder of just how dangerous the icefall can be. Climb fast, but not so fast you lose your footing, lest you become a memory and resurface as the boney topic of someone else's dinner conversation years in the future. Up high on the mountain, a body will not decompose, but down here is just enough warm air and micro-organisms to get that process going, and when coupled with the grinding action of the glacier, bones are all that remain.

May 9 arrived and half the team set off from Base Camp to Camp Two early in the morning. The days of rest allowed certain members to get over yet another bout of intestinal funk and emerge ready, on what we now hoped to be our true summit bid. Erik W would head up early this morning with Jeff, Sherman, Mike O, Chris Morris, and me. Jeff and Sherm would stay with Erik at Camp One, while Mike and I would continue. The rest of the team would follow the next morning, join Erik, Jeff, and Sherm at Camp One, and then proceed to join the rest of us at Camp Two.

The winds, for the time being, have died down, the Sherpas have made it as high as the balcony, and our hopes are even higher as we go up this time. I even start to think of being back down in time for my birthday: May 21. We are being aggressive, given the weather report, but we certainly do not want to be out of position should we get a good window of even just three days, which could mean the difference between making it to the top or coming back another year to try again. Our times up through the icefall continue to improve, a sign that we are all well acclimated and feeling strong. The days are getting a little longer, a little warmer and as always, the sun is as intense as can be at this elevation. Didrik, in fact, had this to say about the sun:

Seeing as my tongue has healed from the vicious sunburn, I am itching to get out of Base Camp and head up the mountain. Note to self and others — under no circumstances expose your tongue to the elements. If you've never had a sunburned tongue, let me explain the process.

First of all, it sneaks up on you. A slight tingling feeling on the tip, like maybe you bit it by accident. The tingling soon turns to an itchy feeling when the little red bumps appear on the tip. The little red bumps begin to grow until they turn white and then, the real pain begins. My drink mix in my water bottle burns. French fries burn. My favorite Nepalese food, momo's — meat or veggie-filled dumplings — which I usually take with horseradish sauce is no longer an option.

I thought I could take it, so I took the sweet little momo between my fingers, swabbed it in the horseradish sauce and gingerly placed it in my mouth, trying to avoid contact with the tip of my tongue. No luck. I used to think I was tolerant of pain. Last year when I was doubled-over in Cambodia with the severest of severe stomach cramps, and my girlfriend was insisting that if I was a girl, it would not be a big deal, I was adamant that my pain tolerance was as high as anyone. But now as the horseradish oozed into the grooves of my tongue, bringing the pain of a thousand bee stings, I relented. The pain in my calves after climbing the Lhotse Face was no match for the 5 square millimeters of sunburned tongue. So anyway, five days later, with the healing process complete, we are here in Base Camp waiting to get up that hill.[2]

Others described this process of waiting as "mastering the hang," meaning learning to live with very little going on, and putting off the goal one more time.

May 10, Day 50 — We arrive at Camp Two, optimistic, hopeful, and energized by the prospect of getting up and off this mountain. Camp Two offered another bad night's sleep at 22,000 feet and one more day of waiting for the rest of the team. We awakened in nervous hope to the thought of going onward and upward to Camp Three, but instead find the mountain in the grips of a brutal storm. At 4:00 a.m., the lightning show was one of the most spectacular I have ever seen, and I have seen a lot.

Once in college, camped near the summit of Mt. Evans at 14,000 feet, I saw our cabin, which had a Faraday Shield (grounded chicken wire placed over the building), glow purple, as my hair stood on end watching bolts dance all around me — spooky! Here, high in the Khumbu, the lightning illuminated the valley below and the sides of the mountain. We were in the clouds that were producing this lightning. Even just lying in the tent I could see these bursts of light like staring directly into a camera flash after just waking up in a dark room.

The occasional rumble of thunder would roll through the valley and it was apparent some of these rumbles were not thunder but avalanches. We just hoped our camp was in the right spot, free from any slide activity. In making communications with people higher up the mountain it became clear this was not the time to mount an attempt. The snow was deep, the winds were blowing hard, waist-deep drifts had formed up higher, and the potential for avalanches on the route was too great. We heard estimates putting the wind at 60 mph and knew that the potential for 100+mph winds was totally feasible. Guess what? It was time to go back down to let things settle.

We all have been climbing long enough in our lives to know, of course, this is what you do in the mountains, but nonetheless, it is like getting a flat tire during a bike race and you can't help but feel dejected. Down we go again after having waited five days. From the looks of the new forecast, we would need to wait another four days, and at 22,000 feet we would just lose too much energy. A number of guys on the team have already withered down to almost nothing from the fact that appetite is lost, huge amounts of calories are burned, and the sicknesses that ravage through camp, making us all at times feel bulimic, take away both muscle and fat. This would be a perfect place for people who are overweight to spend a couple of months — it makes *The Biggest Loser* television show look like a Tahitian vacation.

The demands of the mountain test every bit of a person. It tested me physically, emotionally, spiritually, relationally, and especially, put my patience under fire.

The best thing for me to do was dig deep for that little bit of optimism that still allowed me to feel good about something, joke about it all, laugh with the others, and find ways to persevere. Tell myself again why I am here, what the bigger meaning of it is, and why I want to get up there so badly. The worst thing I could do would be to go down that road of negativity and allow myself to think too much about home, loved ones, food, and what other parts of life I might be missing out on. I couldn't let my attention and feelings become divided, not that I didn't think of and pray for my loved ones — I just couldn't become consumed by the thoughts so much as to lose focus. I would still need to want this.

Pasquale had this to say about our situation and summit attempt:

> To say that the team is impatient is an understatement. After almost two months on this expedition we want to get to the summit. Many of us have been through the Khumbu Icefall five times and are looking forward to our last time through it. With only two weeks left in the climbing season, the opportunity for more than one summit attempt is gone. We have at most one chance to get to the summit of

Everest before we have to head for home. As I said in an earlier dispatch, all of our camps are completely set up and stocked. We have slept at Camp Three at 24,000 feet and have spent over 14 nights at or above 22,000 feet. Originally, we did not want to be the first team on the mountain and "lead" the route up to the summit of Everest. As things worked out, we are the largest and potentially strongest team on the mountain. It appears that when we leave for our final summit push this Saturday, we may well have to lead the route to the summit. No other team has attempted to push the final 3,000 feet of route from the South Col at 26,000 feet, to the summit at 29,035 feet. This means that we must lead. All of the fixed rope that our Sherpas fixed last week to just below the South Summit is now buried under many feet of new snow. It is useless and will have to be re-fixed prior to this coming week's summit attempt. Our current schedule is to climb to Camp One this coming Saturday, Camp Two on May 20, rest day on May 21, Camp Three on May 22, Camp Four at the South Col on May 23 and Summit May 24, with the final push starting at 9:00 p.m. on May 23. In the event of bad weather we will not retreat, but merely remain in our high camps until we either summit or run out of time.[3]

Didrik added his sentiments by saying:

· "I'm trying to keep myself from pulling my hair out. It feels like I've been here for years. . . . About 20 minutes out of Camp One I turned around and saw the most sickening looking black sheet of clouds forming over the summit pyramid of Everest. . . . swarming as fast as the summer fog moves into San Francisco. . . . *Maybe it is a good idea to let this Jet stream peter out before we head up there.*"[4]

We had a good plan on paper and I really prayed that the Lord would grant us passage on what would be our last shot no matter what. Hard to believe after all this time it would come down to this: one shot. My thoughts in this moment: *Dear God: Please Give Us Patience — NOW!!* It is May 18, and in all honesty, I thought by now I'd be sipping champagne on a flight home, upgraded to 1st class, telling lies to anyone who would listen: of how I single-handedly led a team of climbers, including a blind man, up Everest — the biggest, meanest, iciest, windiest mountain on earth — well the tallest anyway . . . telling stories of how I climbed up without oxygen, running up with Erik W to become heroes.

The reality is I am here at Base Camp, looking about as strong, fit, and handsome as a burnt match with sideburns. We left a week ago for what we thought would be our summit bid, but instead we got snowed on, so much so, that at 28,000 feet our tallest Sherpa had snow up to his armpits. We went up the Western Cwm at 22,000 feet in the sunny heat of the day (only avoidable by getting up at the atrocious hour of 3:00 a.m. to leave by 4:00 a.m.). We, however, need our beauty sleep, so we left at 5:30 a.m. As we climbed up in the 100+ degree heat, we were glad to be wearing the warmest boots on the planet. Arriving at Camp Two, we stripped to nothing but our skivvie shorts, and were still too hot.

As the week passed, we experienced weather: snow, wind, heat, avalanches, thunder, and lightning — oh my! We have all been kept safe and healthy thus far, giving me confidence that the prayers of loved ones back home are being answered — now if one-half of y'all would start praying for things like pizza, ice cream, nachos, soda, beer, and tentmates that don't stink, we would appreciate that, too. Soon, we will go up again (as other teams fall apart, pack up, and leave), summiting soon after my birthday, I hope.

Tomorrow, May 19, five teams will start their summit attempts; thus far in the season, not one team has made it to the top, neither from the north nor south sides. It is sad to say we will be on the heels of most of these teams going up and are really hoping not to get involved in a bottleneck situation. The other thing we don't want is for 18 teams to follow us in breaking trail up through the new snow. The games have begun once again as we all jockey for position on the mountain, no one telling the whole truth of their plans so as to keep one step ahead of the other teams.

Due to the storms, much of the fixed rope has been buried and will need to be replaced. Some of ours was taken, we believe, by the Russian team that is climbing a new route on Lhotse, though they deny it. We let them use our tents at Camp Three and in return they stole our rope. There is nothing like being used twice. Steve Gipe had remained at Camp Two through this process and his presence was indeed missed. I, for one, looked forward to having his company again and the peace his nature brings to our dining and climbing experiences. So now, as we prepare to set off for the summit the weather is the biggest question mark and our biggest hurdle, well sort of.

Deadpoint Reflections

Most people never run far enough on their first wind to find out they've got a second.[5]
— William James

Finally, brothers, whatever is true, whatever is noble, whatever is right, whatever is pure, whatever is lovely, whatever is admirable — if anything is excellent or praiseworthy — think about such things.
— Philippians 4:8

Crux: I was going to write something here about quitting, but I lost my motivation; quitting boils down to value. What is the goal worth to you? How bad do you want it? Do you still fight for your wife? How about investing time in your children and their values? Into your fitness, diet, and spiritual well-being, or is it not worth the effort? Is it past failure, obstacles, lack of vision, foresight, funds, confidence? I have to admit, some days I just don't have it. The little blister on my pinky toe takes me out of the race. Usually at that moment I see a double leg amputee run by sweating it out, but grinning ear to ear because he cares. Then I come up with some brilliant excuse — obviously he doesn't have any blisters on his pinky toes. How easy it is to become defensive of that quitting attitude. An unmotivated person with a lack of desire to accomplish a goal will never stand on top of a summit and understand the beauty of effort, the spirit of the fight, the thrill of the victory. This person will understand, however, the want thereof. I believe that quitting is one of the easiest trends to begin, but one of the hardest to end.

Hold: Perseverance: Faith in purpose, stamina, persistence, passion, and risk go down swinging. What makes me want to persevere is not merely seeing the importance of just hanging on; it is letting go of the hold and reaching upward. To stand at the bottom of the cliff looking up, and saying no, not today, is one thing. Being five hundred feet up on the cliff, holding on to edges the size of dimes as tired arms filled with a burn begin to lose their grip and the pain caused by the narrow edge flares up from digging into the tips of the fingers, whose skin is slowly being peeled away and sweat loosens the grip, sending a message to the brain saying move now or fall and lose your progress, is another. Imagine there is no rope. Now, there becomes no choice but to press on. Need necessitates perseverance. In climbing I have a little slogan — "go down swinging." That is to say, I can't just back off out of fear or lack of ability and be lowered down, I have to keep trying, fall though I may. Of course this is done with a rope and partner.

Anchor: *We also rejoice in our sufferings, because we know that suffering produces perseverance; perseverance, character; and character, hope. And hope does not disappoint us, because God has poured out his love into our hearts by the Holy Spirit, whom he has given us* (Romans 5:3–5). Usually this verse reads like this to me in my head: "Why am I suffering, I can't take anymore, I thought I had enough character. Lord, you are disappointing me, though I am thankful for your love, but please, I hope this is it with the character building."

In this world you will have trouble. But take heart! I have overcome the world." — Jesus Christ (John 16:33).

Endnotes
1. Barry Bishop, "How We Climbed Everest," *National Geographic* (October 1963).
2. Didrick Johnck, Everest Live, May 5, 2001, www.2001everest.com.
3. A.V. Pasquale, Everest Live, May 16, 2001, www.2001everest.com.
4. Didrick Johnck, Everest Live, May 17, 2001, www.2001everest.com.
5. www.iwise.com/PDyrf.

Do or Die

[The Hillary Step]
Everest

MORE EVEREST RECORDS

*OLDEST AMERICAN: May 25, 2001
Sherman Bull at 64 yrs

*LARGEST TEAM IN ONE DAY: May 25, 2001
by NFB team, 19 on summit in one day

FASTEST ASCENT: 2004 Pemba Dorje Sherpa who reached the summit from Base Camp in 8 hours and 10 minutes

MOST ASCENTS: 20 by Apa Sherpa as of May 21, 2010

CLIMBER TO CLIMB ALL 4 SIDES: Kushang Sherpa

LONGEST STAY ON TOP: Babu Chiri Sherpa, 21.5 hours

* Our team

Who may ascend the hill of the LORD? Who may stand in his holy place? He who has clean hands and a pure heart, who does not lift up his soul to an idol or swear by what is false. He will receive blessing from the LORD and vindication from God his Savior.   — Psalm 24:3–5

Enjoy the mountains; they have beauty and wisdom for us if we approach them with humility, respect, and knowledge.[1]   — Charles Houston

May 20, Day 59 — It is time. Time to climb toward the dream I have had since being a little kid. It feels like that was right about the time we left Colorado on this expedition — that I have aged while away, it has been so long. One more time up through the icefall, knowing that no matter what, this is it. A sense of urgency and focus comes over the team, and even though we can't see how these next days will play out we can see the end, the light at the end of this mountainous tunnel.

For the first time as we climb there also seems to be a plan that we can follow through on. This time the gear is more quickly prepared, we are faster out of our tents, we know the terrain ahead very well, and our roles are doled out for at least the next three days. Then it will become not a competition — although it can feel that way at times — perhaps rather a test for summit day positions. There are no guarantees as to who will perform well, who will get sick, or who may just decide to back out. Anything can happen and we all need to be ready to be called upon to lead or take a backseat, and not one of us wants to ride in the backseat. For this group, leading comes naturally, and following orders is more of a democratic process of open discussions, which actually worked well, and I think allowed us to make some of the best and safest decisions. It does not, and probably should not, work this way on all teams, but given the years and careers of experience on this team it was a style that suited us well.

Certainly thus far it has not sounded like a pleasure cruise and especially so if you are blind and can't see the beautiful, surrounding, white-capped mountains every day to get you through and help you bide your time — having something to gaze upon and even dream on as you ponder different routes and possibilities. So why climb this? Sure, that is a common question, but why climb this blind? This is a bigger question and mystery for most people. Erik answers with this:

"All I can say is that I use what I have to get enjoyment out of my surroundings. People with sight often neglect their other senses, but I try to use my sense of smell, touch, and sound to the fullest. For example, on rest days coming out of my tent in the morning I love to feel the cold mountain air touched by the warmth of the morning sun. At Camp Two, in a lightning storm I sat at the door of my tent listening to the explosions echoing off the surrounding peaks. Each time the thunder crashed, the echo gave me a view of the massive terrain. When I'm crossing ladders in the icefall there is a satisfaction in moving my foot forward and locking my crampon points on the ladder rungs. All these things for me are scenery — a different kind of scenery than a sighted person might experience, but scenery, nonetheless. I think whether we're sighted or blind we have an obligation to squeeze as much beauty and wonder out of the world that we're born into as we can. Whether we're on a mountain or home playing with our children, there's beauty all around us if we only look for it."[2]

The morning of May 20, those of us remaining left Base Camp after Erik, Jeff, and Sherm had made a 5 hour and 23 minute ascent up to Camp One the day before. A new speed record for Erik, and this did a lot for our confidence in him. Not only was he fast, he kept going, and on that same day advanced to Camp Two, a first for Erik, and a strong effort. So at 5:30 a.m. we all headed up, and before noon we were at Camp Two, eager to see how our time would play out.

A cool and calm morning, the temperature rose to 109 degrees Fahrenheit, and the layers came off quickly. One hundred climbers crowded Camp Two, as every person who was trying to summit Everest from the south side was there — given these numbers, the danger factor rises greatly due to the fact there could be a lot of people vying for space on the same day on a narrow ridge. Our plan still had not changed, nor could it really. Not much.

As we waited, I couldn't help but reflect a little on what makes this team so special. We have our differences at times, but truly what I see as setting us apart from every other team on this mountain comes down to two things: trust and team work, or even better, team spirit. The trust that Eric places in me is extraordinary. After all, with as little as a few words I hold his life in the balance. I liken it to my faith in God and it paints for me a clear picture of what faith is like. Erik can't see my face, yet he takes me at my word and trusts that the path I lead him on is right and true, maybe not always straight and not without its bumps, but the true path nonetheless. Likewise, I can't see God's face, yet I listen for His voice and follow the path He has set before me. It takes faith and it is often only one step at a time that He allows me to advance before speaking illumination onto the next step. Brad Bull eloquently stated this about trust:

"Through the act of progressing up a mountain, a general sense of trust usually develops between expedition team members. Climbing with Erik provides an amazing experience. It may be simply a matter of the people that gravitate to Erik, but this team has cohesion unlike any I have ever climbed with in the past. We have each been involved in some climbing endeavor with him before, so this expedition builds upon trust from previous experiences. Erik has climbed many peaks around the world, but Mt. Everest presents challenges unlike any that he has ever confronted. The Khumbu Icefall is terrain that Everest veterans never get thoroughly comfortable climbing through. Its massive snow and ice formations latticed with seemingly bottomless crevasses are simultaneously awe-inspiring and awful. For all climbers on the mountain, this amazingly dynamic landscape is navigated with extreme caution to get through as quickly and safely as possible.

We take turns climbing with Erik in either daily or twice daily rotations. This typically entails a person in front ringing a bear bell and giving verbal descriptions of the physical forms to be negotiated. Erik travels undaunted by what he cannot see, as he powers his way upward. A third person often climbs directly behind Erik, giving course corrections and additional direction.

This relationship redefines the typical climber trust, for while I can never imagine what exactly goes through Erik's head as we climb, I know that I feel the importance of our connection with every step. We are not and will not be roped together from Base Camp to the summit. There are lengths of fixed lines attached to the mountain that we tie into individually, but for me, the bond between climbers is far stronger. It is this trust and mutual dependency that has already made this a hugely rewarding excursion for me.

By reaching Camp Three, we think Erik has unofficially set a new altitude record for a blind climber, and we have every reason to believe that he will be the first blind climber to stand on the world's highest summit. While the challenges he faces are greater than those of the rest of the team, I am convinced that if Erik does not reach the summit, it will not be due to his blindness, but due to the myriad of reasons that have prevented the thousands of climbers before him from standing at 29,035 feet.

Most of all, I have an incredible appreciation for the intangible connection of trust that is being forged between the members of this expedition and I expect this will manifest itself in life-long friendships."[3]

I think this trust is made up of three essential components that I didn't see on other teams. I didn't see it because most of them were not teams at all; they were just clusters of people from a variety of nations with casual affiliations sharing a permit, most often for the sole purpose of seeing themselves — the individual — stand on top. In this case, egos are not suppressed, nor are selfish ambitions. John Krakauer had this to say in an interview with *Outside* magazine about his team in 1996: "We never became a team. Instead we were a bunch of individuals who liked each other to a degree and got along well enough, but we never had this feeling that we were all in it together . . . we never coalesced as a team, which in turn contributed to the tragedy: we were in it for ourselves when we should have been in it for each other."[4]

The three distinguishing components of trust as I see them are commitment, confidence, and reliance. Erik can rely on me because he knows I am committed, therefore giving him confidence. He can have confidence in the fact that I am committed not just to myself and my team, but to him directly. He knows that should a storm roll in while we are halfway through the icefall, I will not leave his side even though I could get down five times faster without him. I will, even if it means losing my fingers, get him out of the situation. It was not just me who felt this way, the entire team instilled this confidence due to the fact that they were reliable when it mattered most and committed to each other.

I would say that the distinguishing attributes for our successful team could be added to any successful team, and if you lead a team might I suggest that role could be made easier if these attributes are sought after: individual strengths maximized toward a common goal while maintaining a focus on others in a collaborative and cooperative manner so as to feed the underlying shared passion of the team. What every team needs is skilled people who are passionate about what they do, who want to do it, not for themselves as much as for others who share the same goals and passions. The shared goal and desire to contribute ideas for the purpose of success will be the team's triumph.

Truly, I think pastors and teachers, good pastors and good teachers, get this. They want people to succeed. So many people on this mountain and around the world wanted us to fail because in some way our success would diminish their accomplishments. Could you imagine a pastor having this attitude? If people stick to their old habits and sin cycles while I, the pastor, maintain a life of purity and righteousness, I will no doubt look better and better every day while being able to assert my righteous authority over these flailing and ignorant people, who will need to keep coming back to me for a glimpse of who they could and should be.

By contrast, the good teacher is the one who sets students up for success, and sees their success as his own and even encourages them to go beyond what the teacher himself has been able to accomplish. It just seems to go against human nature to applaud the successes of our competitors, spouses, coworkers, etc. Instead of lamenting the fact that a friend of mine got a contract I feel I would have been perfect for, I have to push myself sometimes, while biting my tongue to say, "Good job, you deserve it." It all boils down to humility. By the grace of God I am able to achieve this on occasion and not be a total imbecile all the time, and can applaud the accomplishments of others and adjust the position of my heart to let them know in sincerity they are indeed deserving of the prize.

I have also had the good fortune of having teachers, pastors, and friends who do this for me. So wanting to be more like these people and more like Jesus, I try. It is from the example of others though that I am able to truly apply this and want my friend Erik to succeed more than I want to succeed in summiting myself. Interesting, but I truly believe that by holding my dream a little more loosely and putting my focus on someone else, I in turn became more likely to succeed myself. Gone from the forefront of my mind are the fears and doubts that threaten to rob me of confidence and purpose.

It could be said that the higher one goes, the fewer values one holds. While at Camp Two, we witnessed this phenomenon when a 19-year-old Canadian climber descending from a successful summit of Lhotse lost his footing and went careening down the side of its massive face. It was late in the day and he had lost one crampon, as well as, his ice axe. Now with the sun looming just above the ridge of Nuptse, about to make its exit, we all knew his time was limited. He was calling for help and knew that without his tools he would have no chance of getting back to his camp in one piece.

The word traveled quickly over the radio network and soon spotting scopes, binoculars, and telephoto lenses were all trained upon this climber at 25,000 feet up on the side of Lhotse. Through squinted eyes he looked like a mere dot, hard to discern from a rock as he lay there motionless. From the sound of the chatter, his own team was not prepared to do anything for him in terms of a rescue and, in fact, we could see one of his teammates continuing down the regular route back to camp and not down the path of his fall, which was by no means unclimbable. This kid happened to be a part of one of "those" teams that had casual affiliations and no strong bond or loyalties, beyond sharing the cost of a permit, and because of this, was about to become a victim of what I would term an unconscionable lack of action.

His team flailed around doing nothing, and we could only help coordinate by radio as we were too far away to mount a rescue attempt. He was beginning to panic. It is a dilemma played out season after season in the high mountains, and fewer and fewer seem to be willing to answer this call of moral responsibility. Stopping a climb to aid another climber will most times end ones chance for a summit, perhaps even derail an entire expedition. Sponsor dollars, time, and life dreams are all at risk of being lost for the sake of what is often an ungrateful and complete stranger.

Simone Moro, an Italian uber climber, was setting out to be the first to do a 24-hour link-up of Lhotse and Everest, and had just gotten himself into position for a solo strike on Lhotse. He was set in Camp Four, ready to go to the summit the next day, or the day after, and had been climbing alongside our team much of the season. He had provided lots of useful information as well as, route tips and updates. His quiet, raspy Italian accent, sounding like a soprano version of the Godfather, could easily be heard anytime he entered our camp to shoot the breeze and catch up on all of the goings-on of the mountain scene. He was a delightful person, a colorful character, and extremely capable and comfortable in these high Himalayan peaks.

When Simone got word this climber had fallen and was in need of help just on the other side of a giant rock outcropping from his Camp Four, he thought he could help. He didn't sit and think long; he was soon out of his tent and moving up the mountain and around this rock onto the face. What I saw next was one of the most amazing single rescuer feats I have ever witnessed. Going one hundred meters up, one hundred meters across, and then two hundred meters down, Simone reached this fallen climber in what seemed to be a matter of minutes. At this altitude it would take most people an hour and a half to cover the same ground. What followed was even more amazing. He put this guy on his back for portions of the return to Camp Four and carried him back up, over, and around this rock, all before the sun set, giving him a place to spend the night and a meal to eat.

The output of energy that Simone had used on this effort was so great that he was not able to recover enough to try for his summits. I do not know if his sponsors were pleased or upset, but my thinking is this is exactly the kind of guy I would want to represent my company. There are far too many people seeking individual glory on the sponsor sheets of corporations and not enough of good character. For the next couple days the drama continued to unfold as the climber was carried and then assisted off the mountain, with no lasting injuries from the fall or the cold, largely thanks to Simone. The reward he had offered to anyone who would help was $1,500.

Upon arrival at Base Camp there was no recollection in his mind of ever having made this promise. Not that it mattered that much to Simone, but after all, he did give up his climb completely for this guy. Words are just words, and actions certainly do speak louder. I am indeed a larger fan of Simone from this action than I think I would have been had he summited both peaks in a 24-hour period like he was intending. The mountains will remain, and thanks to the actions of one, so will this young life. The high peaks of the world tend to bring out the best in people, and the worst in people. They almost have an affect on people like alcohol does in that it tends to exaggerate any underlying character or emotional issues, as well as, a person's sense of morality and system of values.

So much of what you do and how you fare on the mountain depends on other teams and other people, and the circumstances and events that tend to surround everyone. The better able a team is to avoid certain situations and drama, the more likely that team is to succeed in reaching the summit. If another team happens to be near you when it all falls apart for them, the more likely it is that you will be sucked into a rescue situation, causing the summit attempt to be forfeited.

For some this is a non-issue because they have no value for human life and no morals by which to climb, so they in turn have no problem leaving someone to die, justifying their climb by time, cost, and the fact that a stranger on the mountain knew well the risk and chose to take it themselves, eschewing any responsibility to the needy party whatsoever. The true heroes then, are the ones who sacrifice personal goals, dreams, finances, and cling to their values to aid a stranger in need. It is called compassion, selflessness, courage, righteous behavior. People that exhibit this at home are the ones you want to make your climbing partners, because you know they won't abandon you when it hits the fan. The high peaks could be likened to a battlefield in this way: when the bullets start flying, some will start running, but it is the band of brothers who stay and fight side by side. In May 2001, I was climbing with this band.

The night of May 21 came while we were at Camp Two. This is my birthday, and easily the most memorable birthday I have ever had. I turned 32 at 22,000 feet, on my way to making history and standing on top of the world. The Sherpas at Camp Two had even made a special cake for me with candles and all. It really is the thought that counts, because at this altitude it was a bit dry and a bit hard, but still the best cake ever! With a bulging belly and a clear forecast, it was hard to sleep knowing that at 4:30 in the morning we would be making our way up to Camp Three on the Lhotse face.

Feeling good this time, I did not think I would have the same problems and had no anticipation of turning back. To redeem myself, from the last time I was on this face, I again said I would take the lead with Erik and bring him up to camp with me. He agreed to it and before the sun was up, after a night of restlessness, we were out of our tents ready to climb. He was first and, as his tent was near mine, I could hear it unzip as I lay still warm and cozy in my sleeping bag. My first thought was, *Oh no. Uggh. Here we go.* Then I could hear a little chatter and Erik's steely crampons crunching on the rock and ice as he clanged his way down to the dining tent. My next thought: *The little guy needs me. He can't do this alone. Time to motivate and be his eyes, we gotta do this together.* In a moment, he had just picked me up.

One of my favorite verses from the Bible is Ecclesiastes 4:9–10 where it says, "Two are better than one, because they have a good return for their work: if one falls down, his friend can help him up. But pity the man who falls and has no one to help him up." Many people think that because Erik is blind he is a little like Mister Magoo, constantly stumbling his way through situations, unaware of the reality around him. This is true in the dining tent when we slip spices and other things onto his meal, without his knowing, but when we are climbing, his balance is on and his senses heightened. Therefore it is rare that he ever falls or needs a hand getting back up.

The reason I like the verse from Ecclesiastes is that I think it applies in spirit, as well as, physically. I had been picked up when my team accepted me back after my fall the previous year, and especially when Erik said he wanted me back. I was lifted up when he was ready to go from Camp Two with a focus for the summit. I think each of us on this team on any given day had that role of friend, encourager, believer, and doer. We picked each other up and only on occasion would yell, "Get up off your lazy butt and get moving!" The mentality of the individualist out for himself never entered this team's dynamic.

With just a hint of light coming from the rising sun, our goal was to move quickly and be at Camp Three before the sun's rays warmed the face and too much thawing could take place, sending debris down from above. The day was clear and calm; perfect for our move up to 24,000 feet — a new personal record, should I make it. By 1 p.m. the entire team had made it to Camp Three, including Erik, even considering that we had to make a few photo stops for Didrik along the way.

The photo stop we made near some shredded old tents later became the cover of *Time* magazine. Had I known, I may have tried harder to get into the frame, but as we stood there on the steep face Didrik kept telling Erik to lean back as he told me to climb higher and out of the frame. The result is a somewhat unnatural hero pose of Erik taking a giant step up the mountain, with the summit just behind and above him. That is the closest I have ever been to the cover of a major news magazine. I looked for my shadow in the photo, but not even that made it in.

Thankfully, this day was uneventful with all of us climbing well, feeling well, and even my breathing and heart rate had resumed something closer to normal. The team was now poised and ready. I would share a tent with Sherman and Brad there on the icy ledge. Crammed in like sardines, we would stay outside as long as we could talking to others, visiting nearby camps and climbers, trying to squeeze out every moment of sun that we could until it got too cold and the only refuge would be the crowded tent.

Camp Three is not immune to avalanches or cascading objects from above, but the biggest danger here is usually a climber's complacency to the exposure and nature of this camp. When nature calls, the easiest thing to do is to quickly jump outside the tent, aim in the direction of down, and let gravity take care of the rest. What a few climbers have done is to engage in this process without boots or crampons. The bottom of an inner boot is typically a slippery, textured plastic that is absolutely useless on snow and ice. A climber on a 45 degree slope has no chance should he take a misstep. The result will be a 2,000-foot rocket sled ride to your death. It has happened more than once.

The wise climber takes an extra moment, even though time is often of the essence and an accident of that nature can't be fixed for a few days — you have to live with your mistakes, in other words, and smell even worse than normal — because at this point all you have are the clothes you are wearing. The wise climber puts on the boots and maybe even the crampons, and lets it go without going for a long walk from the tent. (If I don't answer the question here, I will only have to answer it in front of a group of people.) Sometimes what looks to be a dump truck load of rocks coming down the Lhotse face, may just be a dump of another sort.

I would not want my tombstone in this case to read: "He died doing what he loved." On with the boots, on with the crampons, nature calls and I must answer, never thinking before that it could be a matter of life and death. Thankfully, the time at Camp Three is short, because it is a miserable place. Perhaps one of the best moments of the climb that served to lift our spirits and make this place bearable was when the women of Base Camp, (Reba Bull and Kim Johnson), came on the radio to give us an unforgettable weather report. It wasn't the weather forecast that made it memorable, but rather the delivery. I am not sure if Reba's husband Brad was embarrassed, but let me just say after the weather report and when we got home, we all found out that Brad and Reba had conceived their first child after our ascent and that Chris Morris and Kim would later marry. It was that good.

Above Base Camp there really are no good nights of sleep, and Camp Three is no exception; crowded tents, anxiety, snoring tentmates, bad food, nausea, and periodic breathing all contribute. The cold is not a factor; it is all the other things that keep you from sleep. It is restful though, and that is what we need to bank for the coming days. While at Camp Three, some of the team would sleep on oxygen and even use it for the ascent to Camp Four, which is normal, as is putting on the down suit to climb in.

I was feeling especially good at this point and wanted to prove to myself, and to no one else, that I was going strong. It was almost as though the Lord said, "You have trusted Me this far, trust Me today — I have a surprise for you." I carried a bottle of oxygen on my back but did not use it until late that night after arriving and setting up Camp Four at 26,000 feet (8,000 meters). This was not an extraordinary feat, as a small handful of people have summited Everest without oxygen at all, but it was a huge mental feat for me and a giant step of faith to say, "God, I trust You completely in this venture."

Before departing Base Camp One I had cut off all the strings around my neck and made sure I had no good luck charms or superstitious paraphernalia with me that could in any way cloud my trust in the Lord. I did not care if my team knew that, but I wanted God to know I had not a shred of faith in this stuff, but was wholly devoted to Him. Leaving Camp Three with Chris and Brad, we all made it up over the Yellow band and Geneva Spur without O's, and me, without my down suit until I reached Camp Four.

The pace was steady and slow. Funny how it doesn't feel slow, because at any given moment a part of you is moving and going forward in a rhythm like on an assembly line or a slow-moving locomotive. The left arm goes forward, axe in snow, right leg comes through, goes forward, plants in snow, ascender slides up rope as right hand takes the lead, transfer weight onto new foot, breathe, left leg forward, breathe, repeat. Up the trail we would go, a mix of Sherpas, Americans, Indians, Canadians, Russians, and others, all totaling about 71 people as we made our way to the South Col, all with the same hope and desire.

Erik would come up later with Jeff and Luis, all on oxygen and all in their down suits. The wind picked up that afternoon and, even though it did, those guys were burning up in their suits with the intense radiation hitting them like a laser beam. I was glad to have dressed lighter, but to be safe and warm I had to keep moving, and upon arrival at Camp Four donned my suit immediately as the cold took full advantage of any brief stop.

As I went up, I saw one of our Sherpas coming down the Yellow Band in his corduroys, CB ski jacket, and big old ISKI sunglasses. These guys are amazing and tough. A word of thanks to him for all he had done to make this climb possible for us, and then it was off to the col. A last slow scramble over the loose talus just before camp and then, wow! There it is! I can't believe it at first! I made it! No oxygen yet, feeling great, scattered tents, the summit looming above, the path laid plainly out before me — for the first time I can almost picture it. It now seems more possible than impossible.

The winds are blowing hard against us, and what we thought would be an established camp was actually a pile of gear. The thinking behind this was if the tents stood erect too long in this place, they may tear apart and we would be out of luck. So they had been laid aside, ready for the day we arrived. Thankfully, there was a few of us there to get things rolling, constituting a big effort in the winds of 30 to 50 mph to get these set up. One person would grab the tent, another a pole, while a third began to tie it to a large anchor stone. Slowly, as a team, we were able to set up the tents in this manner, one at a time. Our packs and gear would be thrown inside to act as anchors, too, until it could be tied securely to the ground with heavier, reflective cord than that which comes standard on a tent.

A nice benefit to this is that in the night should a person returning from a climb be unable to locate camp, there is the chance that a beam of light will catch a reflector and guide you back. It also reduces the likelihood of stumbling over a cord in the middle of the night, while walking around camp. Slowly the tents are erected and secured, and slowly the rest of the team trickles in to Camp Four, and finally Erik himself makes it in. Unbelievable! The entire team is here within striking distance. Not one person is missing. This I did not foresee. I was certain it would come down to just a handful of people going for the top and hoped that Erik might be one of them, and if not him, I hoped it would be me; but I did not think after what I had been through there was much of a chance for that. This was absolutely amazing, and I could see the hand of God all over it. Too many things had been going our way, too many obstacles overcome, too much evidence of the divine for me to see it any other way.

Eating, drinking, resting, and plotting became the priorities. It was totally possible that this same night, after having just climbed from Camp Three, that we would continue onward toward the summit. Many teams do this and it was a possibility for us. The weather seemed to be intensifying, as the winds buffeted our tents making conversation inside a bit more difficult and the prospect of the summit less likely this night. Erik was fatigued and the whole team decided a bit of rest and a forecast that was certain enough made the 24th look like it would be our day to make an attempt.

Now at 26,000 feet we would go on and off of the oxygen, trying to conserve our supplies for when it mattered most, and when we did use it, we tried to keep a low flow rate of ½ liter/minute. If using a pulse oximeter, one could immediately see the results of oxygen on that number, raising it from maybe 78 percent to 84 percent in just a minute or two. You have to ask yourself, how many brain cells did I just save by using this, and not venture into the territory of how many have I killed by not using it. Eating, drinking, napping, card playing (yes, the Braille cards made it up to 26,000 feet), then dinner and more rest. We made our final decision that night, as the winds did not abate. We hoped we would not regret this decision to postpone our climb, knowing that our time was very limited and we were now committed to it all coming down to one night and one shot.

For whatever reason, sleep came easy on this night, in spite of the fact that I kept waking up with my oxygen mask over my ear. With a number of us sharing a tent and enough down feathers to fill a barn, we were cozy in spite of the sub-zero temperatures and high winds. We would ration our use of the radios to save batteries, but would tune in to hear what some of the other teams were doing. Many of the others did choose to go for the summit on this night, which solidified our decision of not moving, knowing that so many people on the route could cause greater problems. There is security in numbers up to a point. It also depends on who is in those numbers and the kind of experience they have.

Then, in the midst of all of this, we hear that Austrian climber Peter Ganner had fallen to his death near the Hillary step on the south side of Everest. This is the kind of news that sends doubts and fears rocketing right back into the forefront of your mind, causing you to question, once again, your purpose and intentions on this unforgiving mountain, with a blind man nonetheless.

As the day breaks and the sun began to radiate through the tent walls, a little breakfast somehow got choked down. The uncertainties of yesterday are the first things that you hope to erase from the forefront of your mind. How better to do that than to take a stroll around the South Col and marvel at this high place not too dissimilar to the moon. After all, everyone has on a big puffy suit, is breathing oxygen in an inhospitable environment, and no one on earth who is not already acclimated can come to help you, not even by plane, helicopter, or otherwise.

All I had were the guys around me and my faith, and I knew I could trust them both. A few steps out onto this frozen lunar landscape (150 to be exact) reveals the frozen, dead body of Lhakpa Dorge, a Sherpa who had died in 1988 right here in the South Col from cerebral thrombosis. One of my teammates took a picture of him lying there frozen, face down on the ground. Lhakpa was perfectly preserved, frozen to the place where he took his last breath, with his clothes mostly intact over him, but shredded from the years of raging wind and blowing snow. His body is face down, a sobering reminder of what can happen to even the strongest people who have all five of their senses. What on earth are we doing trying to bring someone up to the summit who is missing one of his? Are we are missing the sixth sense, other-wise known as common sense? Any other team in Everest climbing history would give it their best effort to bring another team member down who was blinded, and consider it a life and death emergency. In a moment like this, I realize again just how big an undertaking this is for Erik and for us as a team who surround him, knowing our fates on the mountain are intertwined. In this, we experience true and deep faith and trust.

The doubts and fears creep up like at no other time as each person looks around the tent at each other, wondering how the events of the next night will unfold. Could one of us end up like Lhakpa or one of the other 120 bodies that are still up on Everest? Many told us we would die. In fact, that very night a guide named Sandy from Scotland came over to the tent that Erik was in. He had just come down from the summit and it was getting dark. He came over uninvited and poked his sunburned, chapped, stubblebearded, bloodshot-eyed face abruptly into the tent with a still-shining headlamp on his head. Startled and quiet, he had everyone's attention. Without many words he simply said, "You guys, you're gonna have a hell of a time gett'n a blind guy up there! You got your work cut out for ya!" Next thing you know Sandy zipped the tent closed, and as quickly as he had appeared, he vanished. As if we didn't know that. As if we didn't have enough on our minds. It was as though a Leprechaun had just come by and peed in our Lucky Charms. Not exactly the pep rally we were hoping for at this point in our climb.

It was about this time that some more news came our way. A call of distress came over the radio. It was a Spanish team who was missing one of their members named Carlos. They had a last-seen point, but in the whiteout he had lost his way and was maybe even a bit disoriented. The Spanish team knew we were a large team at Camp Four and that we would be capable of helping even though it was getting late. Then they asked flat out if we could spare a few people to help mount a rescue effort. The search would take place between Camp Four and the Balcony at 27,500 feet.

A worst case scenario would put Carlos down either the Lhotse or Kangshung Face, most likely resulting in a fall to his death or a miserable night out exposed to the elements. Very few people have ever survived a night like that. To lend a hand would be a very risky thing for us to do. We had to make sure that there were enough of us to remain with Erik and with enough energy to get him back down safely. The first thought is of self and team preservation. The second thought is to think that he'll be fine and we should just give him a little time before we throw it all out the window. The third thought is that maybe we should do something, like maybe send four guys out looking. These four guys would most likely lose any chance at a summit attempt.

We basically had two options: stay put and say we just can't help, or send a small portion of our team to begin a search. I was proud of my team because this team chose to take action. Carlos had become a friendly acquaintance over the last two months, but even if he had been a total stranger, I think the decision would have remained the same. Go search. As we began to put a plan together and organize gear for this effort my tentmate Luis asked me, "Eric, would you pray?"

I thought for a second about his request and said, "I will, but why don't you as well." We prayed silently because communication was made difficult by yelling since the wind was buffeting the tent and making such a loud noise. We continued getting our things together and ten minutes later as boots were beginning to exit the tents, our prayers were answered.

A call in broken English came over the radio saying, "We found Carlos! He is going to be okay. We will make it back to camp! We won't need your help." A collective sigh of relief was exhaled and we rolled back into the tents with the rush of adrenaline slowly fading. Our team was put to the test and I was proud to be with these guys. I was also thankful that everyone would at least get a shot at the summit this night.

When you choose to take on a challenge like this, you will have every opportunity to turn back. Adversity doesn't just come in the form of blindness; it comes in every single other possible way as well. For us it was in the mental doubts, the weather, the rescue attempt, the words of others doubting our climb, and now the news that two climbers on the north ridge had just died, of altitude complications — Mark Auricht of Australia and Alexei Nikiforov, of Russia. Could it get any worse? At what point is it best to say, "enough"? How do you really know when it is time to pull the plug? The collective confidence of the team no doubt helps in making decisions, but what really calmed my nerves and allowed me to take the next step once the clock said 9:00 p.m., and it was time to get going, was knowledge of this:

And we know that in all things God works for the good of those who love him, who have been called according to his purpose. . . . What, then, shall we say in response to this? If God is for us, who can be against us? He who did not spare his own Son, but gave him up for us all — how will he not also, along with him, graciously give us all things? . . . Christ Jesus, who died — more than that, who was raised to life — is at the right hand of God and is also interceding for us. Who shall separate us from the love of Christ? Shall trouble or hardship or persecution or famine or nakedness or danger or sword? As it is written: "For your sake we face death all day long; we are considered as sheep to be slaughtered." No, in all these things we are more than conquerors through him who loved us. For I am convinced that neither death nor life, neither angels nor demons, neither the present nor the future, nor any powers, neither height nor depth, nor anything else in all creation, will be able to separate us from the love of God that is in Christ Jesus our Lord" (Romans 8:28–39).

I knew that death was not the worst thing that could happen to me. I wasn't chasing death by any means. I felt like every decision we made was the best one and I had limited as much risk as possible in this place, but nonetheless, I had confidence and assurance for my soul because of my faith, because it was not in me, it was in Jesus. I often joke that my team had two Christians at Base Camp, eight at Camp Four, and again two when we got back down.

May 24, Day 63, 9:00 p.m. — It was show time. Silently, we all got dressed and ready in the tents. Words were few and action was fast and deliberate. Multiple layers of the best long underwear, fleece, and socks all went on under the down suits. Harnesses were put on over those and then adjusted and tightened. Packs were made ready with extra gloves, snacks, headlamp batteries, and oxygen bottles. Water bottles were placed inside the large pockets of the down suit with a couple of snacks for quick access. Next it was the hat, goggles, boots, gloves, and a step outside to put on steel crampons as the last piece.

For a moment, with all these layers and this big suit I felt like the overstuffed kid in the movie *A Christmas Story.* With all our red and green suits from Mountain Hardwear we also looked as though the Teletubbies had decided to go climb Everest. Ice axes and trekking poles were put in hand as we all gathered and started slowly moving up the mountain away from the South Col at 9:00 p.m. without saying a word.

I normally begin every day of climbing with a prayer; on this day I didn't. The reason? I had never stopped praying. We knew the plan. We were ready. This was not at all like a junior high backpack trip; there were no questions asked and no scrambling for last minute needs. It was a well-disciplined group on a mission and the moment was upon us. Everything had been done, had been spoken, and had been set; we just needed to roll. Funny how this moment almost seemed to be hypnotic or robotic, as it all just fell into place.

Yes, there was adrenaline and nervous excitement, but in the dark of night, all covered up, one nearly distinguishable from the other with oxygen masks and goggles, it was a laser focus that moved us. Then just a few steps away from the col, we got our first big shock. Doctor Steve Gipe made a personal decision. He said, "I have a wife and kid back home; this will have to be my summit." The emotion in his voice was clear and there would be no talking him out of this.

I know we were all sad that our friend Steve would not be going with us after all. He was probably the most loved among us, and many of us had him to thank for the fact we were even still on this expedition; for all the doctoring he had done. His skills were just one more piece that made this team a success. He had been as high as Camp Four once before, but was unable to summit on that attempt as well. Part of me looked back thinking, *He'll be coming up behind us. I know it.* He never did, and as we discovered later, it turned out to be a very good thing. One by one we formed a single file line, working our way up over the ice bulge and into the couloirs of the Triangular Face. Our path was illuminated by little circles of light emitted by our headlamps; well, all of us but one. The joke was, "Hey, Erik, don't forget your batteries!" Ha ha ha, as if he had never heard that before. Somehow at this altitude the dumber the joke, the funnier it was.

A few hours later there was no more laughter when Pasquale, at the front of the pack, slowed, then stopped. I watched as he slowly made his way down the line of climbers wondering what was going on and what kind of problem there must be to stop us all for this length of time. As he progressed down the line he would stop and hug each climber, their headlamps illuminating the moment.

When he got to me near the end of the line, his words were few and to the point. As he lifted his goggles, I could see a tear in his eye and then he said, "Dude, I got nothing left. My feet are frozen and I'm going back down. Gipe is gonna meet me, so I'll be fine." He had told the team to continue, that we had what it takes and to not give up. I thought perhaps in that moment of pause he was going to turn us back due to a bad forecast or some other form of news that would hinder our ascent, but it was a personal decision. When I heard he was going down, I was shocked and my heart sank. Only the realization we were continuing returned the focus to my gaze.

This decision speaks highly of Pasquale and, though it was not his intention, this one decision taught me a lot about leadership. I learned more in that one moment about leadership than I had learned the entire expedition, and perhaps, even for years. I learned that leadership is taking action on a vision, but when it matters most it is backing that up or even building on a platform of character. I say this because a truly selfish person would have said, "Hey, this was my idea and I am going to summit no matter what: I deserve it!" That decision would have ended badly. Loss of life, loss of digits. Pasquale, at best, would have lost his feet and at worst his life. Had he continued, he could have most certainly taken someone down with him.

He did what was best; he made the right call and left the climbing and leadership up to the team. Delegating leadership to no one individual, rather just saying you have what it takes, go and get it done. How many times do leaders stand in the way of their team and the objective merely because they think they must, that they are vital to the success of the mission? Sometimes they don't realize their job is done and those they have been leading no longer benefit, but need to be let go to lead themselves.

I think Pasquale had used up all his energy in planning, prepping, running about, organizing, thinking etc., and when we had gotten this far there was just nothing left in the tank. He has a theory that malaria chose a bad night to revisit him from a past trip to Africa, but I am not sure we will really know. All I know is he had given it his best, he had given his all for this team and this effort, and we were sad and shocked he would be going no farther. Pasquale was one of the strongest guys on the team and had a tremendous resolve to get to the top, both for himself and for Erik. Most amazingly, he would descend into the care of Dr. Gipe at Camp Four, almost as if it had been planned. This allowed everyone to continue, and with much less worry about his well-being.

11:00 p.m. — Up the fixed lines of the Triangular Face we continued, largely without incident, except for the fact that Didrik kept struggling with a funky crampon (of course, there was never a problem until summit day) which he, being the MacGyver that he was, fixed with his camera strap or some other gadget he found to do the job. Once that was set, Mike O'Donnell lost the batteries in his headlamp, but that was no problem because at about that same time, we experienced a complete whiteout and no one could see anyway.

We had reached the balcony at 27,500 feet and once again it was decision time. The wind and snow were blowing so hard that I couldn't see my outstretched hand in front of my face. When I mentioned this fact I heard a little camper's voice say, "That's okay — I haven't seen mine in 20 years. Get over it!" My thought was that he has a point, I shouldn't complain. We huddled together as a team to reach a conclusion about our next steps and to make the best decision. Worried about the weather, our progress, and the loss of two team members, we were wondering how the rest of the night might play out.

It was beginning to look like high drama. The self-assessment again takes place as each person wiggles his toes and fingers, checks his basic body temp gauge, and does some mental math to see how well things are going. With all systems checked, cleared, and no reason other than fear keeping us from one more step, Sherman Bull, with his four previous Everest trips, chimed in and said, "If you want good weather, go to Central Park in June. This is Mount Everest, what did you expect?"

"Good point, Sherm," we said. Perhaps he was just eager and would let nothing stop him at this point, but history has shown on this mountain that weather, and long exposure to it, is a certain killer. His experience here and our collective mountain sense told us to keep going. This was affirmed when we got a call from Base Camp over the radio the clouds were moving out and stars were now visible.

The call moments later was repeated from Camp Two. Hang on. Hang on a little longer. Don't give up just yet. The storm then lifted enough from us to reveal other dangers — thunderheads were forming all around and we could see the magnificent light show exhibiting a wonderful, though scary display of lightning over the world's highest peaks. These were going off all around us and at this elevation, we were as high as the tops of some of these massive storms.

"Ugghh!!" Again, "Do we keep going?! They will pass, have a little faith." A few steps more and we were just below the South Summit, but again at a complete stop.

I had no idea at the time, but what had happened was Jeff Evans and Brad Bull had taken it upon themselves to dig out the fixed lines had been buried by recent snow and wind. It was an exhausting effort I questioned the need for, but soon realized how vital they would be for our safety both up and down. It was difficult to communicate to Erik at this elevation, and without the use of the fixed lines, our need for and dependence on verbal communication would increase fivefold. Even though we could climb this terrain without ropes, if we didn't use them we would tire more quickly and be more inclined to make mistakes or an error in judgment. The ropes were necessary even though at this time it slowed us down.

4:00 a.m. — The main fear in waiting is that your body will become cold as you stand still in the night, and you will waste energy by jumping around. If you don't move, however, the cold will get to you and shivering will soon commence. It was here that the peak of Makalu became visible for the first time as the sun began to give its early light. And though we couldn't feel the heat of its rays, we could feel the warmth that its hope provided. Makalu, the world's fifth highest peak at 27,766 feet, now seemed to be below us. That was a huge boost. For the first time that night I felt like we were about to pull it off. The "impossible" might be done.

The night had been an emotional and mental roller coaster and showed no signs of improving. One minute it looked like we would have to scrap the whole effort; the next minute it would seem that the challenges were easing and that reaching the summit was within our grasp. And, that roller coaster remained with us as we climbed.

The next thing I knew the sun was fully upon us as we hit the South Summit at 28,500 feet, where we again huddled and made plans for continuing.

Aw, nuts! were my unspoken words as I looked across the ridge. *How are we gonna do this!? Too bad we have to turn back here. Good effort though, guys. Well done. No way.* Those were all first impressions that I dared not speak as oxygen bottles were being swapped out and stashed here for the return trip down. That was the story of the night. Obstacles threatened to turn us back at every step. It was over; then it wasn't; it was over; then we kept going. Then it seemed we could go no further, but we did.

So far, climbing up the ridge and through the night, I had been as blind as Erik and had no reason to be too afraid, but now I could see the full consequences of any misstep.

8:30 a.m. — The mountain now dropped on all sides thousands of feet — a vertical mile on either side. Climbing just for myself I think I would not have seen it the same way, but with my blind teammate, I got freaked out a bit. It is a load of responsibility and he is not the only one thinking of his wife and daughter; I was too. If he fell and died here, and I made it home, I was afraid I would die there. Quite honestly, I didn't see the way at first.

This is the best part of being on a team. Someone else might just see a way when you see none. Someone else might dare to take a step forward when you dare not. We lead each other, we inspire each other. "Okay, shake it out, breathe, think, and move — slowly." It was Luis and Jeff who were quick to take over the lead with Erik at this point of descending ten tricky feet down off the South Summit onto the ridge proper. I fell in behind with Ang Pasang Sherpa to be the back set of eyes, making sure Erik would not make a misstep. The result of that here would be either a 6,000-foot fall into Nepal or an 8,000-foot fall into Tibet. Nepal sounds just a little better, but if you fall into Tibet you have a few seconds more of life to make things right with God. That said, every last word could be important; better fall right.

The way across was slow and deliberate. An occasional poke of the ice axe into the drifted and corniced snow would reveal blue sky on the other side when removed. It was like walking on air or cotton candy, with no terra firma beneath if you made the slightest miscalculation. Balance was key, especially for Erik. The snow underfoot was at times sugary and would give way under foot like sand on the slope of a dune. The rocks could be suspect, too. So, if you are blind and you are climbing Everest, you rely on every word of your guide. The only thing is, your guide has a mask on his face and can't be heard, or at least not well, and if you can hear him he sounds like a phone call from a Charlie Brown cartoon. "Did you say left?" Erik might ask. "No, what are you deaf?" one of us might respond. "Now step right, er left, uh, I mean left, no right," would be the next instruction and somehow, miraculously with sugar snow, loose rock, disoriented and poorly oxygenated guides, Erik would not tumble to his death. He would show this amazing ability to stay upright, hear just enough of our voices and commands to know what to do next, all while weeding out properly, what not to listen to and what not to do, taking cues perhaps more from the sound of our boots and equipment than from our voices.

The throat microphones we had gotten from the Navy Seals proved to be mostly useless here, as the condensation and resulting ice forming on our oxygen masks would interfere with them as much as our heavy breathing and muffled voices. We opted instead to keep the masks circulating oxygen just below our chins, off our face, yet near enough to offer some benefit. This way we could just flat out yell when we needed to, and we needed to.

Once this high and exposed ridge had been crossed, the last obstacle remaining was the famed Hillary step. It was the move I had always wondered about. How hard would it be? In my mind this one section, due to its reputation, was almost as big as the mountain itself. In reality, would it be as imposing as the lore around it? Luis went first and handled it with aplomb. Erik came up after Luis, and as he did, he reached for one old rope. You never know what the ropes look like above this point, they could be old and manky and unable to take your weight.

It was actually when I lifted my camera to my eye to take a picture of this that I noticed he was only grabbing one old rope and that caused me to give a heads up. The step was littered with a myriad of old ropes and it was at this spot a climber had died, just the day before. In 1996, a climber got caught in these ropes and died hanging here, only to be cut free some time later. I wouldn't let this happen to Erik. I yelled out, as he moved upward, "Wait! Don't just grab one, Erik, grab them all! So with a quick flick of the arm he reached out and grabbed a handful of ropes and kicked his foot into the drift of hardened snow on the right.

A sense of wonderment and a bewildered puzzled feeling came over me: "Why all these old ropes? We should just cut them out and toss them." A great idea if you had all summer and all the oxygen you might ever need to do this. The real danger in doing this is it is hard to retrace the ropes as they dive under the snow and ice, twist over and under other ropes and then emerge as much as 20 feet later. If one rope is cut above, and not from below because it is frozen in, when an unsuspecting climber comes to grab it after a thaw, it will be just a loose free rope. Sometimes it is possible to remove old ropes in complete sections and this is a good and safe practice as new ropes are being placed all the time.

Expedition style climbing relies heavily on these narrow diameter lightweight fixed lines. Climbing alpine style with a single rope that moves with you would be far too inefficient for the numbers of people who try to summit and the speed required to keep people moving safely. Without the fixed lines we would see fewer attempts, fewer summits, and probably more deaths as bottlenecks and waiting would become the norm. Though some of these ropes are old and weathered, we are thankful for them and the fact that they are poorly anchored into rotten snow. (Another example of that "positive pessimism".) This offers no peace of mind.

A crampon up onto the rock at left, a scan of the hand for a hold, another kick into the cornice at right, a shout from me saying to Erik where to place the next foot, then two more moves and Luis, Erik, and I were scratching our crampons on the rock, having crested the Hillary step. This felt like a summit moment. I knew that now, just before ten in the morning, with the weather holding, the Hillary step below us, feeling strong, climbing well, there was nothing short of a big mistake that would keep us from the top of the world.

The emotions at this moment started to overwhelm me. My eyes watered and my heart, which was already beating fast, beat faster still. A feeling of euphoria welled up inside and tried to burst out and was only kept inside by the fact focus was still needed for every step, both mine and Erik's. By this time, we had also heard over the radio an emotional announcement that Brad and Sherman Bull, along with Chris Morris, had already made the summit. This only caused tears of joy to roll out of my eyes and cloud my vision. Now I was blind, too.

I remember hearing Brad's voice shout it out, his wife Reba's tearful, joyous congratulatory response, and Pasquale and Kami coming on to say well done, as we kept moving slowly upward. They had had more than a half an hour up on top and were able to take some amazing pictures. They then headed down and met us heading up. We hugged, and spoke what few words we could as we wrestled the gear off our faces and fought back the feelings long enough to get out a "Good job!" and an "I love you, man! Be safe! See you back at Camp Four."

In return we got: "You are almost there, good job, keep going, you'll make it!" Next thing you know they were distant specs as we made the last few steps up over the steep part of the ridge, around a corner, and then the low angle slope that led us to the summit. In this brief moment of pause, I thrust the bottom tip of my ice axe heavenward as if to say one hundred different things with that one pumping action of my arm and axe. Luis, Erik, Eric, Jeff, and Ang Pasang now had nowhere left to go. There was no higher place on earth and there was no higher feeling.

May 25, Day 64, 10:30 a.m. — The five of us stood on that snow patch the size of a kitchen table, which is the top of the world. What I wanted was a moment when the earth would stand still, a complete pause and a moment to reflect on life, to take in the view, to celebrate with a shout: "Praise God!" Instead, what I got was a brief celebration with my friends. I was so overcome by emotion and so choked up I could hardly speak, let alone shout. I was indeed moved, not by the beauty, but by the accomplishment. I was moved for Erik, for myself, for Joseph and his family, for those who believed in us and urged us on.

It wasn't that I had done it — no, it was that WE had done it. All of us together had overcome all the obstacles and criticism and doubt and fear and stood courageously on top — TOGETHER. In that moment it was pure team celebration. It was "not me, but you" and that made it all the sweeter. The only thing I can imagine that could be sweeter will be the step that leads through the gates of heaven, and seeing Jesus face to face.

I removed from my left chest pocket a small 2 by 2 laminated photo of my friend Joseph as we posed for a few pictures. My intent was to leave him at the summit — my friend who believed in me more than I believed in myself. I removed my glove, put his picture in my teeth, and then the wind kicked up and blew Joseph into Tibet. It didn't matter; I think he would have preferred it that way, to not be gawked at on display at the summit, or criticized as a piece of garbage, but to be free after having climbed to the top of the world with a good friend, as we had done many times. I know when we meet again in heaven this will provide a laugh, that is, if it even makes conversation due to the glory of that experience. I am sure the mountains Joseph is enjoying in heaven, will to me one day, make Everest look like a windy Kansas wheatfield.

People may be impressed by an Everest summit, but God isn't. After all, He made it. I think what impresses Him is exercising our faith in Him and trusting Him and His strength to get us up to the pinnacle of His creation, not the object itself or the fact that I stood on it. This summit was a gift. It was not a trophy, or a piece of booty, it was indeed a gift. How better to remember the moment than to photograph it — the one picture anyone would want to snap, blow up, and hang on the wall. So I reached into my pocket, pulled out my Olympus point and shoot camera, composed that beautiful shot, pressed the button and . . . it froze up! Noooo! And, all I got out of it was one shot; one picture at the top of the world. It is a fairly decent shot of us together, but it lacks the view and contains only the sky. The picture could have been posed and composed at Base Camp, for crying out loud.

Thank goodness for Michael Brown and his 25 pound video camera, because with that footage, there is proof the summit by this team was for real. The camera arrived, thanks to the help of two Sherpas who assisted Michael to the summit with it, taking turns carrying it and setting it up, and carrying it some more. The emotion was evident in Michael's voice, not that he had summited, but rather of frustration that he wasn't getting the shot he wanted, that we were ready to head down, and that there was a pack of indistinguishable Sherpas standing on the summit, perhaps from our team or perhaps from the north side.

The funny thing was they had been hard to spot throughout the night, mostly because for most of the trip they had been wearing tattered old mountain gear, but on summit day out came the good shiny down suits, which I am sure had been handed down to them from Westerners who had now achieved the dream and no longer had use for the suit, serving perhaps, too, as a tip for getting them to the top. Whatever it was, the situation was bad for video and he was not happy and we knew it. It was fine. Nothing was going to spoil this moment, and now looking back, the video is worth more than I ever thought it could be, and I am grateful for the fact that Michael, Charlie, and Kim had been a part of the expedition and a part of the team.

The biggest moment he did capture at the summit is, however, one that I wish I could relive. I am haunted by my own words and mad at myself for being so influenced by the chatter on the radio instead of what I myself was observing at the summit. The tape was rolling and we were huddled arms over shoulders in a semicircle around the camera at the summit. Luis: "You did it man!"

Jeff: "You are on top of the world. You showed 'em. You did it. On top of the world the center of the Cosmos; apex of the planet. You did it man, you showed 'em!"

Buzzkill Eric Alexander: "We're only halfway there, guys!" What a dork. What a stupid thing to say while we were all in the moment and all on film. Why not say something profound, poetic, meaningful, or thoughtful? Shoot, even funny would have been better than the gloomy black-hole sucker of energy statement I made. I guess what I was thinking was, as the storm appeared to be approaching and those below us could see the mountain being engulfed by storm, that it was still a long way down. More people die on the way down. And honestly, Erik can be really slow going down.

It was 10:30 a.m., which gave us some time, but it had already been 13 hours and I was not ready for 13 more. It is okay. The moment was far more powerful than my words, or any of our words, and it can never be taken away. We persevered. We had a passion for what we were doing, we took the risk, and we persisted over the obstacles with mental stamina, persisting to the end all because we had faith in the purpose for that which we had started. It paid off.

Didrik was next to the summit as we began our descent after roughly 15 minutes at the top. I don't remember the view too well, but that's okay, I can make up whatever I want to describe it to my blind friend. I do remember looking up and seeing a navy blue sky, almost black; a sky that appeared to be tempting me to jump into space itself. Unbelievable. What I will never forget is that feeling of accomplishment, camaraderie, and brotherhood that made it truly worthwhile.

Deadpoint Reflections

I thank my God every time I remember you. In all of my prayers for all of you, I always pray with joy because of your partnership in the gospel from the first day until now.   — Philippians 1:3–5

Finally, my brothers, rejoice in the Lord!   — Philippians 3:1

Crux: Free Solo. How often do we forego any kind of connection with others thinking they will only rob us of our freedom, purpose, and goals? This is typically more a problem for men, but some women struggle with this as well. John Bachar was famous for his death-defying free solos. He could climb the hardest grades in the fastest times because he was fit, and climbed without the hindrance of a rope and climbing partner. His daring method of climbing was a passion of his for years, even though at age 50 he could no longer do 12 one-armed pullups like he could in his younger days. In July 2009, on a solo climb near his home some months after a terrible car accident, John fell to his death. The climb was considered to be an easy grade for him and he was climbing solo even though he had some residual issues from his accident. John loved climbing and loved life, and he knew the consequences of climbing in this style and accepted them for the feeling of freedom it gave him. When I climb, I prefer the shared problem-solving, the shared experience and joy of overcoming an obstacle with a close friend, and the trust that it fosters. What I love about my wife and our marriage is sharing the journey of life together, the laughter, the support when things get tough, and building memories together. When I try to go alone over life's obstacles, I find hurt, distance, and a loss of trust. What keeps us going on is that we are on the same rope and committed to climb through this life together. http://en.wikipedia.org/wiki/Free_solo_climbing.

Hold: Depending on others and seeing the purpose of a team. There is no way that Erik Weihenmayer, being blind, could have summited Mt. Everest without a team. I can say that most likely the same holds true for me. So why would I put myself at a disadvantage in other areas of my life and not seek the benefits of the skills that other people have to offer? I can direct this question to all facets of life — sports, friendship, family, and spirituality. Who is on your team? Are you only looking for superstars? Are you trying too hard to be the standout superstar? Are you able to hand over the lead — the sharp end of the rope, and make the assist instead of the goal? When you do this, you will find that others will show up on your team who offer the same inspiration.

Anchor: Depending on God. Reliance on a team. We need each other by design. My two-year-old twin daughters are completely independent. They don't need my wife or me for a single thing other than providing food, discipline, baths, shelter, love, instruction, medicine, attention, a safe environment, play things, scheduling, conflict resolution, wipes, diapers, entertainment, transportation, and opportunity, to name a few. I have been guilty of the same attitude at times, thinking I need no help, not from others and not from God. I think I have it all under control, when in actuality, God has been dropping manna from heaven to meet my needs while my heart has been hard like that of a calloused desert wanderer ticked off at Moses and God, thinking I could do better. Jesus said, *I am the bread of life* (John 6:48). We need to see Him as this daily sustenance.

Now the body is not made up of one part but of many. If the foot should say, "Because I am not a hand, I do not belong to the body," it would not for that reason cease to be part of the body. And if the ear should say, "Because I am not an eye, I do not belong to the body," it would not for that reason cease to be part of the body. If the whole body were an eye, where would the sense of hearing be? If the whole body were an ear, where would the sense of smell be? But in fact God has arranged the parts in the body, every one of them, just as he wanted them to be. If they were all one part, where would the body be? As it is, there are many parts, but one body.

The eye cannot say to the hand, "I don't need you!" And the head cannot say to the feet, "I don't need you!" On the contrary, those parts of the body that seem to be weaker are indispensable, and the parts that we think are less honorable we treat with special honor. And the parts that are unpresentable are treated with special modesty, while our presentable parts need no special treatment. But God has combined the members of the body and has given greater honor to the parts that lacked it, so that there should be no division in the body, but that its parts should have equal concern for each other. If one part suffers, every part suffers with it; if one part is honored, every part rejoices with it.

Now you are the body of Christ, and each one of you is a part of it. (1 Corinthians 12:14–27)

Endnotes

1. Charles Houston, *K2, The Savage Mountain* (Canada: The Lyons Press, 2000).
2. Eric Weihenmayer, Everest Live, May 18, 2001, www.2001everest.com.
3. Brad Bull, Everest Live, April 27, 2001, www.2001everest.com.
4. Jon Krakauer, "False Summit," *Outside Magazine* (May 1997): p. 61.

Only
Halfway There

[Summit
Everest]

LONGING FOR THE SUMMIT

**1934 -
THE ECCENTRIC
MAURICE WILSON:** Attempts to solo Everest, having no mountaineering experience but possessing an inner faith to succeed. He was found in the remains of his tent; apparently he had died while in the act of taking off his boots. His body was buried in a crevasse and it periodically resurfaces over the years as the East Rongbuk Glacier continues its steady advance downhill.

**1970 -
JAPANESE
SKIERS:** Climbing along with the SW Face expedition, Yuichiro Miura skis from the South Col to the bottom of the Lhotse Face on May 6. Reaching speeds of 100 mph (160 kph), Miura slows himself with a parachute but loses control after hitting some rocks. He slides unconscious about 600 feet (200 meters) down the icy slopes, and fortunately stops just short of a huge crevasse.

**1995 -
GEORGE MALLORY:** Grandson of George Leigh Mallory, reaches the Summit of Everest.

**1996 -
GORAN KROPP
AND BIKE:** For his famous 1996 ascent, Kropp left Jonkoping on October 16, 1995, on a specially-designed bicycle with 108 kg (240 lb) of gear and food. He traveled 8,000 miles on the bicycle and arrived at Everest Base Camp in April 1996. On May 3, Kropp blazed a trail through thigh-deep snow to reach 300 feet from the summit. Kropp decided to turn around, believing he would be too tired if he went up further. While Kropp recovered at base camp, the 1996 Everest Disaster unfolded. He helped bring medicine up the mountain. Three weeks later, on May 23, Kropp successfully summited (without extra oxygen support). He then cycled home.

Let us run with perseverance the race marked out for us. — Hebrews 12:1

Everest is a matter of universal human endeavor, a cause from which there is no withdrawal, whatever losses it may demand.[1] — G.O. Dyrenfurth

I'm not quite sure where everyone went, stayed, or how this happened, but the next thing I knew, after only 20 minutes on the summit, I was taking Erik down off of the mountain by myself. The bell had been lost, the microphones from the Seals were a bust, and I had to think quickly in order to figure out a way to communicate to Erik so we could move efficiently, and more importantly, safely on the way down. I took a few steps and then started to repeatedly hit my ice axe against the carabiners on my harness to make noise for him to follow. It was working, he honed in on the new sound and we were off, away from the top. Just as we were making our way to the transition from the shallow grade of the upper slope to the steeper grade of the slope above the Hillary step, we came across Mike O'Donnell. I can't forget the encounter and I can't believe Mike kept on going. He is one tough dude.

We first saw him cresting the ridge with his arms flailing from side to side acting somewhat exasperated. Next he sat down in a manner that half looked like a fall and half looked like he had passed out. I was indeed alarmed. He rolled a little, sitting on his butt, side to side in a panicky fashion trying to loose his pack, and by the time we got to him he was half-standing again. "Mike, are you okay?" I asked.

He answered in his nearly destroyed, raspy voice, sounding like the guy in the movie *The Princess Bride* when he said, "Welcome to the Pit of Despair." "I need some water. Do you guys have any water?" It was at this point I realized that for this entire day I had only had about half a liter of water and a Twix candy bar. The reason was my zipper had frozen shut, leaving me unable to access the water inside my down suit. By now I had managed to get it open and have some water myself and I could see, as well as hear, that in the condition that Mike was in, he needed it more than I did. So I gave him my remaining water and told him he should think about going back down.

He was only a hundred steps from the summit, but I didn't want those to be his last. I was truly scared for his life at that moment and only continued down because I had Erik with me, but I knew there were others behind us that could, and would help Mike should he need it. I think some rest, water, snacks, and oxygen system rectifications made him feel a lot better and he ended up making the summit. Mike descended with Didrik, Michael Brown, and Luis back to Camp Four.

The Hillary step was again upon us and this time it was very much my responsibility to get Erik down it. "Crabwalk down, or turn in and face the rock?" I asked.

"What feels better? What do you want to do?" Erik turned in, grabbed the ropes as I grabbed at his heels to quickly place his feet in the correct places. A few slow moves later we were down off the Hillary Step and began taking on the traverse, one slow step at a time. My main goal was to keep my left from getting confused with my right, because at this altitude, and as I looked over my shoulder to utter trail directions, this can be more difficult than it seems.

It happens all the time, even at sea level, left becomes right and right becomes left when looking back over the shoulder, and in this instance, it could be fatal if he relied on my words alone. Cautiously, we made it back over the narrow, loose, and snow-covered spine to the south summit. Now with piles of O_2 bottles stashed here, it was hard to determine which ones were full and which ones were empty, and exactly whose bottle was whose. We eventually got it figured out, and it was shortly after that I felt as though I ran out of oxygen altogether. I didn't seem to be affected until my attitude really started going south.

On the way up I had been using a flow rate of about 1.5 liters/minute, which helped a good deal and kept me warm and my spirits up. Now, with the flow cut off I was losing my patience. I really noticed this when I would get to an anchor point where we would have to unclip from one side of the rope, move past the anchor, and then re-clip on the other side. As I would do this, everything behind me would keep moving until I could get my mask off, turn around, catch my breath, and then say stop. Usually about the time I was saying stop I would get a blind man's crampon in my back. It didn't feel good and it wasn't until later I figured out I should tell him first before I get down to change my tether.

The sun was up high and its radiation made my down suit feel like a greenhouse. That's correct; it is not always 100 below wind chill on the summit slopes of Everest. A couple of times I thought it was darn near as hot as Africa. My goggles were fogging and when I switched to glasses, they fogged too. I was hot, crabby, hungry, thirsty, and wondering where everyone else was. Then Charlie Mace appeared. Thankfully, Charlie took up the rear and gave me just enough of a break at times that I could then breathe, talk, walk, lead, and cool down.

It was the whole multiple corded strand thing at work. *Though one may be overpowered, two can defend themselves. A cord of three strands is not quickly broken* (Ecclesiastes 4:12). What took us 13 hours to get up took us only 6 to get down. We were tired, but still very elated. Because of my efforts, and stepping in to lead him back down off the summit, Erik complimented me by saying, "We descended through heavy snowfall but, thankfully, little wind. Eric took over guiding me, down the Hillary step, across the knife edge, and contrary to his fears that he wouldn't be strong enough to make the top, he was stronger and more lucid on the way down from Everest's summit than most were on the top of a peak in Colorado. I hugged Eric and said, 'Today, you were my guardian angel. I'm glad you're here.' "

Luis told my family that my efforts were heroic on that day. I don't know. I think we all played our parts and each one of us had one of those hero moments on May 25, 2001. Maybe I gave it a little extra effort because this day was also my sister Lisa's birthday.

Making our way down the couloirs of the Triangular Face and its steep intermittent rock ledges, I could see in the distance something I did not see on the way up: another corpse; the frozen body of a fallen climber so close to Camp Four. He died maybe an hour or less away from the shelter and warmth of the tents, hot water, a meal, and a new oxygen bottle. In a white-out, however, this distance on this type of terrain could be impossible to cover, especially if in a tired, hypothermic, and delusional state. It is hard to say, as there are so many climbers who have died on the mountain, exactly who it was, but my feeling was that it was the body of guide Scott Fischer who died in 1996 as the lead guide and owner of Mountain Madness. He died in the middle of one of the worst tragedies the mountain had ever seen.

Scott had spent numerous hours exposed to the elements looking out for his clients by coming down behind them as the last one of his team "off" the mountain. He was having problems of his own and there was really no one left to help him down. He was showing signs of being severely disoriented, typical of severe altitude illness, and eventually, collapsed into a coma-like state. He was tied to another climber, Makalu Gau of Korea, by one of his Sherpas and left just below the Balcony as the Sherpa descended to go find additional help.

Scott's companion guide, Anatoli Boukreev, amazingly was able to climb back up to Scott, only to find he was dead. Makalu Gau, however, was dramatically rescued, and not for the first time on a high peak. He was carried down with arms raised high claiming victory and putting others' lives at risk, from the climbers to the pilot of the helicopter that set an altitude record just to pull him off. I can't be certain it was Scott. In the moment I thought for sure it was, but after further reflection I believe it also could have been an Eastern European due solely to the fact the equipment and clothing appeared to be a bit dated and would not be of the sort a guide in 1996 would use.

3:30 p.m. Total time RT = 19 hours: Arriving back at Camp Four, we were reunited as a team. Sherman and Brad, we caught near the ice bulge and Chris, too, somewhere along the way. We would all spend one more night here except for Pasquale, who had already headed down to Camp Two and would soon be off to Base Camp the next day, as we would then move down to Camp Two. Spending one more night at Camp Four was no big deal, we just wanted to get down quickly and celebrate, and be free of the worry that comes with still being so high.

There was some extra relief in the fact that Pasquale was doing better and had good support lower on the mountain. My thoughts turned to Mike O'Donnell due to the fact that the last time I had seen him he looked as though he could expire. Mike was able to get off the summit with the remaining members of the team and when he arrived at camp was immediately checked out by Dr. Gipe. Coming down and seeing Gipe was like a homecoming. His kind, gentle demeanor and soft, slow voice would immediately put you at ease, as would the trust he had garnered over time to let you know you were going to get good help, good answers, and professional help with a little TLC.

That night at Camp Four we got word that another expedition leader at Camp Four had said some pretty disturbing words before he left. He said he had come to Camp Four for the sole purpose of "being the first person to film Erik's body being carried down off the mountain." Unbelievable. How at this point of an expedition could someone have such morbid plans, and such a desire for another person to not only fail, but die? It was purely for financial gain, I am sure. I know he could have sold images like that to magazines and news media, but why would someone who had no reason to dislike Erik, if he even knew him, have any desire for anything other than Erik's success? My theory is it just plain irks some people that a blind person can do what they can do, or maybe what they can't do. Our thoughts were immediately that this guy might instead have footage captured of his body being brought down off the mountain, that is if he was so unlucky as to finally meet us, but wisely he had left camp before our arrival.

Day Seven of our summit adventure arrived gray and stormy — the complete opposite of how I was feeling. I don't think there was anything that could have wiped the smile off my face as we packed up the tents and gear, the bottles empty and those full; time to overstuff the pack and move out. Glad to have summited, and glad to leave this place where only the dead remain. Though there is a bounce in my step, the truth of the moment and reality is I won't be able to count my summit and the climb a success until I reach Base Camp. I found my bottle which I had left at Camp Four, still had some O's in it, so I thought why not take advantage of that, use it up, and feel good on the way down, all while saving some brain cells.

The mountain was now fully engulfed in cloud and storm, and it appeared that what was our only open and available window, was now closed. We had snuck it in. It was hard to keep all the excitement and emotion in check. A huge life dream had just been achieved.

The tendency for a lot of people is to get too caught up in the moment and then let their guard down. More people die on the way down for this, among other, reasons. It is easy to outpace your feet, there is fatigue, accidents happen when you lose focus, and it is easy to overlook equipment as well. Lastly, everything I had brought up with me is now coming down on my back in one heavy load on tired legs. This makes for a dangerous combination and is often deadly. I guess this is what I must have been thinking when I said what I did back on the summit.

I did not realize until we had made it back to Base Camp, and was then informed, that we, as a team, had set five world records. For what was essentially the Bad News Bears on Everest, for those who were supposed to go down in flames to their death, we had "done good." There was Erik, blind; Eric, recovering from HAPE; Jeff, lost 30 pounds to sickness; Sherman, 64 years old; Mike, also sick; Gipe, stayed behind and the list seemed to go on. The records were: 1. The blindest man in the world (this is what the Nepalese called Erik); 2. The oldest man in the world (Sherman's new title). At 64, he became the oldest man to set foot on the summit of Everest. It was on his fifth attempt, which caused him to say: "I didn't plan on being the oldest man to climb Everest, I just got old trying." 3: Sherman and Brad became the first American father and son. 4: The largest team (19) to summit on the same day (11 Americans and 8 Sherpas). 5: The 25-pound camera, which Michael and two Sherpas carried to the top became the biggest piece of video/photographic equipment to be used and/or placed at the summit. The IMAX camera in 1996 was brought as high as Camp Four. Can't blame anyone for not bringing that thing any higher. The HD footage that Michael captured was stunning — almost better than being there. Almost.

Right away our ascent, and this team, was making headlines around the world. Those at home were relaying headlines to us from as far away as Australia, South Africa, and the United States of America. In Nepal, there was a sense of wonder and celebration mixed with doubt and perhaps confusion as to whether or not this was real, true, and maybe just a question of "How blind is he?" Immediately, plans were being made for interviews, press conferences, meetings, possibly even one with the King of Nepal and the royal family.

Coming down off the mountain I think we all had the feeling we were really part of something special, a part of history. The hardest part of the descent was just keeping it all in perspective, not letting this puffiness get too deep into my head. Be real, focus, one step at a time. Having invested a heavy amount of energy into the climb with Erik yesterday, this was my day to be free and descend fast. In our red and green suits, we headed back down over the Geneva Spur, the Yellow band, and it all seemed to go so quickly. The tents of Camp Three were quickly pulled out, with a few being torn out, as they had frozen into the ice.

At this point the Sherpas, who were carrying extra heavy loads and trying to make some extra money, were hauling down monster loads and even jettisoning some of these loads down the entire Lhotse face to be retrieved at the bottom. Other than the poor weather, the descent to Camp Two was uneventful. There was the usual nervousness that the ropes of the 3,700-foot Lhotse face provide, the crevasses of the lower slopes, and then finally, the peace of Camp Two. I had climbed most of the day with Jeff Evans and we both arrived at Camp Two tired and relieved. One night here and then a quick descent to Base Camp, where we would see our friends and engage in a great meal, celebration, a quick packing of all the gear, and then we would fly down the trail to the warmth and comfort of those low elevations like 14,000 feet.

Erik and the rest of the team pulled into Camp Two and there was much rejoicing. The next morning, I again initiated the lead with Erik. Mike O'Donnell, Brad, and Sherm took turns making sure we didn't loose our blind friend on this, our last day on the mountain. Interestingly enough, this last day would provide for us the scariest moment of the entire climb. Near the beginning of our descent into the icefall we all stood huddled together at the top of a giant leaning ice precipice. This was as big and high as a seven million dollar home, and only days before, it had lent us its back to wander up its gentle slopes. Upon our return its back had been broken and that gentle slope that once was, would now have to be scaled by eight ladders leashed together standing vertically to the top. None of this was scary or surprising. The icefall shifts and shakes, moves and breaks, and you just hope you are not there when it does. Well, here was direct evidence of how huge these movements can be, and as we stood at its edge, each awaiting his turn to go down these ladders, the house shifted; a mini earthquake, a small shift in the ice — if ever there was a reason to fill your britches, that was it.

The moment went by somehow in slow motion and though it lasted but a moment, if it would be our last I wanted it to go on much longer. That is, until the part where we all get squished under the ice. That part I hope would play at 32x speed. Here we were, this Cinderella team with a fresh Cinderella story, coming off the mountain unscathed, no deaths, no frostbite, a team with our friendships intact even, only to be crushed in the bright sun under 1,000 tons of ice. When the Lord calls you home, you know it is your time. Thankfully, our phone wasn't ringing and this was not our time, just a check to see if we were listening. We still were.

Certain urgency took over and we all wanted off that giant block as fast as possible without jumping. The moment passed, we did not, and we were down and again on our way. For me, five trips up the icefall and thankfully five trips down. The toughest part was that our hearts and minds were already at Base Camp or even farther away, home already, but we still had a job to do, a pack to carry, a friend to see down. Just a couple more hours of work, focus, and determination, and then the moment none of us will ever forget, and those on my team who have gone back to Everest will never replace with a better one.

The entire Base Camp crew had come up to the edge of the icefall to meet us. U2's "A Beautiful Day" was being blasted over the boom-box as we made our last few steps down, out of the icefall, off the mountain and into the loving arms of friends and family. Pasqualle was there, Reba Bull, to embrace her husband and her father-in-law, Kim Johnson had her arms open to welcome her future husband, Chris Morris. It was hugs and tears all around; again getting so choked up that words could not come out without tears of joy following them. It was a snotty, miserable, happy, skinny mess. P.V. in tears hugging Sherman and Erik, words of congratulations all around. This felt like our true summit!

The feeling is what I like to call "the Ex-Lax effect." You have just spent two nervous months on one of the most dangerous mountains in the world. People are dying, the weather is testing you, there is always the element of fear and the question of what will happen next. Now, it is all behind you and there is such a sweet release of all the pent-up anxiety, nervousness, fear, and doubt — it is like the emotional Ex-Lax just kicked in, and all is well. The celebration went on into the night as Tenzing, our cook, made a special dinner and even had adult beverages brought up to Base Camp. We stayed in the stone kitchen shelter most of the night and celebrated with our Sherpas, and whoever else might want to stop by. A few Russians came over and one of them even tried hitting on Brad Bull. Brad, handsome as he is, was not interested in the advances of the Russian, one because Brad is married, and two, because the old Russian man was well . . . an old Russian MAN. This kept us laughing all the way home.

Once the party was over, it didn't take long to get everything packed up and on the trail down to Kathmandu. This was one of the most joyous days of my life. I can remember almost skipping down the trail breathing in the heavy air, listening to my music (audio adrenaline) louder than usual, and taking note of every living thing I saw. After more than two months on the mountain, a stark, frozen two-tone landscape of white and blue, even the slightest bit of living color would capture my attention. A teeny little yellow flower poking up out of the glacial soil, then some grass, and before I knew it laughing children and blooming rhododendron trees.

I imagine it is a little like being set free from prison. A little bit of that feeling hits now, but in a few weeks will fully set in. A friend had given me this Scripture before the trip and I kept it hanging above my tent floor on a ribbon. It is how I felt on the way out: *You shall go out in joy and be led forth in peace; and the mountains and hills will burst into song before you, and all the trees of the field will clap their hands* (Isaiah 55:12). It is possible to go all the way out to the airstrip of Lukla in a day, but we would take two days to make this journey and the 35 miles downhill was a breeze. Carrying just a light pack, while the yaks were loaded with all the gear, allowed us to put it in cruise control all the way down to Lukla where we would get a nice hot shower, a wonderful meal, a cold beer, and a long night's rest in a warm teahouse.

The next day we would catch our flight down to the city and meet the press, perhaps even the royal family of Nepal. A writer from *Time* magazine was ready to meet us, and we all just reveled in these moments. While resting at the teahouse, I picked up a copy of *Into Thin Air* by John Krakauer, and also the National Geographic book called *Everest* by David Breashears, about the creating of the IMAX film *Everest*. I had read each of these before our expedition and now that it was over had a curiosity to browse through them again.

Our expedition had received such criticism from various elite mountaineers and authors before we left, I couldn't help but wonder what those people were thinking now. Maybe it was, "Well, they just got lucky," or perhaps a humble, "I guess I had that wrong. I am very impressed." I don't really know, but in a way I am thankful for the critics and the fuel they provided for our internal fire. Yes, we wanted to prove them wrong, but more importantly prove ourselves right, that we were not foolish risk-takers, glory seekers, or naïve bumpkins. I know every climb is different and everyone's time on the mountain means something different to them. I can take nothing away from another's experience, and as I read these books, I realized that ours was something all together different from either of these.

I saw Michael Brown working hard and late into the cold nights with his camera, yet never complaining that he had no gloves on. In a way he dispelled many of the myths that certain writers want readers to believe. Yes, it is cold on Everest, but if you have ever spent a long, cold day in high winds at any of North America's ski resorts you have experienced a taste of Everest. The main difference is there is no lodge or warm car to go back to, and no fire or Irish coffee to warm you up. You have to sleep in it, climb in it, eat in it, and do your business in it. Being on Everest doesn't mean you are tough; it is just a tough place to be. Not everyday and every moment, however, is that way. I tried to read on, but somehow just couldn't get through it: I wanted to keep celebrating.

The next morning we all got ready, grabbed our stuff, and looked forward to the Rum Doodle tradition of putting our names on the Summiter's board in that infamous restaurant. Out the door and onto the tarmac, but no planes were flying. Things were at a standstill. The locals were acting more than strange — there seemed to be a panic in the air. "The king is dead!" one Nepalese worker exclaimed. Bewildered looks came across our faces as we looked at each other in confusion. And then a trickle of more comments came through — more chatter, moans, and groans among the locals. Understanding started to settle in and bring us down from our high to more a state of shock.

The royal family had just been assassinated by one of their own. Dipendra, the crown prince of Nepal, while at dinner with his family, unhappy with the bride who had been chosen for him, decided to act out violently. Dipendra left the dinner table only to return with an M-16 and a .38 caliber revolver. He barged into the room and began a 30-second shooting spree that killed eight and critically wounded five more. Among the dead was his father the king, his mother the queen, and his brother and sister. The prince, heir to the throne, then turned the revolver on himself and fired a bullet into his temple, leaving him the new vegetable king of Nepal. The one who murdered the king became king — for a short time.

The citizens went into a panic and directed their accusatory rage toward public officials with the belief that nothing had been done to protect the king. Their tempers flared, fueled by doubt, fear, and suspicion as they acted out questioning their government and its future. This was tragic and could have major implications on us and our ability to leave the country. There could be riots, uprisings, coup attempts, fighting, marshal law, travel prohibitions, and who knows what else.

For us now our goal was to get to a safe hotel, be out of the way, let the people mourn, and get out as soon as possible. A game of tarmac frisbee ensued while we waited, then all of a sudden, we had our chance. There wouldn't be many flights out that day and we were fortunate to be on one of them. Quickly load before any minds are changed, pack out the small twin otter plane, and then down the hill, off the cliff, and up into the air in the midst of the greatest peaks on earth.

Upon landing in Kathmandu, we could immediately see a city in turmoil. From the air there was smoke visible rising from the streets, and on the streets people ran around with their freshly shaven heads as a sign of mourning. Large multi-axel trucks were driving by filled with military and policemen ready to be deployed onto the streets to quell the rioters who were beginning to form large mobs. Martial law was being put into action. Wait a second. Just yesterday I was strolling down pastoral mountain valleys, smelling the flowers and fresh yak dung, saying hello to the school children on the trails, tuning in to my Jesus music as I skipped and frolicked my way down out of the clouds.

What an abrupt shift from feeling like I was at the top and center of the world and its attention, to feeling like I need to run for cover and my life.

Thankfully, we were greeted at the airport by trekking support staff that dodged and weaved piles of burning debris as they shuttled us off to the Marshyangdi Hotel, our fortress of guarded peace and sanity in the middle of this chaos. I guess our meeting with the royal family would be called off. Once we got our wits about us and had received more details on the matters at hand, we figured we could venture out safely enough into the streets to get a picture of what was happening. We would do this as we went over to the U.S. embassy for a meeting with a couple diplomats who now really didn't have time for us or seem to care, since Nepal was in the midst of such great turmoil and unrest. Needless to say, our conversation was short and we felt gypped again.

On our way back to the hotel, a few of the team members, including Erik, got the taste of tear gas that had been deployed on the rioters. I passed by an angry group armed with bricks, signs, flaming tires, and whatever else they could get their hands on. I saw people with bloodied heads who had obviously been a part of an altercation or the recipient of an airborne brick message. In fact, Erik nearly had a brick hit him in the head. Apparently, the people were very confused and divided on the death of the king, as well as, what the government would now look like, and it was this confusion that led to violence. The violence would escalate and the police would later be ordered to shoot to kill, and they did.

Among us there was concern, fear, respect for the people and their outrage and sorrow, and it may sound cold, selfish, and callous, but we didn't want this to keep us from finding a delicious pizza somewhere in the city, and even though a curfew was now in place, we would still find a way to get our names on the board at the Rum Doodle. First, we had that interview with the writer from *Time* over a wonderfully hot and delicious pizza, the kind dreams are made of — at least Everest Base Camp dreams. Later, it was Brad and Sherman who were very resolute and determined about this matter of getting to the Rum doodle.

Rushing through the streets of the Thamel district, they got to the Rum Doodle and found it locked up and closed, but this would not do. They pounded at the door, found someone who answered, told them a story, and the next thing you know, hours later there was a celebration at the Rum Doodle where we were all able to place our names on the revered wall with the likes of our heroes, Sir Edmond Hillary and Reinhold Messner. Another night in the city, packing of gear at the hotel, and then the team signing of oxygen bottles and kata scarves that would serve as souvenirs and mementos of our climb together.

With heaping piles of gear and more than two dozen carts, the expressions on the faces of the airport counter workers was of disappointment and frustration rather than awe. They had seen this hundreds of times, as every expedition that comes through carries the same overloaded bags with the same story, hoping to not get the excess weight charge put on. Our goal was to stick together and overwhelm the system, offer up Erik as a hero of Everest and Nepal to try to get all our gear on the flight with no penalties. Instead, just as we got to the counter and began the long process of checking in, the airport closed — with our passports on the counter.

The workers poured out from behind the walls, computers were turned off, flights in the air were being told they could not land and were redirected. It now seemed that there would be no hope of us getting home anytime soon. Jaws immediately dropped to the floor, dumbfounded looks prevailed. Just when I thought I had overcome my last obstacle, one more appears. "Please Lord, let us get on this flight and safely make it home," I prayed.

Maybe 15 minutes went by and the workers came flooding back to their stations. "We are open!" they exclaimed to hundreds of waiting people, all hopeful to make it onto whatever aircraft awaited to take them out of this fiery city in turmoil. "We have one flight that we can let out today only." Praise the Lord, we were next in line.

Not only did we make it on that last flight out of town, we were upgraded to the free champagne section upstairs, movies and all. In fact, when we got on our flight bound for the United States and again for Denver, the pilot announced our team was on board and what we had been able to accomplish. It was an unbelievable feeling to be applauded by a plane full of people. In Los Angeles, there were news crews that met us. I ran into a friend and ski school client from Beaver Creek named Bob Buckman, whose traveling path crossed ours at that moment. In the chaos, I had a hard time placing him in this seemingly random meeting.

Bob couldn't believe the fanfare. Members of the National Federation of the Blind were there with banners proclaiming: "Greatest team to climb Everest!" I had a quick interview with a writer from Sports Illustrated who wrote an article entitled, "With a Little Help from His Friends," which is now framed on my wall of fame at home. Better than all this was the welcome reception at home in Colorado. All our friends and family had arrived at the airport with anticipation and excitement and joy for us. It seems this is something rare in the world today, and that is the ability to celebrate someone else's achievements or someone else's good work or product.

People in this world tend to want the glory for themselves. I probably have to include myself in that statement if I am to be totally honest. When I see this, and especially in me, I make an effort to turn 180 degrees and celebrate the success of someone else. I want to make an effort to build up my friends, my wife, and others, and let them know just how great they are. Well, those people who were at the airport to meet us were doing exactly that. They were there to let us know they thought this was an historic achievement carried out by people they loved and believed in. The news crews there added to the excitement, but the others who had made the drive all the way to the airport made me feel loved, important, and special. I want to be like that. I want to think of others before myself.

Luis made it a point to tell my brother-in-law John, that I was a hero on summit day. I thought I had just played my part as he did and didn't really see it that way. Erik said, "He was like my guardian angel that day." Even from my team I could see some selflessness and kindness in the moment. I don't want to be a brown-noser when I talk to people; I want to be an encourager, especially to those who are up against it. For those who have an impossible dream, I want to help them see the steps to take to make it a reality. I don't want to be a critic, a naysayer, a voice injecting opinion at strangers I have not met. I want to be a believer and a positive influence for those who dare to live out their dreams even though it is against my human nature.

The following weeks were a blur as I would tell and relive the story over and over again to unsuspecting people and animals. That's right, animals like Goofy, Pluto, Mickey Mouse, and Donald Duck, because we were all invited to Disneyland in California as a reward for our achievement. I don't really know what kind of deal was made for this, but it was great. "Eric, you've climbed Mount Everest. Now what are you going to do?" "I'm going to Disneyland!" That is what it felt like.

We got to preview a lot of the work Michael Brown had done on what was initially called *Vision of Everest*, later to be repurchased and renamed *Farther Than the Eye Can See*.

Upon arriving back home in Vail, I received a phone call from the 4th of July parade organizer asking if I wanted to be the grand marshall of the town's big summer event. I had no idea what that meant and I really didn't want to be waving from some car all alone, so I asked Michael Brown to come join me since he graduated from a local high school. There we were in the back of a convertible on the 4th of July, waving to all the locals and tourists who must have been asking themselves, "Who are those guys, and why are they in the parade?" The sign on the side of the car was difficult to read and it didn't matter. This was an honor and we were proud to have been asked. My dad came to visit and ended up marching with the veterans and nearly got in a fight with "Bob, the Roller Skating Drag Queen," which would have been embarrassing had they slugged it out, but also would have been the funniest memory of all time.

The honors kept rolling in and appearances being made: Erik and P. V. on the *Today Show*, Erik on the *Tonight Show* with Shaq and Jay Leno. The funniest part was Erik saying his pee froze before it hit the ground and then seeing both of these other guys not know exactly how to respond. The last big honor was that the entire team, including Kami Tenzing, our Nepalese sirdar, were invited to the White House, and the Oval Office, for a visit with then President George W. Bush. He had only been in office seven months when we came for our visit and we had already had the opportunity to speak to him from our sat phone at Camp Four. It was at that time he issued an invitation and we didn't forget. I think he did, and he must not have thought we would hold him to it. Many guys on the team are registered Democrats and were not too thrilled to be there, but I was truly excited to have the honor of meeting both the man and the position.

We first went to the senate and were able to meet our state representatives and various other dignitaries before meeting with the president. Many of these representatives we would meet again in Colorado when the State House of Representatives passed a resolution to honor our team, made extra special because we were on the floor of the State Capitol when it happened. I was amazed how well the team cleaned up and even more amazed that everyone in this rowdy bunch passed through security and the background check in order to get in the Oval Office.

First we went through the screening machines, emptying our pockets just like at the airport and then into the board room adjacent to the office. While seated here various dignitaries and even generals would pass through. One was a general whom I recognized as a member of the president's staff. Then our turn came to go into the office and have a chat with President Bush. We all got to shake his hand and have a team photo taken with him while swapping climbing stories for stories of the office décor.

The conversation hit a lull and I took the opportunity to reach my arm out and grab the president's shoulder — a move that I didn't fully think through as I squeezed tightly to get his attention. When he turned rather quickly to look at me, I gulped, thinking the secret service was gonna jump me. Thankfully, they were more relaxed than I was and allowed me to ask my question. Here was my one shot; I could ask the president anything I wanted to ask. What would it be? I said to him that I admired his faith and the fact that he didn't back down in those matters. I told him that I had been praying for him and would like to continue to do so. So I asked "How can I pray for you?" His answer surprised me, especially coming from a newly elected president. He said, "I have twin daughters; I would appreciate it if you would pray for them." I said, "I will." Now, years later, I have twin daughters of my own to pray for, but I still keep Barbara and Jenna in my prayers as well. I was even able to get a personal letter to the president recently to which he responded:

> Your thoughtful letter just reached me in the Oval Office. Thank you for your kind words of support and especially your prayers. One of the most powerful aspects of the presidency is knowing that good people like you care enough to pray for my family and me. Congratulations on the birth of your twins. They are blessed to have been born in the world's greatest country with parents who love them a lot. Laura and I send our best wishes, and we will keep you, Amy, and your daughters in our prayers. May God bless you.
>
> — Sincerely, George W. Bush

Our visit wrapped up and the trip to DC had been quite an honor.

A sweet surprise for me was that my friend Joseph's parents made the drive down to the capitol from Martinsburg, Pennsylvania. We got to hug, share stories, cry, and catch up on all that had gone on. I got to share with them how I left Joseph's picture at the summit and how it was his carabiner that kept me attached to the ropes as I climbed. Meeting the president was the chance of a lifetime, and having friends like the Chonkos would be something even better.

Perhaps everyone who summits Everest gets this, I don't know, but my phone started to ring. It was the local paper, my hometown paper, the Rotary club, and then local schools, businesses, and churches that began calling wanting to hear the story, looking for a little inspiration and wanting to share in the celebration. I obliged and was glad I did because at one of these local slideshows I would get the first glance of a cute blonde gal that would later become my wife. What began as a few slideshows has turned into a career of speaking, and what was just a glance has turned into a family of four.

I now have a professional speaking business called Higher Summits that puts me in front of audiences ranging from military academies to corporations, and even small businesses and community organizations. Michael Brown said, "Climbing Everest will change your life." I laughed because I couldn't really, at the time, possibly see how. It was just another mountain, just another summit. I was just another white, American climber and how could that change my life. I have to say it did. I have had opportunities the world over I would never have otherwise had, met fascinating people, and been able to partner with causes and charities I never would have known even existed. It has opened doors for me because I had a little faith that God was saying go ahead, climb, and trust Me.

I don't believe the mountain created the opportunities; after all, the mountain is God's, for He created it. I believe the mountain and its summit were just the means by which change was delivered by God's providence. He has given me all and it is to Him I owe the thanks. The 29,035 foot summit was sweet. The experience was undeniably one of the best of my life. Looking back now, years later, I can see the summit a little more clearly. The true summit was more than just the little patch of snow, it was a bond forged with friends in trust, and a faith grown out of doubt into the confidence of deeper understanding of how to walk, steep as it may be, with Jesus. The Israelites built an Ebenezer when they crossed the Red Sea to remember the great thing that God had done; I look back and have the summit as my Ebenezer. It is not my faith that got me beyond the doubt; it was and continues to be the Object of that faith.

Deadpoint Reflections

He named it Ebenezer, saying, "Thus far has the Lord helped us."
— 1 Samuel 7:12

And this, our life, exempt from public haunt, finds tongues in trees, books in the running brooks, sermons in stones, and good in everything.[2]
— Shakespeare

Crux: The crux here is the crux itself. Not letting trials, difficulty, or obstacles define you or your attitude. Most of us that have at least a moderate enthusiasm for life have met a person like one I will call Mopey Joe. This person can be seen at local events, church, or the grocery store and you have tried to lend an ear, be helpful, maybe even take them on as a cause — help them change for the better. But after a while you realize their negative attitude is more than just circumstances that have them down, it is an identity. No amount of outside help will do, the change needs to come from the Lord and from within. No matter how great a cause for celebration, Mopey Joe can't even manage a smile. Soon avoidance becomes the key play. When MJ spots you from across the room you try not to make eye contact, and if intercepted on your way for the door, you allow for a one-way conversation, not daring to ask any personal questions, knowing the answers will sour any good momentum that may have been building for the day. Don't let life beat you up so bad that you become a Mopey Joe.

Christ wants us to be lights, regardless of circumstances. *Be joyful always; pray continually; give thanks in all circumstances, for this is God's will for you in Christ Jesus* (1 Thessalonians 5:16–18). Corrie Ten Boom, while imprisoned in a Nazi concentration camp, was challenged by her sister to give thanks to God for everything, including the fleas that infested their living chambers. Corrie said to her sister, "Betsie, there is no way even God can make me thankful for a flea." Betsie replied, ". . . in all circumstances. It doesn't say in pleasant circumstances. Fleas are a part of this place where God has put us." Soon after this challenge was presented to her she found herself thanking God for them because it was the one thing that kept the guards and their harsh treatment away from them and their room, giving them the ability to gather and talk, thereby allowing them to share Jesus in the midst of the horror around them. They saw the greater purpose for being in the situation and thanked God for it.

Hold: There is a song out now that says, "Live like you were dying." I've got news — you are. Live, dream, celebrate as though you are dying. Find ways to stay positive, give thanks, celebrate the joys of life, set goals, and live out a few dreams, and when things go south keep doing it without being phony. Don't let severe trials and hangnails turn you into a crusty, angry, bitter, old wart with a bad attitude and a worse reputation.

Anchor: Prayer. Stay connected to the Lord in good, bad, and ugly times.

Love must be sincere. Hate what is evil; cling to what is good. Be devoted to one another in brotherly love. Honor one another above yourselves. Never be lacking in zeal, but keep your spiritual fervor, serving the Lord. Be joyful in hope, patient in affliction, faithful in prayer. Share with God's people who are in need. Practice hospitality.

Bless those who persecute you; bless and do not curse. Rejoice with those who rejoice; mourn with those who mourn. Live in harmony with one another. Do not be proud, but be willing to associate with people of low position. Do not be conceited.

Do not repay anyone evil for evil. Be careful to do what is right in the eyes of everybody. If it is possible, as far as it depends on you, live at peace with everyone. Do not take revenge, my friends, but leave room for God's wrath, for it is written: "It is mine to avenge; I will repay," says the Lord. On the contrary: "If your enemy is hungry, feed him; if he is thirsty, give him something to drink. In doing this, you will heap burning coals on his head." Do not be overcome by evil, but overcome evil with good (Romans 12:9–21).

Endnotes
1. www.mnteverest.net/quote.html.
2. William Shakespeare, *As You Like It*, act II, scene i.

Epilogue

[Mount Vinson]

ELEVATION: 16,050 feet

HOW LONG TO CLIMB: Two to four weeks weather dependent

HOW MANY IN THE TEAM: Three is preferable

RATING: AD

BEST TO CLIMB DURING: November to February southern summer

ALSO KNOWN AS: Named for Carl Vinson, a Congressman from Georgia who helped fund Antarctic research

Notes:

Only one outfitter in the world does logistics for this climb. Antarctica/Mt. Vinson – 7th and still missing summit. Cost $30,000. Sponsors welcome.

But the fruit of the Spirit is love, joy, peace, patience, kindness, goodness, faithfulness, gentleness and self control. Against such things there is no law. — Galatians 5:22–23

Only on the summit can we straighten our bodies which lean always uphill.[1] — Gaston Rebuffat

Having climbed mountains all over the world as a member of expeditions big and small, I have not only been a part of, but have witnessed, read about, and otherwise studied what I believe are the most common reasons, vices, for failure in the mountains and especially the biggest mountain — Everest. These same vices often derail us in relationships, work, and faith. Having interviewed countless CEOs as a part of my speaking profession as well as being allowed to look over countless mission and vision statements of organizations from the United States Military Academies to the Fortune 500, from schools to churches, I have seen several commonalities rise above all else as we seek formulas and recipes for success and foundations on which to build.

The way I see it, the following are common pitfalls which cause us to fail every time: inexperience, pride, selfishness, fear, and doubt. Personally, at some time in my life I have been derailed by every one of these vices. Thankfully, I know a loving God and am forgiven, but how do we fix these attitudes and conditions of the heart in business, in our families, or in our social groups?

Just as you wouldn't throw a kid in the deep end of a pool for his first swim, it is wise not to jump on Everest as a first climb. God can and will perform miracles in spite of us and the skills we may or may not possess, but He has given us talents and desires, and it is our responsibility to maximize those talents and use them for His glory.

Inexperience does not mean that we can't participate; instead, seek after the desires of your heart that God has given you, and be patient in the pursuit, taking on new challenges one step at a time, in faith, as your skills grow. Want to climb Everest? Go hike, then climb, learn from others, start small, then seek a peak like Mt. Rainier in Washington and take a course on mountaineering. Practice these skills and climb it again. Then go bigger, gaining independence and the ability to think for yourself in the mountains. If you don't know what crampons are or how to put them on, you don't belong on Mt. Rainier, let alone Everest.

I am a new parent, and I have a lot to learn. I am reading a lot of books on babies and kids, and doing loads of research on the web as well as seeking wise counsel from those who have gone before me. I am taking baby steps, just as my girls are, toward a better understanding of parenthood, and it is far more demanding than any mountain I have ever climbed. I think over time my experience will hopefully make me a good parent, but I will never espouse to be an expert. Experience not only improves our abilities, it improves our judgment and will ensure our longevity. Whether it be in business or climbing, it will give us an edge always with more still to glean.

How does one adequately prepare for any type of adventure, whether it be climbing, personal, or professional? Is there a key for understanding our direction, purpose, and place? In the movie *The Rookie*, Jim Morris (played by Dennis Quaid) is told by his father, a conservative ex-military man, when asked what he should do regarding an attempt to make a comeback from high school science teacher and baseball coach to playing in the major leagues, "There's a time to stop doing what you want to do, and do what you were meant to do." It sounds profound, and it is. We all want that answer as we push through our sometimes seemingly meaningless daily lives asking ourselves, "Is this all that there is?!"

We seek to know if we were meant for something greater and bigger and beyond ourselves, and if God has a more wonderful plan for our lives than He has revealed at this time. To know the answer requires faith — great faith — and patience. If these are required, then how does one get these and then find the answer for a more meaningful life? First, it requires a personal relationship with Jesus Christ in which you have surrendered your life to Him completely. After this profession of faith God can more easily begin to work on one's humbled heart. The second step is prayer. This is exciting! How often do I/we look at prayer as a chore or as a thing of routine, merely uttering the words we were taught as a child or in church that are not our own. In prayer we have the opportunity to speak to the one true and living God, one to one. The Creator of the universe is there with open ears hearing our utterances — it doesn't matter if we do say something stupid, He wants to hear our voice, our concerns, thoughts, requests, thanks, and silliness, because He wants to be in a deeper more meaningful relationship with us, and how else can this be done unless there is communication.

Communication — which takes place not at just a certain time of the day or night but rather all day and all night, no matter what we are doing or where we are. Yes it is possible to pray with a mouthful, while driving, or halfway up a frozen waterfall hoping your ice axe only partially placed doesn't pop out as you try the next move. In preparation for my adventures, I always begin with prayer. I seek the Lord and ask for His guidance on how I can serve Him, asking to be used according to my unique design and purpose for the advancement of His kingdom. Wanting to take advantage of opportunities that arise divinely, it becomes time to step out in faith through prayer in order to depend on Him and trust Him so that I may persevere through the trials and doubts that will without a doubt begin to flood my life as this process begins. It involves risk to live by faith and to pray faithfully, because God has high expectations and demands for us and our lives.

Beginning in a place of humility, focused on His plan rather than on our own, is the best place from which to pray. When the disciples asked Jesus how they ought to pray, His reply is to pray as such: "Thy kingdom come. Thy will be done." When praying for the Lord's will to be done, the hard part follows — living expectantly that it will be done. "Okay, God, I have prayed. Now get on with it and get your will done so I can move on with my life," is how we often see this, but it is so much more of a deep, lifelong, patient commitment to Him and His call for us that takes months, oftentimes years, of painful shaping and tooling until He has us right where He wants us.

As the time grew closer for us to go to Everest I spent more and more time in prayer because I was way underprepared for a climb of this nature. I hadn't trained much; I was relatively unhealthy, and most certainly very poor. I had failed my team the year before and lacked major confidence. I began to pray that God would make it clear to me if I could live this lifelong dream, and since I was a bit afraid and intimidated from the year's prior events I asked that he would close doors so that it would not happen. I prayed that as I went to the pulmonologist my answer would come in the negative, and as I asked the team they would make this decision easier by saying no! Of course, how could I climb with no money for the expedition — this was already a no. The doctor said go, the team didn't say no, in came the dough, so . . . what do ya know — it was time for me to take the step of faith, as not only myself but countless others prayed for this journey.

Stepping into the unknown by faith is where God wants us. He doesn't want us to have it all figured out, to know all the answers and outcomes, because if we do where does He fit in? He wants our trust and confidence in Him alone, and this begins by knowing Him and praying — communicating with Him. I would pray my way up the mountain beginning at Base Camp with an Easter service . . . and soon have others on the team praying as well, even those who didn't believe. Praying all the way to Camp Four when we would pray for a Spanish climber and friend lost in the upper reaches of the mountain as darkness set in. Pray without ceasing. Jesus Himself would spend significant time in prayer, not hiding any fears as He spoke with the father, "Take this cup from me" (Mark 14:36).

Our prayers need to be honest, and our hearts need to look at the bigger picture as we look beyond our needs, as Christ did when the cup was not taken from Him, but rather given empty to Him so that He could pour Himself out into it, filling it as a living sacrifice for our sakes. After we pray and we hear, we need to be willing to respond to the Lord's call, not like a Jonah running away, because if we do God will still get His way, and chances are it won't be as pretty. This is not to say that His will is always going to be contrary to our own; no, He will bless us likewise with what is on our own heart when we are seeking Him obediently. Just be ready for anything.

From all the numbers of people (1953–2010) who have stood upon the highest point on earth [*there are still more Superbowl champions than Everest summiters*], three people and their teams stand out as exceptional innovators. These three have provided perhaps the greatest moments in Everest's history: Sir Edmund Hillary's first summit, Reinhold Messner's 1978 summit without oxygen, and the 2001 National Federation of the Blind (NFB) summit with blind climber Erik Weihenmayer.

Listening to, but not being controlled by our fears, the 2001 NFB team, of which I was a part, defied the odds and led our blind friend Erik Weihenmayer to this summit. It was a completely new way of looking at things (or not looking at all). It shattered the mold into which people with disabilities are put. It was an exercise in putting oneself in another's shoes, which let us innovate and forge a new path to the top. The mountain had not changed nor did the route get easier. What had changed was our approach.

Just as unspoken limits are put on a person with disabilities, sometimes we need to step out from fear and limitation and devise new methods to overcome these obstacles. Use your head — simplicity spans the gap as easily as the complex. Just a tweaking of what may already exist. This takes our small steps of progress and transforms them into giant leaps over time, turning what was once thought of as impossible to being totally plausible.

Sometimes simple is not a choice. I remember a time when I was working in the French Alps as a pisteur (ski patrolman) and was dispatched to the scene of an accident at the junction of two icy runs. Still getting a grip on my French skills, I was always nervous as to what I might find and how I would communicate. I wanted to make sure to use and pronounce the words correctly so as not to offend my hosts, like my French counterparts had often offended their guests. (An example of this would be one of the French patrolmen asking a portly English woman with a head injury how long she had been knocked up — meaning, of course, knocked out, and sending the husband standing nearby into a jealous rage.)

I arrived at the scene of the accident and to my horror found a Japanese man who had been hit by an Italian witnessed by a German. I, an American speaking French, was there to sort it all out. The Japanese man spoke no French, English, or German, and to make sure he was not suffering from a head injury I would need to ask him questions — but how? Luckily, the Italian spoke Japanese, the German spoke Italian, and then also spoke French to me — the American. Eventually we got it figured out that the Japanese man had been knocked out. He was also suffering from shoulder and back pain. With this information and help, I was able to use the assets around me to find the problem and make sure he got the proper treatment.

Together we had invented a line of communication where at first it seemed impossible, thus enabling me to figure out what had happened to this man and to give the proper care. If upon arrival I had thrown my arms up in despair and not seen beyond the problem to treat the injury he may have been allowed to ski away, causing him further harm. As it turned out, he was helped by an oddball team building on each others' skills and abilities until the problem was solved by adjusting to what resources were around us to get the most from our situation. I think we were growing in wisdom.

How did the man on top of the proverbial mountain get so wise? He gained wisdom by listening to those who struggled up the mountain, over obstacles, and completed the journey. It is on the way to the top, it is along the journey that we learn, grow, innovate, and adapt. It is not just a lump sum we receive on some given day, on some given summit so that we may sit upon a mountaintop and dispense it to those weary souls tired from the climb. Achieving the summit requires innovation, and like wisdom, it builds one upon another as steps up a mountain, the summation of which gets us to our goal. Innovate your way to success. It may be a small step today, but that small step may open the floodgates to future triumphs over the impossible, often coming from a cooperative effort and collaboration.

We can't be sold out for ourselves, and we have to hold human life in higher esteem than a mountaintop, than money, than political gain. If it will happen in the mountains it can and will happen anywhere. It comes down to one word: humility. Humility to me is the act of serving without want of personal gain or reward. When Samone Moro gave up his summit attempt to rescue this kid on the Lhotse face, he had to put his personal aspirations and ego (if he had an ego) aside, and place the life of another, a stranger at that, ahead of himself and his own desires. This is humility, this is success, and this is the summit.

This is what it is about — knowing what is bigger than yourself and doing anything and everything possible to assure the best possible outcome for all, even if it cost's you your goal. When we see ourselves as "all that and a bag of chips," we invite problems, and when we have that attitude, more often than not we are just one little crumb in the bag of chips. Other than selfishness and pride, fear is the main culprit steering us away from the summit, from our goals, from doing what's right.

Fear can keep us from doing stupid things, but more often than not it keeps us from pursuing our dreams and striving for our goals. There can be that overwhelming fear of failure, the grip of which is irrational, with success begging for an escape from its clutches. This became evident to me after my accident on Ama Dablam where I had pulmonary edema, then pneumonia, then the loss of my best friend. If I ever had reason to fear, if ever I was controlled by fear and doubt, it was then. Fearing failure, injury, illness, and possibly death should I return to altitude? To be concerned would be rational; to live in fear and be controlled by it would serve me in no way.

I'm not saying enter a duel if you can't shoot straight with no fear — you'll get killed. You still must know yourself and the skills you possess. So how then do you overcome it? I don't know that you ever overcome it, or that it just plain goes away. Sometimes this will happen, but the rest of the time we need to hit the problem head-on, do our homework, and address each fear. Look at the systems in place. Look at the support, the skills, and the doctor's reports, whatever, to get yourself back in balance. Most importantly, know that perfect love casts out all fear. I love my wife, I love my kids, I love my friends, and when I choose to serve them in love I forget about the fears I may have. When crossing the ladders of the icefall, because I love my friend, I focus on serving and meeting the needs he has. Before I know it, the ladder that freaked me out previously is now behind me. I have crossed it by not focusing on my fear, but on focusing on the needs of someone else. How much more then, when I love my God and serve Him, will my fears be removed?

The Bible says, *Trust in* LORD *forever, for the* LORD*, the* LORD*, is the Rock eternal* (Isaiah 26:4). "So do not fear, for I am with you" (Isaiah 41:10). As I see it, four things will allow us to fight through fear: love, faith, courage, and hope. "Be strong and courageous. Do not be terrified; do not be discouraged, for the LORD your God will be with you wherever you go" (Joshua 1:9). Does courage defeat fear? I believe it beats it back for a time, making way for progress. It is that which propels us in the presence of fear. Some will see faith as superstition, as a crutch, and ask the question, "What if I put my faith in this religion or that religion, does it really matter so long as I believe?" I'd have to say that just because you believe in something doesn't make it real. Faith alone is not what saves us; it is what is on the other end of that faith. Yet faith is "being sure of what we hope for and certain of what we do not see" (Hebrews 11:1). The evidence should give us the confidence.

Just as faith can set us free, failure can set us back and steal our hope, suffering can cause us to freeze up inside and out and blind us to possibilities. There are some people I know who have been gifted with an indomitable spirit that always sees a way out, that always hopes and that always finds joy in any crummy situation. This can be contagious and it can be really annoying when you're the one who can't get excited about eggs on pizza, like me after summiting Aconcagua, and the person next to you is saying how great it would be if there were more eggs, maybe even uncooked. "We also rejoice in our sufferings, because we know that suffering produces perseverance; perseverance, character; and character, hope" (Romans 5:3–4).

What does it take to persevere? You will never take one step if you are indifferent toward climbing a mountain, and you shouldn't. You have to want the summit, want the experience, want the misery, and desire the joy of hard work that will make it possible. You must be willing to overcome the differences that will arise among team members, because it takes trust, and a root of bitterness is hard to dig out. If your mission is not great enough to help you beyond your differences, your mission is not great enough. Mountains, relationships, or anything you do will put some sweat on your brow if you want them to flourish and succeed. To be complacent in any of these will only keep you from ever experiencing the great reward that is out there to be obtained and enjoyed, growing you in character, wisdom, and strength.

When it comes to the pursuit of dreams, there are most definitely two types of people in this world: those who do and those who doubt. The biggest difference between the two is right there in the spelling: do is doubt without the b-u-t. How many times have you heard, or perhaps even said: "That would be fun *but* . . ." or "That is a great idea *but*. . . ." I think of so many great feats in history and of the specific barriers that had to be removed and of the clouds of doubt that needed to be lifted. In one's struggle to go beyond the ordinary and make a way into the unknown it is hard enough to get beyond one's own doubts, let alone those of countless others in your face telling you what you can't do. In other words, don't let a big "but" get in the way of your vision, whether it be your but or someone else's. The greatest doers are the ones who can typically look beyond themselves and many buts to see greater purpose in their efforts. I saw that in my team, a group of guys that believed, that had separated themselves from the crowd by believing in the possibilities without any buts.

Integrity at our core will keep a team together and give it a solid foundation where word matches action, fostering consistency of character, predictability, and dependability. We can guard our plans and our thoughts, those belong to us, but honesty and transparency will only serve to enhance our reputations and longevity in all we do. And what is beyond that? The true test of character is the ability to forgive. It is easier to forgive the unintentional action than it is the contrived plan of the deceiver. Forgive and love your enemy. This, this is the hardest stance in which to position the heart and our inability to do so is made up for by a merciful God and *His* grace, which covers a multitude of sins, not *mine*.

Summit or plummet! Many live as if to say, "The summit is the most important thing. I will do anything for it; if it were yours and I could take it, I would." The mountain of Everest and "summit fever" blinds people with desire: desire for fame, for notoriety, for bragging rights, for sponsorships, contracts, endorsements, enlightenment, and the list goes on for a mile. It instills even the lust to be envied. What I noticed too is that those with this attitude could not handle a blind man in their sacred club, because a blind man on Everest would diminish the accomplishment and the chance at being the envy of all men.

Instead of harboring an attitude such as this, we should encourage others on to great things, even when we wish it was us. G.K. Chesterton said, "The truly great man is the man that makes every man feel great." Encourage and inspire greatness in others, allowing them to shine without expectation of gain or reward; to succeed in this takes moral strength, integrity, and character. Truly it is our character that defines us, and should that not be our most distinguishing attribute? Character is something that man may not see, that is not always immediately evident, but it is something God will not miss. Character is something that trials or an attempt on a prized summit will drive to the surface. To lead is to cast a vision, inspire by conduct, act in selfless integrity, delegate task and authority, and take action with character as the denominator. At times, leadership is letting someone else do just that, knowing when you no longer can, even if it means giving up the summit.

What is the summit? It is the right thing. It is the right decision, made in character, at the right time that proves our mettle. It is more than just a mountaintop; it is any high point in a person's life that we can celebrate. Maybe it is something great that God has done. It is achievement, passion, longing, striving, always seeking something higher than ourselves, a higher way, a higher road or path, the climb that never gives up hope. The summit is the blind kid that gets up, gets out, and never gives up. The summit is belief. The summit is faith. God occupies the summit; no, not of Everest, of all creation, and what we strive for is His loving kindness, His likeness, His grace, His kingdom, and to know Him and be known by Him.

The first question which you will ask and which I must try to answer is this: "What is the use of climbing Mount Everest?" and my answer must at once be, "It is no use." There is not the slightest prospect of any gain whatsoever. Oh, we may learn a little about the behavior of the human body at high altitudes, and possibly medical men may turn our observation to some account for the purposes of aviation. But otherwise, nothing will come of it. We shall not bring back a single bit of gold or silver, not a gem, nor any coal or iron. We shall not find a single foot of earth that can be planted with crops to raise food. It's of no use. So if you cannot understand that there is something in man which responds to the challenge of this mountain and goes out to meet it, that the struggle is the struggle of life itself upward and forever upward, then you won't see why we go. What we get from this adventure is just sheer joy. And joy is, after all, the end of life. We do not live to eat and make money. We eat and make money to be able to enjoy life. That is what life means and what life is for.[2]

— George Leigh Mallory

If I have a faith that can move mountains, but have not love, I am nothing. — 1 Corinthians 13:2

I tell you the truth, if you have faith as small as a mustard seed, you can say to this mountain, "Move from here to there" and it will move. Nothing will be impossible for you. — Matthew 17:20

Your righteousness is like the mighty mountains, your justice like the great deep. O LORD, you preserve both man and beast. — Psalm 36:6

"Though the mountains be shaken and the hills be removed, yet my unfailing love for you will not be shaken nor my covenant of peace be removed," says the LORD, who has compassion on you. — Isaiah 54:10

Endnotes
1. Thomas Hornbein, *Everest: The West Ridge* (San Francisco, CA: Sierra Club-Ballantine Books, 1966), p. 125.
2. Ibid., p. 24.

Appendix

Mount Everest Expedition Equipment List

Ice axe w/leash: General mountaineering tool. Sizing is important: under 5'7" use a 60cm tool; 5'7"–6'1" use a 65cm tool; over 6'1" use a 70cm tool. (Too short is preferable to too long.) Make sure you have a leash that is designed for use on a glacier axe. Please, no technical leashes.

Crampons: With "step in" bindings and flat rather than "cookie cutter" frame rails; anti-balling plates okay. Keep in mind that ice-specific crampons are for technical ice climbing and are not recommended for glacier travel.

Alpine climbing harness: Harness should fit over all clothing, have gear loops, adjustable leg loops, and be reasonably comfortable to hang in. Make sure you can get into the harness without having to step through any part of it.

Carabiners: 3 locking, 3 regular, 2 twist lock, and 1 small screw gate locker; 3 standard ovals recommended.

Ascender: One right or one left.

Rappel/belay device.

Prussiks: Or bring 40 feet of flexible 6mm perlon to make into prussiks.

Adjustable 3-section ski or trekking poles: Optional but highly recommended. Helpful for non snow-covered ascents and descents if you have knee problems.

Footwear

Light hiking boots or trekking shoes: For day hikes and trek to Base Camp. The trail to Base Camp is rocky and rough. Shoes that are lightweight, high comfort, plenty of room in the toe bed, with good support are important.

Tennis shoes or low top shoes: For international travel and town days. Optional.

Booties: Optional.

Camp boots: Optional. Insulated boot for Base Camp.

Double plastic climbing boots w/ altitude liners: Good quality plastic shells with inner boots. Avoid tight fit with heavy socks.

Fully insulated overboots: Not needed with Millet Everest or Olympus Mons Boots.

Gaiters: Please make sure your gaiters fit around the boot without being too tight around your leg. Gaiters should have cordura on the inside of the leg. No lightweight hiking gaiters. Not needed with One Sports or Olympus Mons.

Trekking socks: 3 pair.

Wool or synthetic socks: 4 pair heavyweight wool or synthetic socks (wool is warmer) to be worn over the liner socks. When layering socks, check fit over feet and inside boots. Remember to keep one fresh, dry pair of socks available at all times. It is best to bring new socks, as they lose their cushioning over time. Socks with padded shins are especially nice with plastic boots.

Liner socks: 4 pair of smooth, thin wool, nylon, or Capilene to be worn next to the skin. This reduces the incidence of blisters and hot spots and makes the outer sock last longer before needing to be changed. They should fit well with your heavyweight socks.

Vapor barrier socks: Optional. Helps reduce moisture buildup in your boots, also keeps your feet a little warmer.

Technical Clothing

Lightweight long underwear: 2–3 pair tops and bottoms, Capilene, other synthetic, or wool. No cotton. Lightweight is preferable as it is more versatile (worn single in warmer conditions and double layer for colder conditions.) Zip-t-neck tops allow more ventilation options. One set of white for intense sunny days on the glacier and one pair of dark for faster drying gives the most versatility.

Heavyweight long underwear: 1 pair. Expedition weight Capilene (alternative: a one-piece suit).

Lightweight nylon pants: 1–2 pairs.

Short sleeve synthetic shirt: 1–2.

Synthetic/soft shell jacket: A full-zip version is easier to put on and has better ventilation than a pullover.

Insulated synthetic pants: Full separating side zippers. This is very important for ventilation. Full side zips also allow pants to be taken off without having to remove boots.

Down pants: To fit over insulation layers; outer shell must be windproof.

Expedition down parka: Fully baffled, expedition weight, must have good hood.

Insulated synthetic Jacket: Optional. Allows you to leave your down parka up higher on the mountain as we establish higher camps.

Hard shell jacket w/ hood: We recommend a waterproof, breathable shell material with full front zipper, underarm zips, and no insulation. This outer layer protects against wind and rain.

Hard shell pants. Waterproof, breatheable. Full-length side zippers preferred because it allows easy removal of pants, 7/8th zippers allowed but is more difficult to remove pants. No short lower leg zippers allowed.

Handwear

Lightweight synthetic gloves: 1 pair. Should fit comfortably inside mitts or gloves. Lighter Capilene preferred.

Heavyweight synthetic/soft shell gloves: 1 pair. Windstopper is helpful.

Expedition shell gloves w/ insulated removeable liners: 1 pair. For use lower on the mountain when expedition mitt is not needed.

Expedition shell mitts: 1 pair. Should be big enough so that synthetic gloves fit inside pile liners.

Hand warmers and toe warmers: 3 sets of each. Toe warmers are different than hand warmers because they are formulated to work in a lower oxygen environment, like the inside of a boot; they also burn out more quickly.

Headwear

Headlamp: Bring plenty of spare bulbs and batteries. Halogen bulbs are not necessary.

Glacier glasses (w/ side covers or wrap around): 100 percent UV, IR, high quality optical lenses designed for mountain use, must have side covers, leashes, and a nose guard is particularly helpful. No more than 8 percent light transmission. If you wear contact lenses we recommend packing a spare pair of glasses. If you wear glasses we recommend prescription glacier glasses (gray or amber). Talk to your eye care professional to find out where prescription glacier glasses are available.

Baseball cap/sun hat: One with a good visor to shade the nose and eyes.

Ski goggles: 1 pair. 100 percent UV & IR.

Balaclava: 1 heavyweight, 1 lightweight. Heavyweight must fit over lightweight.

Warm synthetic/wool hat.

Bandanas: 2. Used to shade your neck.

Neoprene face mask: Optional

Personal Equipment

Expedition backpack: 3,500–4,000 cu. in. There are many great packs.

Trekking backpack: 2,000–2,500 cu. in. Optional.

Sleeping bag: Expedition quality rated to at least -40°F. Goose down preferred over synthetic for bulk and weight. If well-cared-for, a down bag will last much longer than a synthetic bag. Needs to be long enough that your feet are not pressing out the foot box, which will make you colder. It should be roomy enough for comfortable sleeping but snug enough for efficient heat retention.

Sleeping Bag: Expedition quality rated to at least -20°F. A second bag for Base Camp. This avoids the carrying of the Expedition Bag up and down the mountain after the higher camps are established.

Self Inflating pads: Two 3/4 or full-length pads. One for use at Base Camp and one for camps higher on the mountain. If you are over 6' a long is recommended. Make sure to include a repair kit.

Closed-cell foam pad: Full-length closed cell is recommended, used while staying at camps higher than Base Camp and to be used in combination with your self-inflating pad.

Cooking gear: Cup: 16 oz. plastic insulated mug with snap-on lid (retains heat well and is spill-resistant in the tent). Some prefer a non-insulated mug for warming hands. Spoon: Good quality tough plastic (lexan). Bowl: Plastic Tupperware type with 2–3 cup capacity and lid.

Sunscreen: SPF 40 or better, 2 small tubes. Make sure that you have new sunscreen.

Lipscreen: SPF 20 or better, at least 2 sticks. Make sure your lipscreen is new.

Water Bottles: 2 to 3 wide mouth bottles with minimum 1 liter capacity per bottle. No water bag or bladder systems, they freeze or are hard to fill.

Water bottle parkas for the big bottles.

Toiletry bag: Include toilet paper, hand sanitizer, and small towel (as well as toothbrush, toothpaste, etc.).

Pee bottle (1 liter): Large mouth, clearly marked water bottle for use in tent.

Pee funnel (for women): It is a good idea to practice, practice, practice. For use in tent.

Camp knife or multi tool: Medium sized. Keep the knife simple.

Thermos: 1 liter capacity. Needs to be strong. Stainless steel vacuum bottle.

Trash compactor bags: 4. To line stuff sacks to keep gear dry and one large enough to line pack. At minimum 3 mil. thick.

Camera gear: Optional. We recommend a small digital point and shoot camera above BC. Simple and light. For more information, see recommendations on the FAQ page of our website (www.AlpineAscents.com/faq.asp).

Compression stuff sacks: Especially for sleeping bags and clothing.

Traveling

Large duffel bags w/ travel locks: 2. Used for transporting your gear.

Base Camp items: It is good to bring additional items you have found to be useful on previous expeditions. For example: paperback books, playing cards, MP3 flash player, shortwave radio, game boys, musical instruments, ear plugs, lots of batteries, etc.

Travel clothes: A set of clean clothes is nice to have to change into after the trip.

First Aid

Small personal first aid kit (simple and light): Aspirin, moleskin, molefoam, waterproof first-aid tape, athletic tape, Band-Aids, personal medications, etc. The guides will have extensive first-aid kits, so leave anything extra behind. Let your guide know about any medical issues before the climb.

Drugs/medications/prescriptions: Climbers should bring Mupirocin (Bactroban) cream, excellent topical antibiotic for scrapes and cuts. Cirpro-floxin (Cipro) 500 mg tablets for traveler's diarrhea and for urinary tract infections. Loperamide (Lomotil) or Immodium for diarrhea. Azithromycin (Z-pak) 250 mg tablets for non-gastrointestinal

infections. Acetazolamide (Diamox) 125 or 250 mg tablets for alltitude sickness. Ibuprofen (Advil, Motrin) 200 mg tablets for altitude headaches, sprains, aches, etc. Excedrin, Acetaminophen (Tylenol) 325 mg tablets for stomach sensitivity.
*Basic gear list provided by Alpine Ascents International

Glossary

acclimatization — to become accustomed to a new climate or environment. The process of adjusting to higher elevations.

anchor — any device that keeps an object in place. A point to which a climber's rope is attached, (e.g., on a rock face or in ice).

belay — to fasten or control the rope to which a climber is attached by wrapping it around a metal device or another person

bivouac — a very simple temporary camp that is set up and used by soldiers or mountaineers.

bivy sack / bivouac sack — thin Gore-tex sac for impromptu camps.

breakover — the point where the ice ends and the gentler slopes begin.

camber — a slightly arched surface

chorten — a Tibetan Buddhist shrine used for ceremony and remembrance.

choss — loose, dirty, and rotten rock.

col — a high mountain pass or saddle.

Cordillera Blanca — Peruvian mountain range meaning white mountains containing parallel ridges.

couloir — a broad mountain gully, especially prone to avalanches.

crampon — a framework of metal spikes fastened to the sole of a boot or shoe to provide better traction on ice or snow.

crux — the most demanding part of a climb up a mountain or rocks.

dacha — a house in the countryside in Russia that someone lives in on weekends or during vacations.

deadpoint — a climbing move where momentum is used to achieve a higher handhold.

dropping trou — a potty break.

epistaxis — nose bleed.

fourteeners — mountains over 14,000 feet high.

Gamow-bag — (pronounced Gam-Off) is an inflatable polyethylene/PVC bag large enough to accommodate one person inside. Inflatable pressure chamber primarily used for treating severe cases of altitude sickness. Named after its inventor, Dr. Igor Gamow.

guanacos — one of the largest mammals of South America, this camelid *(Lama guanicoe)* is related to the llama, alpaca, and vicuna, and is found in the high mountains of the Andes. When domesticated, it is used for fine wool.

HAPE — High Altitude Pulmonary Edema — a serious medical condition resulting from the accumulation of fluid in the lungs, caused by the lower barometric pressure and decreased oxygen levels that exist at high altitude.

hold — transitive verb to take something firmly and retain it in the hand or arms. In climbing it is the object that is grasped.

katas — Tibetan, Nepalese, or Buddhist scarves, given at the embarkation of a journey, or as a welcome.

nak — female yak

O's — oxygen

pancha manca — Peruvian feast where meat is cooked in the ground with vegetables.

ptarmigan — a wild bird of the grouse family, that has feet covered with feathers and white plumage in the winter. Native to mountainous regions. Genus: Lagopus

puja — the act of showing reverence to a god, a spirit, or another aspect of the divine through invocations, prayers, songs, and rituals.

pulse oximeter — an instrument that measures a person's pulse rate and the amount of oxygen in the blood.

rick-shaw — a human-powered taxi where the driver is on foot.

rupees — the main unit of currency in India, Mauritius, Nepal, Pakistan, the Seychelles, and Sri Lanka.

Sagarmatha — Sherpa name for Everest meaning mother goddess of the earth.

Seven Summits — The highest peak on each of the seven continents.

Sherpa — a member of a people originally from Tibet who live on the southern slopes of the Himalayan range in Nepal and Sikkim. Sherpas are noted for their mountaineering skills. *Sher* means "east" and *pa* means "people."

simul-climb — climbers ascend in unison on a rope foregoing a belay.

sirdar — or sardar, is a Sherpa mountain guide who manages all the other Sherpas and expedition logistics in a climbing expedition or trekking group.

summit — the highest point or top of something, especially a mountain.

Super Seven — the most difficult mountain to climb on each continent.

trek — to make a long, difficult journey, especially on foot and often over rough or mountainous terrain.

tuk-tuk — a small, motorized three-wheeled vehicle often used as a taxi in developing nations.

tumpline — a band or strap strung across the forehead or chest to support a backpack.

Western Cwm — the high glacial valley on Mt. Everest's south side above 20,000 feet.

white-out — a situation in which there is so much snow and low cloud that you cannot see clearly.

yak — related to a bison

Yosemite Decimal System — a three-part system used for rating the difficulty of walks, hikes, and climbs. Used by trekkers and mountaineers, the Class 5 portion of the class scale is a rock climbing classification system. Ex: 1 - walk; 2 - hike; 3 - scramble; 4 - scramble with rope; 5.0–5.15 - steep climbing with ropes and equipment.

zopkio: a small mountain beast; a cross between a yak and a cow.

About the Author

Eric Alexander is a skier, climber, and mountaineer who has lived in the Vail Valley for 20 years. He is married to Amy Alexander and has twin daughters, Karis and Aralyn. Born in Indiana, Eric moved west with his family at the age of four to Evergreen, Colorado, where he gained his first experiences in the outdoors with his church youth group. His mentors there, with world-class credentials, gave him a passion for the outdoors and for the Lord, which continues today.

With a BA degree in environmental science from the University of Denver, Eric was a member of the school's Alpine Club, Ski Team, and was president of Intervarsity Christian Fellowship on campus. In Vail, Eric has worked for the Vail Ski Patrol (including one year in France), Ski School, Vail Mountaineering, and now his own business. On May 25, 2001, Eric defied the odds and scaled Mt. Everest, guiding his blind friend Erik Weihenmayer to its 29,035-foot summit. He has continued to climb and lead others, particularly those with disabilities, on trips around the world. Eric has climbed the highest point on six of the seven continents, which is a feat in and of itself. However, what makes this accomplishment even more notable is that Eric has led a person with a disability to the summit of each continent's highest peak.

From these experiences he has been able to build a business called Higher Summits, allowing him to share an inspirational message with people all over the world, opening the door to share his faith in Christ and the true meaning of purpose in life.

Eric continues to climb and lead expeditions throughout Europe, Africa, North and South America, the Himalayas, and other mountainous regions of the globe with disabled teens and adults. He is always looking for new mountains to climb, both personally and in the outdoors, while challenging people to overcome the "Everest" in their own lives.

Connecting...
WITH ERIC

facebook ➡	www.facebook.com/highersmmits
twitter ➡	www.twitter.com/highersummits
BLOG ➡	www.highersummits.com